Just Memos

Aspen Coursebook Series

Just Memos
Preparing for Practice

Fourth Edition

Laurel Currie Oates
Professor of Law
Seattle University School of Law

Anne Enquist
Professor of Lawyering Skills
Director, Legal Writing Program
Seattle University School of Law

Wolters Kluwer
Law & Business

Published by Wolters Kluwer Law & Business in New York.

Wolters Kluwer Law & Business serves customers worldwide with CCH, Aspen
Publishers, and Kluwer Law International products. (www.wolterskluwerlb.com)

To contact Customer Service, e-mail customer.service@wolterskluwer.com
call 1-800-234-1660, fax 1-800-901-9075, or mail correspondence to:

  Wolters Kluwer Law & Business
  Attn: Order Department
  PO Box 990
  Frederick, MD 21705

Printed in the United States of America.

4 5 6 7 8 9 0

ISBN 978-1-4548-3101-3

Library of Congress Cataloging-in-Publication Data

Oates, Laurel Currie, 1951- author.
 Just memos / Laurel Currie Oates, Professor of Law, Seattle University School
of Law, Anne Enquist Professor of Lawyering Skills, Director, Legal Writing
Program, Seattle University School of Law. -- Fourth edition.
    p. cm.
 Includes bibliographical references and index.
 ISBN 978-1-4548-3101-3 (alk. paper)
 1. Legal composition. I. Enquist, Anne, 1950- author. II. Title.
 KF250.O178 2014
 808.06'634--dc23
                                                        2014006307

About Wolters Kluwer Law & Business

Wolters Kluwer Law & Business is a leading global provider of intelligent information and digital solutions for legal and business professionals in key specialty areas, and respected educational resources for professors and law students. Wolters Kluwer Law & Business connects legal and business professionals as well as those in the education market with timely, specialized authoritative content and information-enabled solutions to support success through productivity, accuracy and mobility.

Serving customers worldwide, Wolters Kluwer Law & Business products include those under the Aspen Publishers, CCH, Kluwer Law International, Loislaw, ftwilliam.com and MediRegs family of products.

CCH products have been a trusted resource since 1913, and are highly regarded resources for legal, securities, antitrust and trade regulation, government contracting, banking, pension, payroll, employment and labor, and healthcare reimbursement and compliance professionals.

Aspen Publishers products provide essential information to attorneys, business professionals and law students. Written by preeminent authorities, the product line offers analytical and practical information in a range of specialty practice areas from securities law and intellectual property to mergers and acquisitions and pension/benefits. Aspen's trusted legal education resources provide professors and students with high-quality, up-to-date and effective resources for successful instruction and study in all areas of the law.

Kluwer Law International products provide the global business community with reliable international legal information in English. Legal practitioners, corporate counsel and business executives around the world rely on Kluwer Law journals, looseleafs, books, and electronic products for comprehensive information in many areas of international legal practice.

Loislaw is a comprehensive online legal research product providing legal content to law firm practitioners of various specializations. Loislaw provides attorneys with the ability to quickly and efficiently find the necessary legal information they need, when and where they need it, by facilitating access to primary law as well as state-specific law, records, forms and treatises.

ftwilliam.com offers employee benefits professionals the highest quality plan documents (retirement, welfare and non-qualified) and government forms (5500/PBGC, 1099 and IRS) software at highly competitive prices.

MediRegs products provide integrated health care compliance content and software solutions for professionals in healthcare, higher education and life sciences, including professionals in accounting, law and consulting.

Wolters Kluwer Law & Business, a division of Wolters Kluwer, is headquartered in New York. Wolters Kluwer is a market-leading global information services company focused on professionals.

In memory of my mother, Lucille Currie,
who led a full life and taught me to do the same.

To my family, Steve, Matt, Mary, and Jeff Enquist, and Ilana Stern
for their love, support, and patience.

Summary of Contents

Contents

List of Electronic Supplement Sections

See http://www.aspenlawschool.com/books/oates_legalwritinghand book.

Preface

This book, the fourth edition of *Just Memos*, sets out the materials that are in Books I and III of the sixth edition of *The Legal Writing Handbook*: It helps students make the transition from other types of writing to legal writing, it provides students with an introduction to the U.S. legal system and legal analysis and reading, and it walks students through the process of writing objective memoranda, opinion letters, e-memos, and email.

As you work through the materials in this book, keep in mind that writing a memo is a complex task. To do a good job, you must understand our legal system; you must know how to locate, select, and read the applicable statutes and cases; and you must be able to construct and evaluate each side's arguments. In addition, you must be a good writer. You must be able to use the conventional organizational schemes to present the law, the arguments, and your predictions clearly, precisely, and concisely. Finally, writing a good memo requires the exercise of judgment. You must exercise judgment in deciding when to stop researching, in determining which information the attorney needs, and in evaluating each side's arguments.

Instead of presenting each of these skills in isolation, *Just Memos* presents them in context. Chapter 6 shows five sample memos. Later chapters walk you through the process of writing a statement of facts, an issue statement and brief answer, a discussion section using different organizational schemes, and a conclusion. As you read through these chapters, keep your goal in mind. Instead of working to get an "A" on a particular assignment, use your assignments to learn how attorneys think and write about legal issues. By learning how to think and write as a lawyer, you will be a good student and you will develop the skills that you need to be a good attorney.

Acknowledgments

In writing this book, we have been fortunate to have had the critiques and counsel of numerous colleagues who have taught legal writing. A heartfelt thank you to our longtime colleagues Lori Bannai, Mary Bowman, Janet Dickson, Connie Krontz, Susan McClellan, Chris Rideout, and Mimi Samuel. We would also like to thank our newer colleagues, Merryn DeBenedetti, Kirsten Schimpff, and Denis Stearns for their help in drafting the chapters on e-memos. Merryn helped prepare the first draft of the chapter, Denis provided the problem that we have used as the primary example, and Kirsten shared her experiences from practice. In addition, we would like to thank our alum, Dan Brown, for giving us permission to use one of the e-memos that he drafted; Cheryl Kringle, Matthew Cram, and Peggy Graham for their insights about how e-memos are used in practice, and countless other attorneys for providing us with information about how they use e-memos. Thanks also go to Patrick Brown for his guidance on the section about the writing of philosophy majors, Eric Easton for his insights about journalism majors, and Theo Myhre for his invaluable help on the section about the writing of science majors and scientists.

Perhaps the most important collaborators in this project have been our students. Their writing appears throughout the book, and they were our first readers. So many made recommendations and allowed us to use their writing that we cannot mention them all, but we want them to know how much we appreciate their part in what we think of as "their book."

Just Memos

Introduction

Making the Transition

Everyone comes to law school with some writing experience. Whether you were an undergraduate or graduate student at a university, a business person, scientist, poet, paralegal, student, or attorney from a country other than the United States, you have come to a U.S. law school with a range of writing skills and experience that shape who you are as a writer.

For example, if you are coming to law school immediately after receiving your undergraduate degree, you have undoubtedly been shaped as a writer by the expectations of your undergraduate professors, particularly those in your major. Consciously or subconsciously, you have absorbed some of the customs and conventions of academic writing and the specific conventions of your major's discipline.

Similarly, if your most recent writing experiences have been from work, whether it be as a businessperson, social worker, police officer, or other professional, you too have absorbed the writing conventions of your field. The various writing projects and reports you wrote and read for work have shaped your beliefs about what is "good writing" and how it is done.

Even if you wrote for a living—as a novelist, journalist, poet, technical writer—or perhaps we should say, especially if you wrote for a living, you have been shaped as a writer by the work you did before law school. As a writer, you are more likely to be consciously aware of the conventions of the genre in which you were writing before entering law school, and you have undoubtedly honed the writing skills necessary to write successfully in that genre. The challenge, of course, will be to adapt those writing strengths to a new genre, legal writing, and to new readers, lawyers and judges in the U.S. legal community.

Whatever you were doing before law school, you were part of a specific culture — whether it be the world of health care, the world of school children, the world of wildlife biologists — and the writing that was done in those cultures was tailored for specific purposes and specific readers. The change to legal writing will require an adjustment.

Those of you who are coming to a U.S. law school from another country may have a more obvious cultural adjustment to make when it comes to writing. In some cases it will include the challenge of learning the writing conventions of another language, but even in cases in which the language of your home country is English, there will undoubtedly be cultural differences in what your new readers will expect from your written work.

In short, everyone coming to law school is making a transition from the writing he or she did before law school to the writing of the U.S. legal community. The trick will be to figure out what are the obvious and subtle similarities and differences between the writing culture you are coming from and the writing culture you are joining. Even if you were a paralegal before law school, you will have to figure out what was specific to the firm or legal setting in which you worked and what is generally true about writing for the larger, more generic legal community. At the very least, your specific role as a writer will have changed from paralegal to attorney, and that change alone will make a difference in the expectations your readers will have for your writing.

This chapter is designed to help law students make the transition to legal writing as smoothly and painlessly as possible. Several concepts are the keys to a successful transition: (1) understand the purpose of the new type of writing you are learning; (2) know what your new readers want and need from what you write; (3) understand your role as the writer in this genre; and (4) learn the specific conventions of the new type of writing you are adding to your writing repertoire.

§ 1.1   Understanding the Purpose of a Piece of Legal Writing

Here's an important truth that will help you make effective choices as you work as a writer: Once you understand what a piece of writing is supposed to accomplish — its purpose — you will have a sound basis for the many decisions you as the writer will make in creating a document. Put another way, you have about 90 percent of the information you need for creating a document once you know

- why you are writing something,
- what the document is supposed to do, and
- what the reader hopes to achieve by reading it.

Like other types of writing, legal writing exists to communicate. Lawyers write because they want to communicate information to their readers. But the broad term "communicate" is not specific enough to be particularly helpful as you transition to the new genre of legal writing.

Most legal writing exists for one or more of these three specific reasons:

1. to explain,
2. to persuade,
3. to memorialize.

Whether you are writing a letter to a client, an office memo for a senior partner, or a brief for a judge, you will undoubtedly have as one of your primary purposes the goal of explaining. You might be explaining to the client that the law is on her side and therefore she is likely to be successful if she sues her employer. You might be explaining to a partner how the courts have interpreted a statute and why that interpretation means the firm's biggest client should not include a particular term in a contract. You might be explaining to a judge why an application of the law to your client's facts would lead to a just result.

If clear explanation is the first goal of most legal writing, then the goal of effective persuasion is not far behind. Sometimes the persuasion is subtle. In writing an opinion letter, you may be persuading a client to see the strengths and weaknesses of his or her legal position. You may also be subtly persuading that client to see not only the limitations of his or her options but also the wisdom of adopting one particular option.

Persuasion is also part of legal memoranda. Although you will see in Chapters 11-14 that an office memorandum should be an objective assessment of the law and its application to a case, a good office memo also includes persuasion in the sense that it anticipates the arguments each side is likely to make and, in doing so, showcases which ones will be more or less persuasive.

The goal of persuasion is most obvious, and important, in brief writing. When writing to a court, you will be working to get a judge or justice to see the law, precedent, the facts, and the arguments from your side's point of view. You will want that judge or justice to view the case from your perspective so he or she will rule in your favor. When you write for a court, you will have clear-cut evidence of whether you succeeded or failed in your goal to persuade, and that will be what the court decides as a result of reading your writing.

The third goal of most legal writing — to memorialize — is especially evident in documents like contracts and wills. The document exists as a statement of what the contracting parties agreed to or how the deceased person wanted his or her assets distributed. Opinion letters, office memos, and briefs also have a goal of memorializing the work an attorney has done. Because the work is preserved in writing, the client can go back over a letter and review the advice. An office memo written for one client's case may be used by other attorneys in the office working on that case. Undoubtedly, it will be filed for future consideration, and it might be reviewed and used again, at least in part, if the client has a similar problem or even if another client has a similar problem. In litigation, a brief written in support of or opposition to a pretrial motion can become part of the record on appeal, recording what the parties did, or did not argue, to the trial court.

Before leaving the topic of purpose in legal writing, let's think again about the transition most new law students are making from writing they did before they came to law school to writing they will do as lawyers. Note how different the purposes of student writing are from the purposes of "real world" legal writing. Student writers write to prove that they have learned something. They write to demonstrate knowledge and mastery of a subject, and quite frankly, to get a good grade. As a general rule, readers of student writing (professors) do not read student essays, reports, and research papers to gain information or learn anything new. Because professors are already experts in the subject matter, their purpose in reading is to evaluate how well the writer has learned the material. This difference between student writing and real world writing is actually a rather profound one, and one that accounts for many of the other differences between writing that is done for class and writing that is done for professional reasons.

Keep in mind, then, as you work on the assignments for your legal writing and research classes that, even though the assignments are part of a law class, in almost every case, the writing tasks are intended to simulate real world practice situations. In other words, you are not supposed to be writing like you are a student with the purposes of a student writer. You are supposed to be writing as if you are a practicing lawyer with one or more of the real world goals of explaining, persuading, and memorializing. Even though you are still a student learning how to write like a lawyer (and hoping for a good grade), stay focused on key concept number 1: Know your purpose for writing.

> ### COMMON MISTAKE 1
>
> Some students in legal writing courses mistakenly assume that their legal writing professors will be reading and evaluating their papers as though they, the professors, are the real readers. Consequently, these students leave things out of the writing on the assumption that "my professor already knows that." While it is true that your professor undoubtedly researched the problem and knows the analysis inside out, he or she will be evaluating your writing from the point of view of a "real world" reader—someone who is depending on the writer's research and analysis and who was not in class and participating in the class discussions on the issues.

> ### COMMON MISTAKE 2
>
> Some new legal writers make the "undergraduate mistake" when they are writing their first office memos: They want to make sure their legal writing professor or their supervising attorney knows how much work they did and how thoroughly they researched the problem. Consequently, they include far more cases than are necessary to understand the analysis or make the arguments. This mistake often comes directly from their undergraduate experience. As undergraduates, many of us were rewarded for writing papers that showed how much work we had done. Length often translated into high grades. Law school and law firm writing is different. Legal writers should adopt the real world reader's point of view about length, which is "I'm busy. Tell me what I need to know and then stop writing."

§ 1.2   Writing for Legal Readers

Closely related to understanding your purpose in writing is understanding who your reader or readers are. In legal writing, the goal is not just to explain or persuade in the abstract. Instead, you are writing to real readers, readers who need your writing with all of its research, analysis, arguments, citations, conclusions, and insights in order to do their jobs.

Real legal readers include both lawyers and nonlawyers. When writing for a reader who is not a lawyer, keep in mind how much or how little experience that person may have with law and legal matters. For example, clients who are not lawyers and are not experienced in matters related to law may need explanations in lay terms. Other nonlawyer readers may have a sophisticated understanding of law and their legal issues and would find a watered down explanation condescending. The point, of course, is that an effective writer will adjust his or her approach accordingly.

To some extent, you may have to make similar adjustments for readers who are lawyers.[1] All lawyers do not have the same background or practice experience. In some situations, a senior partner who is the reader for a given memo about a tax issue may be the firm's tax expert. In such a situation, the writer can assume much more knowledge and start the discussion further into the law and analysis. Writing a memo for a different reader, maybe someone who hasn't looked at tax law since law school, would require an adjustment. In this second situation, the smart writer will give a quick refresher and enough background to get that kind of reader up to speed quickly so that he or she is ready to follow the analysis.

Anticipating your reader's knowledge base is only the beginning of writing for legal readers. Most legal readers, whether they are senior partners or judges, tend to have a few common characteristics, and these characteristics have shaped their notions of what is good legal writing. First, they tend to be very busy. Consequently, they appreciate writing that gets to the point quickly and lays out information clearly. They don't want writers to take them down every blind alley the writer had to explore before figuring out that information was irrelevant. They don't give extra credit for discussing additional cases or extra arguments if those cases or arguments aren't needed. They are annoyed, not impressed, if they think the writer is padding the document. Therefore, before including something in a piece of legal writing, ask yourself, "does my reader need to know this?" Notice that this question is different from "did I need to know this in order to analyze the problem?" Legal readers will expect legal writers to be selective about what they include in the document and to synthesize the relevant material. They will expect legal writers to understand that their time is valuable and to write, and edit, with that in mind.

Second, legal readers appreciate — actually demand — clear organization. They want the information they need laid out in a well-structured, easy-to-follow fashion. They appreciate roadmaps that give them an overview of the analysis and signposts that guide them through it, all the while focusing their attention on "where the fight is." They like transitions that help them see the connections between ideas and follow the writer's line of reasoning. They appreciate mini-conclusions that summarize a section and macro conclusions that summarize all the main pieces of a large document. In short, it is hard to over-emphasize how important a clear and explicit organization is to most legal readers.

---

1. The generalizations in this section about legal readers refer to U.S. legal readers.

The fact that experienced, sophisticated attorneys want such explicit organization and analysis may come as a surprise to some new legal writers. After all, not all cultures value explicitness in the same way the U.S. legal culture does. In fact, leaving things unsaid and for readers to figure out is a mark of sophisticated writing in some academic cultures and in some Asian and Middle Eastern cultures. Stating one's point so directly may be considered not just unsophisticated but also brash and even rude. For writers coming from these backgrounds, it may feel unnatural at first to spell out points so clearly and explicitly, but over time it will become second nature as these writers better understand how writing works in the U.S. legal culture.

Third, because legal readers need the writing they read in order to do their jobs well, they insist on the highest levels of professionalism. This means that accuracy and precision are critical virtues in legal writing—no playing loose with the facts or the law. Legal readers depend on their writers to get the facts and law right and to be strictly accurate in how they are represented.

The emphasis on professionalism also means that mistakes such as poor citation form; the misspelling, especially of a name; and grammar, punctuation, and proofreading errors matter more than they do in other kinds of writing. Being accurate, precise, and polished in written documents are all critical parts of being professional that legal readers expect.

If accuracy, brevity, clarity, precision, and professionalism are high priorities for legal readers, then the next obvious question is what isn't such a high priority for them? Unlike a great deal of undergraduate writing, legal writing places less emphasis on creativity. While the professor reader in an undergraduate course in poetry or creative writing might reward an unusual approach to a topic or a novel twist in a plot, readers of legal writing tend to prefer writing that is far more conventional. Creativity is nice, especially if a creative argument turns out to be a winning argument, but remember that legal readers are not reading to be entertained. The writing is all about work and getting a job done, so creative introductions or unusual analytical approaches take a back seat to accuracy, brevity, and clarity for legal readers.

Similarly, legal readers resent unnecessary complexity. Consequently, when it comes to things like sentence structure and word choice, the acronym KISS for "keep it simple stupid" is useful advice. Legal readers do not want to puzzle over a sentence or word. For them, the sign of a well-written sentence is one that can be understood the first time they read it. For them, the well-chosen word is, more often than not, one they already know. If an unfamiliar word is required in a given instance, they expect the writer to define it immediately within the writing. Legal writers don't need to worry that they are "dumbing down" the writing when they present information as simply as possible. For legal readers, clear communication is the goal; they don't want to be dazzled by the writer's vocabulary or convoluted syntax.

Does this mean that legal readers are incapable of handling complexity or that they have weak vocabularies? Certainly not. The appreciation for simplicity goes back to the initial point about how busy legal readers are. The legal issues are often so inherently complex that no one wants added unnecessary complexity that will simply take up time and attention.

> **COMMON MISTAKE 3**   Some new legal writers make the mistake of "dressing up their ideas." They fear that if they state things simply they will seem unsophisticated. Here again, the mistake may be the result of an undergraduate writing experience that rewarded students for making simple ideas seem complex. The opposite is true in legal writing: You will be rewarded and appreciated if you can make complex ideas seem simple.

§ 1.3   Understanding Your Role as a Legal Writer

When a junior associate or a legal intern is assigned to research and write a client letter, office memo, or brief, the expectation is that the associate or intern will spend many hours researching and analyzing the legal problem and then write up that work in a document that will take the client, assigning attorney, or judge approximately fifteen minutes to read and understand.

An underlying assumption of the U.S. legal culture, then, is that the reader's time is more valuable than the writer's time. Legal readers, including supervising attorneys, partners in law firms, and judges, tend to have positions of authority over the writers of legal memos. Consequently, writers are expected to expend their time and energy writing clearly so that readers do not have to spend extra time and energy understanding what they are reading.

This does not mean, then, that the writer's role is unimportant — far from it. As the writer, your role is to become the expert on a given case. Through careful study of the facts and thorough research, you will be the one who knows what law is the controlling law and which cases are the key cases. In addition, after reading the arguments set out in the cases and the courts' evaluation of those arguments, you will be the one who is in the best position to predict what each side will argue and how the court will view those arguments.

Ultimately, your role as the writer of a client letter is to be the one who advises the client about what he or she should do next and why. Your role as the writer of an office memo is to give your educated opinion about what the court is likely to do in the current case and be clear about how you reached that opinion. Your role as the writer of a brief is to figure out what approach and arguments will persuade the court to rule in your client's favor. In short, your role is to exercise expert judgment, and in fact, that is exactly what you are paid to do when you are assigned to write a client letter, office memorandum, or brief.

You need to exercise judgment

- about what are the legally significant facts,
- about what statute(s) or common law doctrine will govern,
- about which cases are the key analogous cases, and
- about which arguments the court will find persuasive.

As new attorneys or law students, many find the legal writer's role a bit intimidating. It can be hard enough to be confident that you have found the right law and key cases without trying to create brand new, never-seen-before arguments, or worse, predicting what a court will do or convincing a court what it should do. Take heart, though. Many of the arguments will be variations of ones you see in the cases (no one is expecting you to make this all up from scratch), and law school is exactly the right place to learn and practice these skills.

A key part of your role as well will be to cite authority (at least in office memos and briefs) to support each of the points you make. The citations show that you have the support of the law, other courts, and other legal minds behind your analysis. Furthermore, by including the source for the facts and correctly citing the record, statutes, cases, books, law review articles, and other secondary sources, you create a document in which everything about the case comes together. Thus, one major aspect of your role as a legal writer is to be the synthesizer — the one who brings all the relevant material together and presents it in a way that gets the job done.

One final point about your role as a legal writer: Every piece of writing you create in your role as a lawyer reflects on your professionalism. Words are the tools of your trade, so how you use words represents how seriously you take your work. In the heat of the moment or in the thick of an argument, it can be tempting to slip into a sarcastic or denigrating tone. Resist the temptation. Be particularly careful to maintain a professional tone in all the writing you do. As a lawyer, your writing, including the tone you use, is a big part of how you are representing your client and yourself.

§ 1.4   Learning the Conventions of Legal Writing

In the earlier discussion of the purposes of legal writing, legal readers, and the writer's role, a number of the common practices and conventions of legal writing have already been mentioned:

1. a high priority on clarity, brevity, precision, and organization
2. an appreciation for explicit roadmaps, signposts, topic sentences, and transitions
3. an expectation for easy-to-read sentences and paragraphs, but not bullet points or charts
4. a requirement for citations to authority
5. an expectation about professional tone.

In addition, new legal writers may be struck by a number of other conventions of legal writing. For example, specific formats are often expected and sometimes required in legal writing. Legal readers expect an office memo to have an issue statement, sometimes called a Question Presented, which seems to be an artifact from an earlier time. Briefs have required cover pages, tables of authorities, argumentative headings, and page and paragraph numbering systems. Therefore, when you are assigned a new type of legal writing, check to see whether there are court rules governing the format and review some samples or models of that type of writing. Knowing format requirements before starting to write is more efficient than spending a lot of time creating a format only to find it does not meet expectations.

Less surprising is the convention to set out a rule before applying it to the facts or making an argument using the rule. Also not surprising, at least for some, is the custom of setting out general rules before more specific rules. In fact, throughout legal writing the convention is to organize material from general to specific.

Writers of academic prose may be immediately comfortable with other conventions, such as the tendency not to use contractions or the use of the third person rather than the first person "I" or "we" or the second person "you." The practice of staying in the third person means that language such as "I think," "I believe," or "I feel" is not typically used in legal writing. Rather than write "I think the court is unlikely to find," most lawyers write "the court is unlikely to find." Some firms do make an exception and use the first person "our" when referring to "our client" or "our case," but others maintain the more formal "the client" or the client's name when referring to the case.

§ 1.5   Advice for Specific Groups

Even though it can be a bit risky to generalize about the customs and conventions of any given community of writers, knowing about some patterns in different writing cultures can ease a writer's transition into legal writing. Making that knowledge more explicit can help a writer look at his or her assumptions about "good writing" and see which assumptions apply and which do not apply to legal writing.

Below is a list of different communities of writers and some of the common assumptions those communities have about writing and how those assumptions are similar to or different from the underlying assumptions that shape legal writing. In creating this list, however, we do not mean to suggest that legal writing is somehow "right" in its assumptions about what makes good writing and these other fields or cultures are somehow "wrong." In fact, we would argue that the differences make sense given the differences in readers, purpose, and culture. Nor do we mean to suggest that writers need to erase and replace what they know about how to write for the communities they were part of before joining the legal community. Instead we would suggest that writers think of the experience of learning to do legal writing as adding a new category or genre of writing to their writing repertoire.

One final point: Although we cannot discuss every undergraduate major, previous profession, or culture, we hope that the insights about how different disciplines and cultures view writing will help you make a smooth transition into legal writing.

§ 1.5.1   English Majors

Most English majors come to law school believing that they will do exceptionally well in their legal writing classes. In most cases, this proves to be true, but their success tends to happen more toward the end of the course rather than at the beginning. Early in the course, English majors may resist what they consider the formulaic and restrictive nature of legal writing. They complain that it "stifles their creativity," and they are frustrated because they cannot show off their vocabularies and sophisticated writing style. Once they accept the idea that they are learning a new genre, in much the way a poet would adapt when learning to write screenplays, they stop resisting, start adapting, and then gradually see how they can channel some of their earlier skills into legal writing. Their storytelling ability helps them write the facts; they apply their creativity to constructing arguments; and they bring the close reading skills they developed for literature and poetry to their reading of statutes and rules.

§ 1.5.2   Philosophy Majors

Like English majors, philosophy majors are likely to feel that their creativity is stifled and their analytic ability tightly restricted by the standard modes of legal analysis. In their doctrinal courses, they may be initially surprised by the heavy emphasis on precedent and the layers of doctrine, as well as disappointed by what may appear to them to be the law's emphasis on rhetoric.

As they learn to write office memos, philosophy majors are likely to find the construction of rules paragraphs to be arbitrary; their natural instinct will be to think about the validity of the rules rather than simply lay them out for the readers. Once they get to the arguments, philosophy majors are likely to feel at home, and it is here that their background in logic can give them an edge.

§ 1.5.3   Journalism Majors and Journalists

Like their "cousins" the English majors, journalism students and journalists bring an interesting combination of advantages and disadvantages to legal writing. Perhaps most important is the simple fact that they have fresh writing skills. They come to law school and the practice of law with their writing skills honed by lots of practice. In addition, journalists are already well schooled in the concept of writing for a specific audience. Many of them have learned to adjust their style to the varying demands of straight news reporting to the specific conventions of the sports page, the op-ed page, the lifestyle and feature sections, or a blog. Initially some journalists may resent having to tone down their style a bit for legal writing, particularly if they have grown accustomed to writing "zinger" sentences or writing with vivid language and extended metaphors for the sports page.

Yet another advantage that journalists bring to legal writing is their thoroughness and accuracy with the facts. They are used to answering the questions "who," "what," "when," "where," and "how," and they are also used to being required to state the source for the facts.

Organization and paragraph length are usually the two areas in which journalists will have to adjust. The typical journalism piece is written in an inverted-pyramid, front-loaded style so the editors can cut the piece from the end to fit space limitations and, if a reader loses interest and stops reading midway in a story, he or she still will have gotten the key ideas in the opening sentences. While much of legal writing also puts key points (rules, the best cases, and arguments) up front, the organizational structure is shaped by very different considerations and reader expectations. A threshold issue will almost always be treated first, even if it is relatively easy to resolve. Even though legal readers are busy, most will read a memo through to the end and not treat the last pages or lines as optional. For the most part, true paragraphs do not exist in journalism. Because of the narrow width of many newspaper columns, the convention in journalism is to write mostly one-sentence paragraphs. Journalists transitioning into writing about law have to learn to write longer paragraphs.

Finally, most journalists have learned to be extraordinarily careful with spelling, particularly the spelling of proper names, which is an asset that carries over nicely into legal writing. Punctuation, however, may be a different matter. Journalism prefers "open punctuation," which means using as little punctuation as the rules will allow; legal writing, by contrast, tends to used "closed punctuation," which means that lawyers lean in the other direction and use commas when the rules give them the option to do so. The serial comma, for example, is generally omitted in journalism (no comma before the "and" in "red, white and blue") but is included in legal writing ("red, white, and blue").

§ 1.5.4   Science Majors and Scientists

Science majors and scientists bring a strong set of skills in critical thinking and formal analysis that individuals in many other professions or disciplines may lack. The ability to evaluate evidence, make logical connections, and draw plausible conclusions forms the very basis of substantive legal analysis. However, legal writing diverges from scientific writing in several ways that may prove challenging or even frustrating.

In terms of writing style, legal writing favors active voice sentences, not the passive voice sentences used as the professional standard in scientific writing. Formal organization of various legal writing projects requires a different organizational structure than scientific writing (e.g., title, hypothesis, materials, methods, observations, results, conclusion), although experience working with any formal structure will be of help in legal writing.

In terms of substantive analysis, deriving governing rules and tests from case law precedent or statutory language is similar to formulating the hypothesis and methods sections of a scientific paper. However, on a practical level jurisprudence has little in common with scientific laws and validity studies. Science majors and scientists may find their experience similar to the frustration experienced by philosophy students. "Law" is not created by systematic application of the scientific method in order to discover logically necessary, objective truths with universal application that can be repeated and verified by any scientist in a variety of conditions. Rather, "law" is created by a combination of individual circumstances, public policies, concepts of fairness, tradition, emotion, credibility, economic realities, political considerations, and persuasive argument, among other factors.

In fact, legal reasoning and persuasive argument may represent the greatest challenges to science majors and scientists engaged in legal writing. Although persuasive argument skills have a subtle use in the results and conclusion parts of a scientific paper, the rhetorical strategies and skills necessary for legal writing will likely draw on a legal writer's experience in non-scientific areas of life. Consequently, science majors and scientists transitioning into writing about law should be prepared to merge an "objective" approach with a more subjective "relational" approach.

§ 1.5.5   Writers from Other Cultures

Each of us absorbs the writing preferences of our first language and our native culture. Those preferences are often so deeply embedded in the many aspects of writing that they are hard to see and even harder to articulate. Often we are unaware that different cultures (and different professions) have different ideas about what makes something "good writing."

The U.S. culture, and specifically the U.S. legal culture, is no different from any other professional culture. It has expectations and preferences that have developed over time about how something should be written. Students who come to U.S. law schools wanting to learn U.S. legal writing may find it useful to begin by examining the cultural preferences related to writing from their native cultures and languages and then compare those preferences with those of the U.S. legal culture.

The United States Legal System

The United States system of government. For some, it is the secret to democracy, the power to elect one's leaders and the right to speak freely. For others, it is a horrendous bureaucracy, a maze through which one must struggle to obtain a benefit, to change a law, or to get a day in court. For still others, it is more abstract—a chart in an eighth-grade civics book describing the three branches of government and explaining the system of checks and balances.

For lawyers, the United States system of government is all of these things and more. It is the foundation for their knowledge of the law, the stage on which they play out their professional roles, the arena for the very serious game of law.

No matter which metaphor you prefer—foundation, stage, arena—the point is the same. To be an effective researcher, you must understand the system. You must know the framework before you can work well within it.

Like most complex systems, the United States system of government can be analyzed in a number of different ways. You can focus on its three branches—the executive branch, the legislative branch, and the judicial branch—or you can focus on the system's two parts, the federal government and the state governments.

In this chapter we do both. We look first at the three branches, examining both their individual functions and their interrelationships. We then examine the relationship between state and federal government, again with an eye toward their individual functions and powers.

§ 2.1   The Three Branches of Government

Just as the medical student must understand both the various organs that make up the human body and their relationship to each other, the law student must understand both the three branches of government and the relationships among them.

§ 2.1.1   The Executive Branch

The first of the three branches is the executive branch. In the federal system, the executive power is vested in the President; in the states, it is vested in the governor. (See Article II, Section 1 of the United States Constitution and the constitutions of the various states.) In general, the executive branch has the power to implement and enforce laws. It oversees public projects, administers public benefit programs, and controls law enforcement agencies.

The executive branch also has powers that directly affect our system of law. For example, the President (or a governor) can control the law-making function of the legislative branch by exercising his or her power to convene and adjourn the Congress (or state legislature) or by vetoing legislation. Similarly, the President (or a governor) can shape the decisions of the courts through his or her judicial nominations or by directing the attorney general to enforce or not to enforce certain laws.

§ 2.1.2   The Legislative Branch

The second branch is the legislative branch. Congress's powers are enumerated in Article I, Section 8, of the United States Constitution, which gives Congress, among other things, the power to lay and collect taxes, borrow money, regulate commerce with foreign nations and among the states, establish uniform naturalization and bankruptcy laws, promote the progress of science and the useful arts by creating copyright laws, and punish counterfeiting. Powers not granted Congress are given to the states or left to the people. (See the Tenth Amendment to the United States Constitution.) The state constitutions enumerate the powers given to the state legislatures.

Like the executive branch, the legislative branch exercises power over the other two branches. It can check the actions of the executive branch by enacting or refusing to enact legislation requested by the executive, by controlling the budget and, at least at the federal level, by consenting or refusing to consent to nominations made by the executive.

The legislative branch's power over the judicial branch is less obvious. At one level, it can control the judiciary through its power to establish courts (Article I, Section 8, grants Congress the power to establish inferior federal courts) and its power to consent to or reject the executive branch's judicial nominations. However, the most obvious control it has over the judiciary is its power to enact legislation that supersedes, or replaces, a common law or court-made doctrine or rule.

The legislative branch also shares its law-making power with the executive branch. In enacting legislation, it sometimes gives the executive branch the power to promulgate the regulations needed to implement or enforce the legislation. For example, although Congress (the legislative branch) enacted the Internal Revenue Code, the Internal Revenue Service (part of the executive branch) promulgates the regulations needed to implement that code.

§ 2.1.3   The Judicial Branch

The third branch is the judicial branch. Article III, Section 1, of the United States Constitution vests the judicial power of the United States in one supreme court and in such inferior courts as Congress may establish. The state constitutions establish and grant power to the state courts.

a.   The Hierarchical Nature of the Court System

Both the federal and the state court systems are hierarchical. At the lowest level are the trial courts, whose primary function is fact-finding. The judge or jury hears the evidence and enters a judgment.

At the next level are the intermediate courts of appeals. These courts hear the majority of appeals, deciding (1) whether the trial court applied the right law and (2) whether there is sufficient evidence to support the jury's verdict or the trial judge's findings of fact and conclusions of law. Unlike the trial courts, these courts do not conduct trials. There are no witnesses, and the only exhibits are the exhibits that were admitted during trial. The decisions of the appellate courts are based solely on the written trial record and the attorneys' arguments.

At the top level are the states' highest courts and the Supreme Court of the United States. The primary function of these courts is to make law. They hear only those cases that involve issues of great public import or cases in which different divisions or circuits have adopted or applied conflicting rules of law. Like the intermediate courts of appeals, these courts do not hear evidence; they only review the trial court record. See Exhibit 2.1.

An example illustrates the role each court plays. In *State v. Strong*, a criminal case, the defendant, Mr. Strong, was charged with possession of a controlled substance. At the trial court level, both the State and the defendant presented witnesses and physical evidence. On the basis of this evidence, the trial court decided the case on its merits, with the trial judge deciding the questions of law (whether the evidence should be suppressed) and the jury deciding the questions of fact (whether the State had proved all of the elements of the crime beyond a reasonable doubt).

Both issues were decided against the defendant: The trial court judge ruled that the evidence was admissible, and the jury found that the State had met its burden of proof. Disagreeing with both determinations, the defendant filed an appeal with the intermediate court of appeals.

In deciding this appeal, the appellate court could consider only two issues: whether the trial court judge erred when he denied the defendant's motion to suppress and whether there was sufficient evidence to support the jury's verdict.

Because the first issue raised a question of law, the appellate court could review the issue de novo. The court did not need to defer to the judgment of the trial court judge. Instead, the appellate court could exercise its own independent judgment to decide the issue on its merits.

The appellate court had much less latitude with respect to the second issue. Because the second issue raised a question of fact rather than law, the appellate court could not substitute its judgment for that of the jury. It could only review the jury's findings to make sure that they were supported by the evidence. When the question is one of fact, the appellate court may decide only (1) whether there is sufficient evidence to support the jury's verdict or (2) whether the jury's verdict is clearly erroneous. It may not substitute its judgment for the judgment of the jury.

Exhibit 2.1	**The Roles of the Trial, Intermediate, and Supreme Courts**

Trial Court

■ The trial court hears witnesses and views evidence.
■ The trial court judge decides issues of law; the jury decides questions of fact. (When there is no jury, the trial court judge decides both the questions of law and the questions of fact.)

Intermediate Court of Appeals

■ The intermediate court of appeals reviews the written record and exhibits from the trial court.
■ When an issue raises a question of law, the intermediate court of appeals may substitute its judgment for the judgment of the trial court judge; when an issue raises a question of fact, the appellate court must defer to the decision of the finder of fact (the jury or, if there was no jury, the trial judge).

Supreme, or Highest, Court

■ Like the intermediate court of appeals, it reviews the written record and exhibits from the trial court.
■ Like the intermediate court of appeals, it has broad powers to review questions of law: It determines whether the trial court and intermediate court of appeals applied the right law correctly. Its power to review factual issues is, however, very limited. Like the intermediate court of appeals, it can determine only whether there is sufficient evidence to support the decision of the jury or, if there was no jury, the decision of the trial court judge.

Regardless of the type of issue (fact or law), the appellate court must base its decision on the written trial court record and exhibits and the attorneys' arguments. Consequently, in *Strong*, the intermediate court of appeals did not see or hear any of the witnesses. The only people present when the appeal was argued were the appellate court judges assigned to hear the case and Strong's and the State's attorneys. Not even the defendant, Mr. Strong, was present.

If Mr. Strong lost his first appeal, he could petition the state supreme court (through a petition for discretionary review) and ask that court to review the intermediate court of appeals' decision. If the state supreme court granted the petition, its review, like that of the intermediate court of appeals, would be limited. Although the supreme court would review the issue of law de novo, it would have to defer to the jury's decision on the questions of fact.

Most of the cases that appear in law school casebooks are appellate court decisions, for example, decisions of the United States Court of Appeals or the United States Supreme Court or decisions from state appellate courts. These cases, however, represent only a small, and perhaps not representative, percentage of the disputes that lawyers see during the course of their practice.

Accordingly, as you read the cases in the casebooks, remember that you are seeing only the proverbial tip of the iceberg. For a case to reach the United States Supreme Court, the parties must have had the financial means to pursue it, and the Court must have found that the issue raised was significant enough to grant review.

> **PRACTICE POINTER**
>
> As you will learn in Civil Procedure, to hear a case a court must have both subject matter jurisdiction and personal jurisdiction. Stated very simply, a court has subject matter jurisdiction when it has power to hear a particular type of case. For example, the federal courts have subject matter jurisdiction to hear cases involving the United States Constitution and United States statutes, state courts of general jurisdiction have subject matter jurisdiction to hear cases involving the state constitution and state statutes, and municipal courts have subject matter jurisdiction to hear cases involving city ordinances. It is not, though, enough that a court has subject matter jurisdiction. The court must also have personal jurisdiction or the power to hear and decide cases involving the parties to the case or controversy.

b.   The Federal Courts

In the federal system, most cases are heard initially in the federal district courts, the primary trial courts in that system. These courts have original jurisdiction over most federal questions and have the power to review the decisions of some administrative agencies. Each state has at least one district court, and many have several. For example, Indiana has the District Court for Northern Indiana and the District Court for Southern Indiana. Cases that are not heard in the district court are usually heard in one of several specialized courts, for example, the United States Tax Court, the United States Court of Federal Claims, or the United States Court of International Trade.

In the federal system, the intermediate court of appeals is the United States Court of Appeals. There are currently thirteen circuits: eleven numbered circuits, the District of Columbia Circuit, and the Federal Circuit. See Exhibit 2.2. The Federal Circuit, which was created in 1982, reviews the decisions of the United States Court of Federal Claims and the United States Court of International Trade, as well as some administrative decisions.

> **PRACTICE POINTER**
>
> For an electronic copy of a map showing the federal circuits, see *http://www.uscourts.gov/court_locator.aspx*

| Exhibit 2.2 | The Thirteen Federal Judicial Circuits |

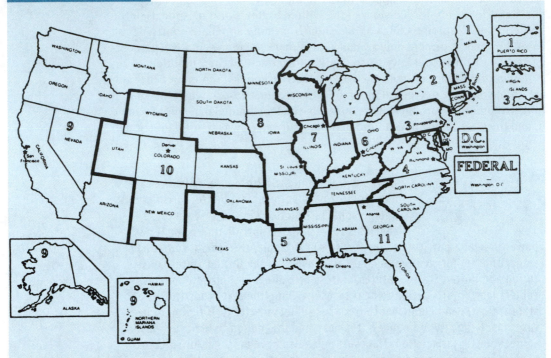

Reprinted from *Federal Reporter* (West's National Reporter System) with permission of West, a Thomson Reuters business.

The highest federal court is the United States Supreme Court. Although many people believe that the Supreme Court is all-powerful, in fact it is not. As with other courts, there are limits on the Supreme Court's powers. It can play only one of two roles.

In one role, the United States Supreme Court is similar to the state supreme courts. In the federal system, the United States Supreme Court is the highest court, the court of last resort. In contrast, in its other role, it is the final arbiter of federal constitutional law, interpreting the United States Constitution and determining whether the federal government or a state has violated rights granted under the United States Constitution.

Thus, although people often assert that they will take their case all the way to the Supreme Court, they may not be able to. As a general rule, the Supreme Court may hear a case only if it involves a question of federal constitutional law or a federal statute. The Supreme Court does not have the power to hear cases involving only questions of state law. For example, although the United States Supreme Court has the power to determine whether a state's marriage dissolution statutes are constitutional, the Court does not have the power to hear purely factual questions, such as whether it would be in the best interests of a child for custody to be granted to the father or whether child support should be set at $300 rather than $400 per month.

Each year the United States Supreme Court receives more than 7,000 requests for review (writs of certiorari). Of the approximately 100 cases that the Court actually hears, the overwhelming majority are appeals from the federal courts.

Exhibit 2.3 illustrates the relationships among the various federal courts.

Because the United States District Courts and Courts of Appeals hear so many cases, not all of their decisions are "published." When they are published, decisions from the United States District Courts are published in either the *Federal Supplement*, or *Federal Rules Decisions*, and decisions from the United States Courts of Appeals are published in the *Federal Reporter*. (Decisions from the specialized courts are published in specialized reporters.

> **PRACTICE POINTER**
>
> A "published" decision is a decision that is published in a set of books called a "reporter." (For more about reporters, see §4.2.4b.) Thus, decisions that appear on Lexis Advance®, WestlawNext™, Bloomberg Law, or a free website but that are not in a reporter are not published decisions. They are unpublished, or unreported, decisions. In some jurisdictions, you cannot cite to an unpublished decision in a brief to that jurisdiction's courts. To find out whether you can cite to an unpublished decision, see your local court rules.

All United States Supreme Court decisions are published. The official reporter is *United States Reports*, and the two unofficial reporters are *Supreme Court Reporter* and *United States Supreme Court Reports, Lawyers' Edition*.

Exhibit 2.3   The Federal Court System

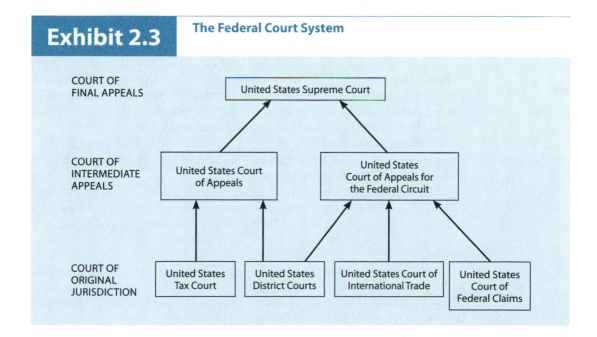

Exhibit 2.4	**The State Court System**

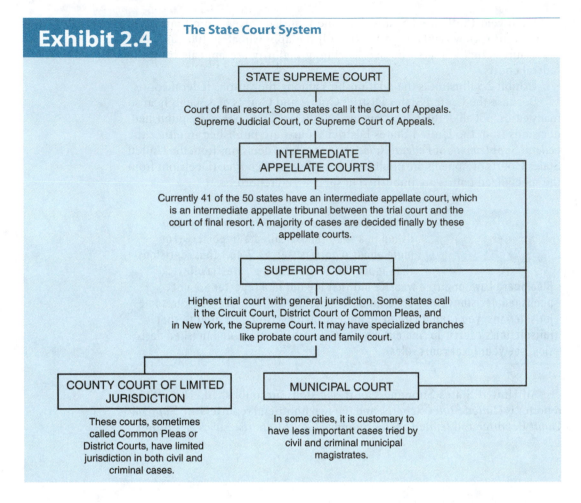

c. **State Courts**

A number of courts operate within the states. At the lowest level are courts of limited jurisdiction. These courts hear only certain types of cases or cases involving only limited amounts of money. Municipal or city courts are courts of limited jurisdiction, as are county or district courts and small claims courts.

At the next level are courts of general jurisdiction. These courts have the power to review the decisions of courts of limited jurisdiction and original jurisdiction over claims arising under state law, whether that law is the state constitution, state statutes, or state common law.

About three-quarters of the states now have an intermediate court of appeals. These courts hear appeals as of right from the state courts of general jurisdiction, and the bulk of their caseload is criminal appeals. Because of the size of their workload, many of these courts have several divisions or districts.

Every state has a state "supreme" court. These courts review the decisions of the state trial courts and courts of appeals and are the final arbiters of questions of state constitutional, statutory, and common law. Exhibit 2.4 illustrates the typical relationship among the various state courts.

Decisions of state trial courts are not usually published. In addition, because of the volume, not all decisions of intermediate state courts of appeals are published. Those that are, and all decisions of the state supreme court, appear in one of West Publishing Company's regional reporters and, if the state has one, the state's official reporter.

d. Other Courts

There are also several other court systems. As sovereign entities, many Native American tribes have their own judicial systems, as does the United States military.

§ 2.2   The Relationship Between the Federal and State Governments

It is not enough, however, to look at our system of government only from the perspective of its three branches. To understand the system, you must also understand the relationship between the federal and state governments.

§ 2.2.1   A Short History

Like most things, our system of government is the product of our history. From the early 1600s until 1781, the "united states" were not united. Instead, the "country" was composed of independent colonies, all operating under different charters and each having its own laws and legal system. Although the colonies traded with each other, the relationship among the colonies was no closer than the relationship among the European countries prior to 1992. It was not until the Articles of Confederation were adopted in 1781 that the "states" ceded any of their rights to a federal government.

Even though the states ceded more rights when the Constitution became effective in 1789, they preserved most of their own law. Each state retained its own executive, its own legislature and laws, and its own court system.

Thus, our system of government is really two systems, a federal system and the fifty state systems, with the United States Constitution brokering the relationship between the two.

§ 2.2.2   The Relationship Between Laws Enacted by Congress and Those Enacted by the State Legislatures

As citizens of the United States, we are subject to two sets of laws: federal law and the law of the state in which we are citizens (or in which we act).

Most of the time, there is no conflict between these two sets of laws: federal law governs some conduct; state law, other conduct. For example, federal law governs bankruptcy proceedings, and state law governs divorce.

Occasionally, however, both Congress and a state legislature enact laws governing the same conduct. Sometimes these laws coexist. For example, both Congress and the states have enacted drug laws. Acting under the powers granted to it under the Commerce Clause, Congress has made it illegal to import controlled substances or to transport them across state lines. The states, acting consistently with the powers reserved to them, have made illegal the possession or sale of controlled substances within the state. In such instances, citizens are subject to both laws. A defendant may be charged under federal law with transporting a drug across state lines and under state law with possession.

There are times, however, when federal and state law do not complement each other and cannot coexist. An act can be legal under federal law but illegal under state law. In such instances, federal law preempts state law, provided that the federal law is constitutional. As provided in the Supremacy Clause, laws enacted by Congress under the powers granted to it under the Constitution are the "supreme Law of the Land; and the Judges in every State shall be bound thereby . . . ."

The issue is different when the conflicting laws are from different states. Although there are more and more uniform laws (the Uniform Child Custody Act, the Uniform Commercial Code), an activity that is legal in one state may be illegal in another state. For instance, although prostitution is legal in Nevada as a local option, it is illegal in other states.

§ 2.2.3   The Relationship Between Federal and State Courts

The relationship between the federal and state court systems is complex. Although each system is autonomous, in certain circumstances the state courts may hear cases brought under federal law, and the federal courts may hear cases brought under state law.

For example, although the majority of cases heard in state courts are brought under state law, state courts also have jurisdiction when a case is brought under a provision of the United States Constitution, a treaty, and certain federal statutes. Similarly, although the majority of cases heard in the federal courts involve questions of federal law, the federal courts have jurisdiction over cases involving questions of state law when the parties are from different states (diversity jurisdiction).

The appellate jurisdiction of the courts is somewhat simpler. In the federal system, the United States Court of Appeals has appellate jurisdiction to review the decisions of the United States District Courts and certain administrative agencies, and the United States Supreme Court is the court of last resort, having the power to review the decisions of the lower federal courts. Similarly, if a state has an intermediate court of appeals, that court has the power to review the decisions of the lower courts within its geographic jurisdiction, and the state's highest, or supreme court, is the court of last resort.

§ 2.2.4   **The Relationship Among Federal, State, and Local Prosecutors**

The power to prosecute cases arising under the United States Constitution and federal statutes is vested in the Department of Justice, which is headed by the Attorney General of the United States, a presidential appointee. Assisting the United States Attorney General are the United States Attorneys for each federal judicial district. The individual United States Attorneys' offices have two divisions: a civil division and a criminal division. The civil division handles civil cases arising under federal law, and the criminal division handles cases involving alleged violations of federal criminal statutes.

At the state level, the system is slightly different. In most states, the attorney for the state is the state attorney general, usually an elected official. Working for the state attorney general are a number of assistant attorneys general. However, unlike the United States attorneys, most state attorneys general do not handle criminal cases. Their clients are the various state agencies. For example, an assistant attorney general may be assigned to a state's department of social and health services, the department of licensing, the consumer protection bureau, or the department of workers' compensation, providing advice to the agency and representing the agency in civil litigation.

Criminal prosecutions are handled by county and city prosecutors. Each county has its own prosecutor's office, which has both a civil and a criminal division. Attorneys working for the civil division play much the same role as state assistant attorneys general. They represent the county and its agencies, providing both advice and representation. In contrast, the attorneys assigned to the criminal division are responsible for prosecutions under the state's criminal code. The county prosecutor's office decides whom to charge and then tries the cases.

Like the counties, cities have their own city attorney's office, which, at least in large cities, has civil and criminal divisions. Attorneys working in the civil division advise city departments and agencies and represent the city in civil litigation; attorneys in the criminal division prosecute criminal cases brought under city ordinances. State, county, and city prosecutors do not represent federal departments or agencies, nor do they handle cases brought under federal law.

§ 2.3   Deciding How Much Weight to Give to a Particular Authority

Not all enacted and common law is given equal weight. In deciding which law to apply, courts distinguish between mandatory and persuasive authority.

Mandatory authority is law that is binding on the court deciding the case. The court must apply that law. In contrast, persuasive authority is law that is not binding. Although the court may look to that law for guidance, it need not apply it.

Determining whether a particular statute or case is mandatory or persuasive authority is a two-step process. You must first determine which jurisdiction's law applies (that is, whether federal or state law applies and, if state law applies, which state's law); you must then determine which of that jurisdiction's statutes and cases are binding on the court that will be deciding the case.

§ 2.3.1   Which Jurisdiction's Law Applies?

Sometimes determining which jurisdiction's law applies is easy. For example, common knowledge (and common sense) tells you that federal law probably governs whether a federal PLUS loan constitutes income for federal income tax purposes. Similarly, you would probably guess that a will executed in California by a California resident would be governed by California state law. At other times, though, the determination is much more difficult. You probably would not know which jurisdiction's law governs a real estate contract between a resident of New York and a resident of Pennsylvania for a piece of property located in Florida.

Although the rules governing the determination of which jurisdiction's law applies are beyond the scope of this book (they are studied in Civil Procedure, Federal Courts, and Conflicts), keep two things in mind.

First, remember that in our legal system, federal law almost always preempts, or takes precedence over, state law. Consequently, if there is both a federal and a state statute on the same topic, the federal statute will preempt the state statute to the extent that the two are inconsistent. For example, if a federal statute makes it illegal to discriminate on the basis of familial status when renting an apartment but under a state statute such discrimination is lawful, the federal statute governs — it is illegal to discriminate on the basis of familial status. There are a few instances, however, when a state constitutional provision or a state statute will govern. If the state constitution gives a criminal defendant more rights than does the federal constitution, the state constitution applies. While states can grant an individual more protection, they cannot take away or restrict rights granted by the federal constitution or a federal statute.

Second, in the federal system there is not the same body of common law that there is in the states. Unlike the state systems, in the federal system there are no common law rules governing adverse possession or intentional torts such as assault and battery, false imprisonment, or the intentional infliction of emotional distress. As a consequence, if the cause of action is based on a common law doctrine, the case is probably governed by state and not federal law.

§ 2.3.2   What "Law" Will Be Binding on the Court?

Within each jurisdiction, the authorities are ranked. The United States Constitution is the highest authority, binding both state and federal courts. Other federal and state law is under the United States Constitution.

In the federal system, the highest authority is the Constitution. Under the Constitution are the federal statutes and regulations, and under the federal statutes and regulations are the cases interpreting and applying them.

In the state system, the ranking is similar. The highest authority is the state constitution, followed by state statutes and regulations and the cases interpreting and applying those statutes and regulations and state common law.

In addition, the cases themselves are ranked. In both the federal and state systems, decisions of the United States Supreme Court carry the most weight: When deciding a case involving the same law and similar facts, both the courts of appeals and the trial courts are bound by the decisions of the supreme, or highest, state courts. Decisions of intermediate courts of appeals come next; the trial courts under the jurisdiction of the intermediate courts of appeals are bound by the courts of appeals' decisions. At the bottom are the trial courts. Trial court decisions are binding only on the parties involved in the particular case.

Statutes and cases are also ranked by date. More recent statutes supersede earlier versions, and more recent common law rules supersede early rules by the same level court. Courts are bound by the highest court's most recent decision. For example, if there is a 1967 state intermediate court of appeals decision that makes an activity legal and a 1986 state supreme court decision that makes it illegal, in the absence of a statute, the 1986 supreme court decision governs. The 1986 decision would be mandatory authority, and all the courts within that jurisdiction would be bound by that decision.

§ 2.4   Exercise

1. In 1930, in Case A, the Supreme Court of your state set out a common law rule. In 1956, in Case B, the Supreme Court of your state changed that rule. In your state, which case would be binding on a trial court: Case A or Case B?

2. Same facts as in Question 1 except that in 1981, in Case C, the Supreme Court of your state modified the rule set out in Case B, adding a requirement. In your state, which test would a trial court use: the test set out in Case A, the test set out in Case B, or the test set out in Case C?

Case A	State Supreme Court	1930
Case B	State Supreme Court	1956
Case C	State Supreme Court	1981

3. Same facts as in Question 2 except that in 1983 your state legislature enacted a statute that completely changed the common law rule. What is now binding on the trial court: the cases or the statute?

Case A	State Supreme Court	1930
Case B	State Supreme Court	1956
Case C	State Supreme Court	1981
State Statute		1983

4. Same facts as in Question 3 except that in 1985, in Case D, a case involving the application of the 1983 statute, the Court of Appeals of your state gives one of the words in the statute a broad interpretation. (The word was not defined in the statute.) In applying the statute, which courts are bound by the Court of Appeals' decision in Case D: a trial court within the Court of Appeals' geographic jurisdiction? A trial court outside the Court of Appeals' geographic jurisdiction? The division of the Court of Appeals that decided Case D? A division of the Court of Appeals other than the division that decided Case D? Your state's Supreme Court?

State Statute		1983
Case D		1985

5. In 1995, in Case E, a different division of the Court of Appeals applies the 1983 statute. In reaching its decision, the court declines to follow the decision in Case D. Instead of interpreting the word broadly, the court interprets it narrowly. The losing party disagrees with this decision and files an appeal with your state's Supreme Court. In deciding the appeal, is the Supreme Court bound by the Court of Appeals' decision in Case D? The Court of Appeals' decision in Case E?

State Statute		1983
Case D	Court of Appeals	1985
Case E	Court of Appeals	1995

6. Same facts as in Question 5 except that in 1999 the state legislature amends that statute, explicitly defining the word that was the subject of debate in Cases D and E. The legislature elects to give the word a very narrow meaning. In Case F, which is brought before a state trial court in 2008, what would be controlling: the 1983 version of the statute? The 1985 decision in Case D? The 1995 decision in Case E? The amended version of the statute?

   Note: In Case E, the Supreme Court reversed the Court of Appeals and interpreted the term broadly.

State Statute		1983
Case D	Court of Appeals	1985
Case E	Court of Appeals	1995
Case E	Supreme Court	1996
Amended State Statute		1999

Chapter 2 Quiz

Draft answers for each of the following questions. Make your points clearly and concisely, and write sentences that are easy to read and that are grammatical and correctly punctuated.

1. Which branch of the federal government has the power to enact statutes?
2. Which branch of the federal government is responsible for enforcing federal statutes?
3. Which branch of the federal government has the power to determine whether a federal statute is constitutional?
4. What is the difference between a statute and a regulation?
5. At trial, what is the role of the judge? The role of the jury?
6. What role do the appellate courts play?
   a. Do they hear testimony?
   b. Do they decide issues of fact?
   c. Do they determine whether there was sufficient evidence to support the trial court's judgment?
   d. Do they determine whether the trial court applied the right law and applied that law correctly?

7. In the federal system, what is the name of the trial court? The intermediate court of appeals? What courts operate in your state? (To find this information, you will need to do an Internet search.)
8. What do lawyers and judges mean when they say that a federal statute "preempts" a state statute?
9. What do lawyers and judges mean when they say that a court has "jurisdiction" to hear a particular type of case?
10. Are all of the court decisions that appear on the Internet (for example, on Lexis Advance and WestlawNext) "published" decisions? What makes a decision a "published opinion"?

Understanding Statutes

The last fifty to eighty years have seen a fundamental change in American law. In this time we have gone from a legal system dominated by the common law, divined by courts, to one in which statutes, enacted by legislatures, have become the primary source of law. The consequences of the "orgy of statute making," in Grant Gilmore's felicitous phrase, are just beginning to be recognized. The change itself and its effect on our whole legal-political system have not been systemically treated.

Guido Calabresi,
A Common Law for the Age of Statutes

The "orgy of statute making" Guido Calabresi described has created a legal system dominated by statutes. Although no one knows for sure how many statutes there are, one fact is certain: The ability to read and analyze statutes is a skill that every attorney needs.

§ 3.1   How Statutes Are Enacted

Because attorneys are sometimes called upon to make arguments based on a statute's legislative history, we begin this chapter by briefly describing the processes through which federal and state statutes are enacted. If you are already familiar with this process, you can skip to section 3.2. If, however, you are not familiar with the process, or if all you remember is the song from the "Schoolhouse Rock" video, *I'm Just a Bill*, then read the following two subsections, noting both how complex the process is and the names of the documents that are created at each stage.

§ 3.1.1   Federal Statutes

In the United States, federal statutes are enacted by Congress, which is made up of two houses, the House of Representatives and the Senate. See section 2.1.2. All federal statutes begin as a bill, which is the name used to refer to proposed statutes. Although a bill may be drafted by anyone, only a member of Congress can introduce, or present, a bill to Congress. The member of Congress who introduces the bill becomes the bill's sponsor and usually works to get the bill passed into law.

For the purpose of this example, presume that the bill's sponsor is a member of the United States House of Representatives. To introduce the bill, the sponsor places a copy of the bill in the "hopper," which is a box located on the platform where the Speaker of the House of Representatives sits. After the bill is placed in the hopper, the Clerk of the House assigns the bill a number that begins with "H.R.," which stands for House of Representatives, and the bill is sent to one of the House of Representatives' twenty standing committees, for example, the Committee on Agriculture, the Committee on Homeland Security, or the Committee on International Relations.

The standing committee reviews the bill, debates its merits and, if it chooses, makes changes to it. If, after debating the bill, a majority of the members of the standing committee believe that the bill is unnecessary or unwise, the standing committee can vote to table the bill or can let the bill "die in committee." If, however, the standing committee decides that the bill has merit, the committee will usually refer it to a subcommittee for further study and debate. The subcommittee may conduct hearings, during which experts, supporters, and opponents may testify or speak about the need for the bill and its effect. After these hearings and debate, the members of the subcommittee can vote to table the bill, let the bill die, or vote to send the bill back to the standing committee for further action. If the subcommittee sends the bill back to the standing committee, the standing committee can vote to table the bill, let it die, or release the bill and send it, along with a committee report that explains the bill, back to the full House of Representatives.

When the House of Representatives receives a bill from a standing committee, the Clerk of the House places the bill on the House of Representatives' calendar, scheduling it for consideration by the membership of the House of Representatives. During these public debates, members of the House of Representatives can offer amendments, which will be voted on by all of the members of the House of Representatives. At the close of the debates, the bill is placed before the membership for a vote. If a majority of the House of Representatives approves the bill, the engrossed bill, which is the version of the bill passed by the House of Representatives, is sent to the Senate for its consideration.

When the Senate receives a bill, or act, from the House of Representatives, it refers it to one of the Senate's sixteen standing committees. This standing committee will consider the bill and do one or more of the following: (1) approve the bill as it was passed by the House of Representatives and send it back to the full Senate for a vote; (2) send the bill to a Senate subcommittee for further consideration, including additional hearings; (3) send the bill to a joint subcommittee made up of members of the House of Representatives and the Senate, which will attempt to draft a compromise bill that is acceptable to both the members of the House of Representatives and the Senate; or (4) let the bill die. If the Senate standing committee recommends passage of the bill as it was passed by the House of Representatives, it will release the bill and send it to the full Senate for its consideration and its vote. If, however, the Senate subcommittee sends the bill to a joint committee, any compromise bills that are drafted must be approved by the membership of both the House of Representatives and the Senate.

Once a bill has been approved by both the House of Representatives and the Senate, the enrolled bill, which is a bill that has been passed by both houses, is sent to the President. If the President signs the bill, the bill is assigned a public law number (beginning with "P.L."). If, however, the President vetoes the bill, the bill does not become law unless both the House of Representatives and the Senate override that veto by a two-thirds vote. Chart 3.1 summarizes the process and lists the documents that are created at each stage in the process.

Chart 3.1	How a Bill Introduced in the United States House of Representatives Becomes a Law

Step	Document
1. A member of the House of Representatives introduces the bill.	• Bill
2. The bill is referred to a committee. The committee may then refer the bill to a subcommittee. (Most bills die in committee.)	• Transcripts from Committee Hearings • Committee Print
3. If the bill does not die in committee, the committee submits its report on the bill to the House.	• Committee Report
4. The bill is presented to the House for debate, amendments, and a vote.	• Engrossed Bill
5. If bill is approved, it is sent to the Senate. The Senate repeats steps 1-4.	• Engrossed Bill
6. If the Senate passes the bill, it returns the bill, with any amendments, to the House. The House then approves the amendments, determines that the amendments are unacceptable, or creates a Conference Committee to create a compromise bill	• Conference Committee Report • Enrolled Bill
7. If both House and Senate pass the same version of the bill, the bill is sent to the President for signature. If the President signs the bill, it becomes law.	• Presidential Statement • Public Law

The process is the same if a bill is introduced in the Senate. The only difference is that when a Senator introduces a bill, the bill is assigned a number that begins with an "S." and if the majority of the Senate approves the bill, it is then sent to the House of Representatives for consideration.

Once a bill has been signed into law, it is assigned a public law number, and the law is codified, or placed into the appropriate section or sections of the *United States Code* (U.S.C.).

PRACTICE POINTER	For a more detailed explanation of how federal statutes are enacted, see *http://beta.congress.gov/legislative-process.*

§ 3.1.2   State Statutes

In the forty-nine states that have a bicameral legislature — a legislature with two houses or chambers — the process is similar. A member of one of the state's two houses will introduce a bill, the bill will be read and referred to a committee, and the committee will debate the bill and either let it die or send it back to the house in which the bill originated. If that chamber approves the bill, the bill will be sent to the other chamber for its consideration. If the other chamber approves the bill, the bill will be sent to the governor, who can either sign the bill, making it law, or veto the bill. If the governor vetoes the bill, the state legislature can overturn that veto by a two-thirds vote. The exception is Nebraska: The Nebraska legislature has only one house.

§ 3.2   How Regulations Are Promulgated

In enacting statutes, the legislative branch can give the executive branch the power to promulgate regulations implementing the provisions set out in the statute. If the executive branch does not exceed the powers granted to it by the legislative branch, these regulations have the force of law. For example, in enacting the Clean Air Act, a federal statute, Congress gave the Environmental Protection Agency, an agency created by the President, the power to promulgate regulations implementing the Clean Air Act.

The process of promulgating a federal regulation is relatively straight-forward. The federal agency that has been given the power to promulgate regulations publishes proposed regulations in the *Federal Register* and invites comments from the public. After the comment period ends, the agency considers the comments and prepares the final version of the regulations. The final versions of federal regulations are published in the *Federal Register* and then in the *Code of Federal Regulations* (C.F.R.), which is republished each year.

At the state level, the process is similar. The state agency that has been given the power to promulgate regulations publishes proposed regulations in some type of state register, and invites public comment. When the comment period ends, the state agency considers the comments and then publishes the final version of the regulations in its state administrative code.

§ 3.3   The Relationship Among Statutes, Regulations, and Cases

The relationships among statutes, regulations, and cases are both simple and complex. They are simple in the sense that there is a hierarchy: Statutes, which set out the law, are at the top; regulations, which implement the law, are in the middle; and cases, which apply the statutes and regulations, are at the bottom.

Statute
↓

Regulations Implementing Statutes
↓

Cases Applying the Statute and Regulations

The relationships are, however, also complex in that they involve both the federal government and the state governments and, within each of those governments, the system of checks and balances that the drafters of our Constitution created. See section 2.2.

Federal Statutes	**State Statutes**
Statutes (Legislative Branch)	Statutes (Legislative Branch)
Regulations (Executive Branch)	Regulations (Executive Branch)
Cases (Judicial Branch)	Cases (Judicial Branch)

We start with two simple examples and then move to some of the more complex situations that you may encounter.

§ 3.3.1   Federal Statute Governs

Presume for a moment that you have been asked to research an immigration issue. Historically, there was no common law governing immigration and, under the United States Constitution, only the federal government has the power to regulate immigration. Thus, immigration issues are governed by federal statutes, federal regulations, and federal cases that have applied those statutes and regulations.

Because the statutes are the "highest authority," you will want to start your research, and your analysis, with these statutes. You will, however, also need to look for federal regulations. While the federal statutes will set out the general principles and rules, the federal regulations will provide more specific information, for example, definitions, standards, and procedures. If the statute and/or regulations are ambiguous, you will also want to look for cases that have applied the statutes and regulations. In looking for cases, look first for mandatory authority: a United States Supreme Court decision or, if there are no United States Supreme Court decisions, for a decision from the court of appeals for the circuit that will hear the case. If there are no court of appeals decisions from the circuit that will hear the case, look for decisions from other circuits and for district court decisions. For more on mandatory and persuasive authority, see section 2.3.

Immigration Issue

Federal Statutes Governing Immigration
Title 8 of the *United States Code*
See, for example, 8 U.S.C. § 1551 (2012)
↓

Federal Regulations Governing Immigration
Title 8 of the *Code of Federal Regulations*
See, for example, 8 C.F.R. § 2.1 (2012)
↓

United States Supreme Court Cases
↓

United States Court of Appeals Cases
↓

United States District Court Cases

In reading federal statutes, regulations, and cases, keep the following "checks and balances" in mind. First, in promulgating regulations, a federal agency cannot exceed the authority granted to it by Congress. Therefore, a federal agency cannot promulgate regulations unless Congress has authorized it to do so, and the regulations that it promulgates cannot contradict the statute. Second, while the federal courts have the power to hold that a federal statute is unconstitutional, if the statute is constitutional, the courts must interpret and apply the statute in a way that is consistent with the statutory language and Congress's intent.

§ 3.3.2   State Statute Governs

Now presume that you have been asked to work on a landlord-tenant case involving a house located in California. Because the United States Constitution does not give the federal government the power to regulate relationships between landlords and tenants in California, the case will be governed by California law. Although historically, most state law was common law, today much of that common law has been replaced by enacted law, that is, by statutes. Consequently, you would begin researching a California landlord-tenant issue by looking for California statutes.

While in some instances state legislatures give state agencies the power to promulgate regulations implementing a state statute, the California legislature has not authorized a state agency to promulgate regulations relating to landlord-tenant issues. Therefore, your issue will be governed by the California statutes and by the California cases that have applied those statutes. Although a California court might, in some circumstances, look to court decisions from other states, those decisions will never be more than persuasive authority. For more on mandatory and persuasive authority, see section 2.3.

Landlord-Tenant Issues in California

California Landlord-Tenant Statutes
↓
California Supreme Court Cases
↓
California Court of Appeals Cases

§ 3.3.3   Both Federal and State Statutes Govern

Sometimes an issue will be governed by both federal and state law. For example, a company operating in New York will have to comply both with federal statutes governing employment and with New York laws governing employment.

In general, federal laws establish the minimum standards. For example, there is a federal statute that establishes the federal minimum wage, a federal statute that establishes minimum safety standards, and a federal statute that guarantees family leave benefits to some classes of employees. While a state cannot enact a statute that reduces these benefits, it can enact a statute that gives employees additional benefits. For example, a state can enact a statute that provides for a higher minimum wage than that provided for by the federal statute, a state can enact a statute that imposes additional safety standards, and a state can enact a statute that provides additional classes of employees with family leave benefits.

When there is both a federal and a state statute that govern, you will need to look not only for the federal statute, federal regulations implementing that federal statute, and federal cases interpreting and applying that statute but also for the state statute, any applicable state regulations, and state cases interpreting and applying the state statute and state regulations.

Federal Statute Sets Minimum	State Statute Provides Additional Benefits
Federal Statutes	State Statute
↓	↓
Federal Regulations	State Regulations
↓	↓
Federal Cases	State Cases

In working on cases that are governed by both federal and state law, keep the following in mind.

1. In general, federal law preempts, or takes precedence over, state law. (See United States Constitution, Article VI, Clause 2, which states that laws enacted by Congress under the powers granted to it under the Constitution

are the "supreme Law of the Land; and the Judges in every State shall be bound thereby . . . .")

Thus, if the state statute provides fewer benefits or protections, it will not be enforced. In some instances, however, a state can provide its citizens with additional benefits.

2. Federal regulations implement federal statutes, and state regulations implement state statutes.
3. In most instances, it is the federal courts that interpret and apply federal statutes and the state courts that interpret and apply state statutes.

§ 3.3.4   Party Argues that a Statute Is Unconstitutional

Occasionally, a party will argue that a statute is unconstitutional either because the legislative body that enacted the statute did not have the authority to enact the statute or because the statute is unconstitutionally vague and/or overbroad.

When the statute at issue is a federal statute, it is the federal courts that must decide whether the statute is, or is not, unconstitutional. While most of these cases are first heard in a United States District Court, a party who loses at the District Court level can file an appeal, asking the appropriate United States Court of Appeals to review the District Court's decision. In addition, the party losing at the United States Court of Appeals level can file a petition for a *writ of certiorari* with the United States Supreme Court, asking the United States Supreme Court to review the United States Court of Appeals' decision.

When the statute is a state statute, the issue is a bit more complicated. If the party challenging the statute alleges that the statute violates the state's constitution, then the challenge will be decided by the state's courts. While initially the issue will be decided by a state trial court, the party that loses at the trial court level can appeal to the state's intermediate court of appeals, if the state has such a court, or to the state's highest appellate court. If, however, the party challenging the statute alleges that the statute violates the federal constitution, the party can raise the issue in either a state court or a federal court. In such instances, the final arbiter is not the state's highest court but the United States Supreme Court.

§ 3.3.5   Party Argues that an Agency Exceeded Its Authority in Promulgating a Particular Regulation

Some cases involving federal regulations are first heard, not in the federal courts, but by an administrative law judge who is employed by the executive branch of the federal government. For instance, an individual who believes that the Social Security Administration has incorrectly denied his or her claim for disability benefits can appeal the agency's decision, asking a federal administrative law judge to review that decision. In these cases, claims that a regulation is invalid because the agency that promulgated it exceeded the authority granted to it by Congress will be decided by the administrative law judge. The losing party can, however, appeal the administrative law judge's decision. These appeals are heard initially by a United States District Court.

However, the party losing at the District Court level can ask the United States Court of Appeals to review the District Court's decision, and the party losing at the United States Court of Appeals level can ask the United States Supreme Court to review the United States Court of Appeals' decision.

In other cases, for example, cases in which an individual or a company has been charged in a United States District Court with violating a federal statute and regulation, the individual or company can, as part of its defense, argue that the regulation is invalid. In this situation, the United States District Court will make the initial decision about whether the regulation is invalid, and the losing party can appeal the decision to the United States Court of Appeals, and the party that loses at the United States Court of Appeals can file a petition for a *writ of certiorari*, asking the United States Supreme Court to review the United States Court of Appeals' decision.

Likewise, some cases involving state regulations are heard first by state administrative law judges who are employed by the executive branch of the state government. For example, an individual who believes that the state has improperly denied his or her claim for state worker's compensation benefits can ask a state administrative law judge to review the agency's decision. In these situations, an individual's claim that a state regulation is invalid will be decided by the state administrative law judge, subject to review by the state's courts. In contrast, in cases in which an individual has been charged in a state court with violating a state statute and regulation, the state courts will decide whether or not the regulation is invalid. The only time that a federal court will review a state regulation is when a party claims that the state regulation violates the United States Constitution.

PRACTICE POINTER	Given the relationships between federal and state statutes and regulations and the relationships among the various branches, the statements set out in the left-hand column are **incorrect**.
The state statute **preempts** federal statute	If there is a conflict between a state statute and federal statute, the federal statute governs unless the state statute provides additional protections.
The court **overruled** the statute	Although courts can hold that a statute is unconstitutional, they cannot **overrule** a statute. If a statute is constitutional, the court must apply that statute.
The regulations **supersede** the statute	Although the regulations are promulgated after the statute is enacted, the regulations **do not supersede** the statute. In promulgating regulations, administrative agencies can only exercise the authority granted to them by the legislative branch. Regulations implement, but do not add to, subtract from, or change the statute itself.

§ 3.4   Reading and Analyzing Statutes

Statutes can be difficult to read. Sometimes, a statute is difficult to read because the person or group that drafted the original bill did not do a good job drafting the bill; more often, though, a statute is hard to read because statutes are the product of a system that requires compromise to get a bill enacted into law. Although the initial bill may have been well written, during the legislative process the bill was amended one or more times to get the votes needed to get the bill out of committee, to get the votes needed to have the first house or chamber approve the bill, to get the votes needed to have the second house or chamber approve the bill, and/or to ensure that the President or governor will sign and not veto the bill.

Although reading and analyzing statutes is time consuming, it is time well-spent. When an issue is governed by a state statute, that statute is the "highest" authority: The regulations must be consistent with the statute and, unless the courts decide that the statute is unconstitutional, they must apply the statute as it is written and not as they wish it had been written.

The following subsections walk you through the process of finding, reading, and analyzing a statute.

§ 3.4.1   Finding Statutes Using the Citation

If you have been given the citation to the applicable statute, finding the statute is easy. Simply locate the statute in the book version of the applicable code, on a free website, or on a fee-based service (e.g., Lexis Advance or WestlawNext).

PRACTICE POINTER   You can find federal statutes on the following free websites:

- *http://uscode.house.gov*
- *http://www.law.cornell.edu/uscode*

You can find state statutes on the following free websites:

- *http://www.law.cornell.edu/states/listing*
- *http://www.llsdc.org/state-legislation*
- Each state's official website

Although the citation formats vary from jurisdiction to jurisdiction, most citations to statutes contain three types of information: (1) an abbreviation that identifies the name of the code in which the statute can be found, (2) the title and section number, and (3) the year of the code. Look at the following citation, which is a citation to a federal statute.

42 U.S.C. § 12101 (2012)

In this citation, the letters "U.S.C." identify the code: "U.S.C." stands for *United States Code*, which is the official code for federal statutes. The number before "U.S.C." is the title number; the cited statute is in Title 42 of the *United States Code*. The number following "U.S.C" is the section number: The cited statute is section 12101 of Title 42 of the *United States Code*. The final number, which is in parentheses, is the year of the code. To find the cited statute, you need to look at the 2012 version of the *United States Code*.

42	U.S.C.	§ 12101	(2012)
Title	Name of Code	Section	Year of Code

Now look at the following citation, which is the citation to the Florida statute governing service of process.

Fla. Stat. § 48.031 (2012)

In this citation, "Fla. Stat." is the abbreviation for Florida's official code, which is called the *Florida Statutes*. The number that follows that abbreviation is the title and section number; the number before the period, the "48," is the title, and the number following the period, "031," is the section number. The last number, the number in parentheses, is the year of the code.

Fla. Stat.	§ 48.031	(2012)
Name of Code	Title and Section Number	Year of Code

> **PRACTICE POINTER**
>
> To find the name of each state's code or codes and the abbreviations that are used for the codes, see Appendix 1 in *ALWD Guide to Legal Citation, Fifth Edition,* or Table 1 in *The Bluebook, A Uniform System of Citation, Nineteenth Edition.*

If you have not been given the citation to the statute, finding the applicable statutory section or sections can be more difficult. If you are using books, the easiest way to find a statute is to use the index that comes with the book version of the code. (This index is usually set out in a separate volume at the end of the code.) If you are using a fee-based service, such as Lexis Advance or WestlawNext, the easiest way is to use either the table of contents option or the index option. If you are using a free source, use the table of contents or index option if the source offers that option. Otherwise, locate the applicable sections using the search text box.

For more information on finding state statutes and regulations, see Chapter 4 in *Just Research*, and for more information on finding federal statutes and regulations, see Chapter 5 in *Just Research*. For more information on finding county and city ordinances, see Chapter 6 in *Just Research*.

§ 3.4.2   Distinguishing Between the Text of the Statute and Other Material Provided by the Publisher

What you find when you look up a statute will depend on the source that you use. If you use a free website, more likely than not, you will find only the text of the statute, credits, and historical notes. If, however, you use a fee-based service or the book form of an annotated code, you will find not only the text of the statute, credits, and historical notes but also other material provided by the publisher, for example, cross-references to other sources and notes of decisions/ case notes that you can use to locate cases that have applied the statute. See the screen shot below from the Westlaw version of Fla. Stat. § 48.031 (2012).

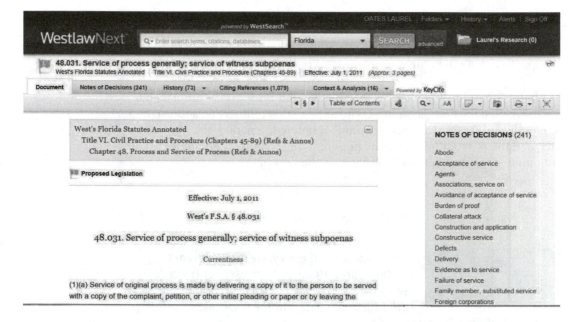

§ 3.4.3   Making Sure You Have the Right Version of the Statute

Before spending time reading and analyzing a statute, make sure that you are reading the right version of the statute. If the issue that you have been asked to research involves an event that happened in the past, you will need to find the version of the statute that was in effect at the time that event occurred. In contrast, if the client has asked you to determine what he or she can do next month, you need to find the version of the statute that will be in effect next month.

To determine whether the version of the statute that you have found is the right version, use the credits and historical notes that are set out after the text of the statute. If the statute has been amended since your cause of action arose, use the version of the statute that was in effect on the applicable date. If you are advising a client about what it can or cannot do in the future, use an online source to see if there is pending legislation.

§ 3.4.4   Identifying the Elements or Requirements

While some disciplines and cultures focus on the "whole," as law is practiced in the United States, the focus is on the "parts." Thus, in reading a statute, most United States attorneys are looking for the elements, that is, for the requirements set out in the statute. For example, in reading the following Florida statute dealing with substituted service of process, an attorney would try to identify the elements, or requirements, for substituted service of process.

> **Fla. Stat. § 48.031. Service of process generally; service of witness subpoenas**
>
> (1)(a) Service of original process is made by delivering a copy of it to the person to be served with a copy of the complaint, petition, or other initial pleading or paper or by leaving the copies at his or her usual place of abode with any person residing therein who is 15 years of age or older and informing the person of their contents. . . .

While sometimes Congress or the state legislature sets out the elements in a list, most of the time the elements are embedded in the text of the statute. In these situations, you will need to read and reread the statute, determining, as best you can, what the elements are. One of the easiest, and most reliable ways of doing this type of analysis is to do a form of sentence diagramming. Begin by identifying each clause and phrase. For example, in analyzing Fla. Stat. § 48.031(a)(1) (2012), you find the following clauses and phrases.

> **Fla. Stat. § 48.031(a)(1) (2012)**
>
> *Service of original process is made*
>
> by delivering a copy of it
> to the person to be served
> with a copy of the complaint, petition, or other initial pleading or paper
> or by leaving the copies at his or her usual place of abode
> with any person residing therein
> who is 15 years of age or older
> and informing the person of their contents.

Once you have listed the clauses and phrases, look at the words that the legislature used to connect those clauses and phrases and the words in those clauses and phrases. In particular, note whether the clauses, phrases, and words are connected with "and" or with "or." In addition, try to determine what modifies what.

In our example, the statute begins with a subject, "service of original process," and a verb, "is made." This subject and verb are followed by two phrases that begin with the word "by": "by delivering" or "by leaving." Thus, it appears that service of process can be made either (1) by delivering a copy of the process to the person to be served or (2) by leaving a copy at his or her usual place of abode. A close reading of the language used to describe the second option suggests that there are four sub-elements or requirements: (a) the process must be left at the person's usual place of abode, (b) the process must be left with a person residing therein, (c) the person with whom the process is left must be fifteen years or older, and (d) the person serving the process must inform the person served about "their contents." By reformatting your first list of phrases and clauses, you can see the two options and the requirements for each option.

Service of original process is made

(1) **by delivering** a copy of it to the person to be served with a copy of the complaint, petition, or other initial pleading or paper

or

(2) **by leaving** the copies at
    (a) his or her usual place of abode
    (b) with any person residing therein
    (c) who is 15 years of age or older

    and

    (d) informing the person of their contents.

The next step is to look for other statutory sections that are on point. Begin by looking for statutory definitions. Are the terms in the subsection that you just read defined in a different subsection of the same statute or in a different section of the same chapter or act? If there are statutory definitions, you need to use those definitions. If the statutory language is ambiguous, also look for a findings and purpose section that explains why the statute was enacted and what drafters hoped to accomplish. Finally, if your statute contains cross references to other statutes, look up and read those cross references.

Once you have done your own analysis of the statute, check your analysis against the analysis that others have done. For example, have the courts, in interpreting and applying the statute, listed the elements and does their list match yours? In cases in which a jury would decide whether the statute has or has not been violated, are there any pattern jury instructions, and how are the elements listed in those jury instructions? Is the statute discussed in a practice manual, a treatise, a law review article, or other secondary source and, if it has, how has the source listed the elements?

If your list matches the list set out in the cases, the jury instructions, and secondary sources, you can be confident that you have read the statute correctly. If your list does not match those lists, you will usually want to go with the list set out in a case that is mandatory authority or in the pattern jury instructions unless that reading of the statute does not favor your client and you can make a good faith argument that the courts or the authors of the pattern jury instructions have misread the statute.

§ 3.5　Exercise

Read the following statute and then answer the questions.

Text of statute:

Wash. Rev. Code § 9A.46.110 (2012):

(1)　A person commits the crime of stalking if, without lawful authority and under circumstances not amounting to a felony attempt of another crime:

(a)　He or she intentionally and repeatedly harasses or repeatedly follows another person; and

(b)　The person being harassed or followed is placed in fear that the stalker intends to injure the person, another person, or property of the person or of another person. The feeling of fear must be one that a reasonable person in the same situation would experience under all the circumstances; and

(c)　The stalker either:

(i)　Intends to frighten, intimidate, or harass the person; or

(ii)　Knows or reasonably should know that the person is afraid, intimidated, or harassed even if the stalker did not intend to place the person in fear or intimidate or harass the person.

(2)　(a)　It is not a defense to the crime of stalking under subsection (1)(c)(i) of this section that the stalker was not given actual notice that the person did not want the stalker to contact or follow the person; and

(b)　It is not a defense to the crime of stalking under subsection (1)(c)(ii) of this section that the stalker did not intend to frighten, intimidate, or harass the person.

(3)　It shall be a defense to the crime of stalking that the defendant is a licensed private investigator acting within the capacity of his or her license as provided by chapter 18.165 RCW.

(4)　Attempts to contact or follow the person after being given actual notice that the person does not want to be contacted or followed constitutes prima facie evidence that the stalker intends to intimidate or harass the person. . . .

. . .

(6)　As used in this section:

(a)　"Follows" means deliberately maintaining visual or physical proximity to a specific person over a period of time. A finding that the alleged stalker repeatedly and deliberately appears at the person's home, school, place of employment, business, or any other location to maintain visual or physical proximity to the person is sufficient to find that the alleged stalker follows the person. It is not necessary to establish that the alleged stalker follows the person while in transit from one location to another.

(b)　"Harasses" means unlawful harassment as defined in RCW 10.14.020.

. . .

(d)　"Repeatedly" means on two or more separate occasions.

Questions:

1. How would you determine whether the statute above governs acts that occurred in April 2014?
2. To convict an individual of stalking, what does the State have to prove? List the elements.

3. What is and is not a defense to the crime of stalking?
4. What other types of statutory sections would you want to look for?
5. What other statutory sections would you want to read and analyze?

Understanding Judicial Opinions

lthough sometimes a statute will answer the question that you have been asked to research, more often than not you will also need to look at judicial decisions, which are also called judicial opinions or, more simply, cases. If the issue is governed by common law, you will be looking at the cases to find the common law rule and examples of how that common law rule has been applied in analogous cases. In contrast, if the issue is governed by a statute, you will be looking at the cases to determine how the courts have applied the statute, or a particular part of the statute, in cases that are analogous, or similar to, your client's case.

§ 4.1 Which Cases Are Binding on Which Courts

The image created by most casebooks, TV shows, and news articles is that all cases are created equal. Nothing could be further from the truth. Even though a criminal law casebook may set out cases from United States District Court for the Northern District of California, from the United States Court of Appeals for the Third Circuit, and from the Mississippi Supreme Court, in practice your search for cases will be more focused. While casebooks are designed to illustrate the historical development of a rule or the ways in which different jurisdictions have approached the same issue, as a practicing attorney you will look first for cases that are mandatory authority, that is, cases that are binding on the court that will be deciding your case. You will look at persuasive authority, for example cases from outside your jurisdiction, only when there is no mandatory authority or when you are asking a court to overrule, or invalidate, one of its decisions.

Three examples illustrate when cases from a particular court are mandatory authority. In the first example, the issue is governed by a state statute and the cases that have interpreted and applied that statute. In the second example, the issue is governed by federal statutes and regulations and the cases that have interpreted and applied those statutes and regulations. The third example involves an issue governed by common law.

§ 4.1.1   Issue Governed by State Statute and Cases that Have Interpreted and Applied that Statute

Presume for a moment that the State of Oregon has charged Martin Obote with assault under an Oregon statute. Because Mr. Obote has been charged under an Oregon statute, the case will be heard by the Oregon courts and, in deciding whether Mr. Obote is guilty, the Oregon courts will apply the Oregon statute and Oregon cases that have interpreted and applied that statute.

Initially, the case will be heard by one of Oregon's circuit courts, which are trial courts that have jurisdiction to hear cases in which the defendant is charged under an Oregon statute with a misdemeanor, gross misdemeanor, or a felony. Mr. Obote can choose to have a bench trial or a jury trial. If Mr. Obote chooses to have a bench trial, there will not be a jury, and the trial court judge will decide both issues of fact and issues of law. If, however, Mr. Obote chooses a jury trial, the judge will decide issues of law, and the jury will decide issues of fact. Under both options, the State has the burden of proof and must prove each element of the crime beyond a reasonable doubt.

At the trial court level, the Oregon statute, Oregon Supreme Court cases, and Oregon Court of Appeals cases are mandatory authority. Thus, in deciding issues of law, the trial court must apply the Oregon statute in a manner that is consistent with the ways in which the Oregon Supreme Court and Oregon Court of Appeals have applied that statute in analogous cases. The only exception is for issues that involve a right guaranteed by the United States Constitution, for example, an individual's Fourth Amendment right to be free from unreasonable searches and seizures. When the issue involves a right guaranteed under the United States Constitution, United States Supreme Court decisions are mandatory authority.

If, after hearing the witnesses and viewing the exhibits, the judge or jury finds that Mr. Obote is guilty, Mr. Obote can file an appeal, which in most instances will be heard by the Oregon Court of Appeals, which is Oregon's intermediate court of appeals. The Oregon Court of Appeals does not conduct trials. Instead, it reviews the written record from the trial conducted before the circuit court and any exhibits that were admitted at trial. With only a few exceptions, the Oregon Court of Appeals can hear and decide only four types of issues: (1) whether a statute is constitutional, (2) whether the trial court applied the right law and properly instructed the jury, (3) whether the trial court judge abused his or her discretion in granting or denying a motion or granting or denying an objection, and (4) whether there is sufficient evidence to support the trial court judge's findings of fact or the jury's verdict.

In deciding these issues, the Oregon Court of Appeals must apply mandatory authority. Consequently, if the issue is an issue of state law, the Oregon Court of Appeals must apply the rules set out in decisions by the Oregon Supreme Court. In contrast, if the issue involves a right guaranteed under the United States Constitution, the Oregon Court of Appeals must apply the rules set out by the United States Supreme Court. While most of the time the Oregon Court of Appeals will follow its own prior decisions, it is not required to do so.

If the Oregon Court of Appeals affirms Mr. Obote's conviction, Mr. Obote can file a petition for discretionary review, asking the Oregon Supreme Court, which is Oregon's highest court, to hear his case. If the Oregon Supreme Court grants Mr. Obote's petition, it will review his conviction; if it denies his petition, it will not review the conviction, and the Oregon Court of Appeals' decision is the final decision.

Like the Oregon Court of Appeals, the Oregon Supreme Court does not conduct trials. Instead, like the Oregon Court of Appeals, it reviews the written record from the trial court and reviews exhibits introduced at trial. In addition, like the Oregon Court of Appeals, it can decide only certain types of issues. With just a few exceptions, it can determine only (1) whether the statute is constitutional; (2) whether the trial court applied the right law and correctly instructed the jury; (3) whether the trial court judge abused his or her discretion in granting or denying a motion or granting or denying an objection; and (4) whether there is sufficient evidence to support the trial court judge's findings of fact or the jury's verdict.

Just as the Oregon Court of Appeals is not bound by its earlier decisions, the Oregon Supreme Court is not bound by its earlier decisions. Thus, in cases heard by the Oregon Supreme Court, the only mandatory authority are United States Supreme Court decisions, and those decisions are only mandatory authority insofar as they involve rights guaranteed by the United States Constitution.

Although the names of the courts will vary from state to state, for example, in New York the trial court is called the "Supreme Court," the roles that trial courts, intermediate courts of appeal, and the highest court play are the same in each state. Chart 4.1 summarizes the role that each court plays and lists the authorities that are mandatory authority.

Chart 4.1	**Role Each State Court Plays and List of Authorities that Are Mandatory Authority**	
Court	**Role**	**Mandatory Authority**
State trial courts	• Conducts trial • In a bench trial, the judge decides questions of law and questions of fact and enters findings of fact and conclusions of law.	• If the issue is governed by a state statute, the state statute and decisions of the state's highest court and, if it has one, intermediate court of appeals are mandatory authority.

(continues)

Court	Role	Mandatory Authority
	• In a jury trial, the judge decides questions of law, and the jury decides questions of fact and enters a verdict.	• If the issue is governed by the United States Constitution, United States Supreme Court decisions are mandatory authority.
State intermediate courts of appeals Note: Some of the smaller states (e.g., Nevada) do not have an intermediate court of appeals.	• Does not conduct trials, hear testimony, or accept new evidence. • Reviews trial court record to determine whether (1) the statute is constitutional, (2) the trial court applied the right law and correctly instructed the jury, (3) the trial court judge abused his or her discretion in granting or denying a motion or granting or denying an objection, and (4) there is sufficient evidence to support the trial court judge's or the jury's findings of fact.	• If the issue is governed by a state statute, the state statute and decisions of the state's highest court are mandatory authority. • If the issue is governed by the United States Constitution, United States Supreme Court decisions are mandatory authority. • Although a state's intermediate court of appeals will usually follow its own prior decisions, those decisions are not mandatory authority.
State's highest court or court of last resort Note: In many states this court is called the Supreme Court.	• Does not conduct trials, hear testimony, or accept new evidence. • Reviews trial court record to determine (1) whether the statute is constitutional; (2) whether the trial court applied the right law correctly; (3) whether the trial court judge abused his or her discretion in granting or denying a motion or granting or denying an objection; and (4) whether there is sufficient evidence to support the trial court judge's findings of fact or the jury's verdict.	• If constitutional, the state statutes are mandatory authority. • For issues governed by United States Constitution, United States Supreme Court decisions are mandatory authority. • Although the state's highest court will usually follow its own prior decisions, those decisions are not mandatory authority.

§ 4.1.2   Issue Governed by a Federal Statute and Regulations and Cases that Have Interpreted that Federal Statute and the Federal Regulations

In our second example, Sanjee Singh wants to sue her employer under the Family and Medical Leave Act (FMLA) on the grounds that her employer illegally fired her after she took three weeks off from work to care for her dying mother. Because the FMLA is a federal statute, the issue is governed by the FMLA, the regulations that implement the FMLA, and the federal cases that have applied the FMLA.

If Ms. Singh does sue her employer, her case would be heard by a United States District Court. As in the state system, Ms. Singh can ask for a bench trial, in which the trial court judge will decide both issues of fact and issues of law, or a jury trial, in which the judge would decide issues of law, and the jury would decide issues of fact. As the plaintiff, Ms. Singh would have the burden of proof. At the District Court, or trial court level, the FMLA, the applicable federal regulations, United States Supreme Court decisions, and United States Court of Appeals decisions from the same circuit as the circuit in which the District Court is located are mandatory authority.

If Ms. Singh loses at the district court level, she can appeal that decision to the United States Court of Appeals for the circuit in which the District Court that heard the case is located. Similarly, if Ms. Singh wins, her employer can file an appeal. Like state intermediate courts of appeals, the United States Court of Appeals does not conduct trials, hear witnesses, or admit new exhibits. Instead, it just reviews the written record from the trial court and the exhibits admitted at trial. In addition, just as the state intermediate court of appeals can decide only certain types of issues, the United States Court of Appeals can decide only certain types of issues: (1) whether the statute is constitutional, (2) whether the regulations are valid, (3) whether the district court judge applied the right law and correctly instructed the jury, (4) whether the district court judge abused his or her discretion in granting or denying a motion or granting or denying an objection, and (5) whether there is sufficient evidence to support the trial court judge's findings of fact or the jury's verdict. When a case is heard by a United States Court of Appeals, the statute, the regulations, and United States Supreme Court decisions are mandatory authority.

Although the United States Supreme Court hears relatively few cases each year, the party that loses at the Court of Appeals level has the right to file a petition for a *writ of certiorari* asking the United States Supreme Court to review the United States Court of Appeals' decision. If the United States Supreme Court accepts review, it would review the trial court record and determine (1) whether the statute is constitutional, (2) whether the regulations are valid, (3) whether the district court judge applied the right law correctly and correctly instructed the jury, (4) whether the trial court judge abused his or her discretion in granting or denying a motion or granting or denying an objection, and (5) whether there is sufficient evidence to support the district court judge's findings of fact or the jury's verdict. The only mandatory authority would be statutes and regulations, and those statutes and regulations are only mandatory authority if the statute is constitutional and the regulations are valid.

Chart 4.2 summarizes the role each federal court plays, and it identifies the authorities that are mandatory authority.

Chart 4.2	Role Each Federal Court Plays and List of Authorities that Are Mandatory Authority

Court	Role	Mandatory Authority
United States District Court (trial court)	• Conducts trial. • In a bench trial, judge decides questions of law and questions of fact and enters findings of fact and conclusions of law. • In a jury trial, judge decides questions of law, and the jury hears questions of fact and enters verdict.	• Federal statutes.* • Federal regulations.** • United States Supreme Court decisions. • United States Court of Appeals decisions from same circuit in which District Court is located.
United States Court of Appeals	• Does not conduct trials, hear testimony, or accept new evidence. • Reviews trial court record to determine whether (1) the statute is constitutional, (2) the regulations are valid, (3) the district court judge applied the right law and correctly instructed the jury, (4) the district court judge abused his or her discretion in granting or denying a motion or granting or denying an objection, and (5) whether there is sufficient evidence to support the district court judge's or the jury's findings of fact.	• Federal statutes.* • Federal regulations.** • United States Supreme Court decisions. • Although the United States Courts of Appeals will usually follow their own prior decisions, those decisions are not mandatory authority.
United States Supreme Court	• Does not conduct trials, hear testimony, or accept new evidence. • Reviews trial court record to determine (1) whether the statute is constitutional, (2) whether regulations are valid, (3) whether the trial court applied	• Federal statutes.* • Federal regulations.** • Although the United States Supreme Court will usually follow its own decisions, those decisions are not mandatory authority.

Court	Role	Mandatory Authority
	the applicable law correctly, (4) whether the trial court judge abused his or her discretion in granting or denying a motion or granting or denying an objection, and (5) whether there is sufficient evidence to support the trial court judge's findings of fact or the jury's verdict.	

* If constitutional
** If valid

§ 4.1.3   Issue Governed by Common Law

For this last example, presume that you represent Mr. Garcia, who is concerned that a group that runs a summer camp has obtained, through adverse possession, title to land that he owns in Washington. Because adverse possession is a common law doctrine, the only statute that is on point is a Washington statute that sets out the statutory period for adverse possession.

Because the land is located in Washington, the case would be heard by one of Washington's trial courts, the Superior Court. In hearing the case, the Superior Court would apply the common law rules set out in Washington cases and the statutory time periods set out in Washington statutes. Because Washington has an intermediate court of appeals, the decisions of that court, the decisions of the Washington Supreme Court, and Washington statutes are mandatory authority.

The party that loses at trial can file an appeal with the Washington Court of Appeals. At the Washington Court of Appeals, the only mandatory authorities are decisions by the Washington Supreme Court and the Washington statutes that set out the length of time a person must possess the property to establish title through adverse possession. Although in most situations the Washington Court of Appeals would follow its own earlier decisions, those decisions are not mandatory authority. The party that loses at the Court of Appeals level can ask the Washington Supreme Court to review the Washington Court of Appeals' decision. If the Washington Supreme Court accepts review, the only authority that is mandatory authority is the statute that sets out the time limits.

§ 4.2   How Attorneys Use Cases

Attorneys use cases in two ways: (1) as authority for a common law rule or for a rule that the courts have created in interpreting and applying a statute or regulation and (2) to illustrate how the courts have applied a common law rule or a statute or regulation in analogous cases.

> **PRACTICE POINTER**   Sometimes an attorney will use one case as authority for a rule and another case to illustrate how that rule has been applied. At other times, an attorney will use the same case both as authority for a rule and as an analogous case to illustrate how that rule has been applied.

§ 4.2.1   Case as Authority for Rule

When an issue is governed by a common law rule, you will cite to one or more cases as authority for that common law rule. For instance, in the adverse possession case described in section 4.1.3, you would need to cite to a case or cases for both the general rules, that is, for the test the courts apply in determining whether an individual has gained title to land through adverse possession, and for the specific rules, that is, for the tests that the courts apply in determining whether a particular element is or is not met.

EXAMPLE 1   **Author Cites Cases as Authority for the Common Law Rule**

To establish title through adverse possession, the claimant must prove that its possession was (1) exclusive, (2) actual and uninterrupted, (3) open and notorious, and (4) hostile for the statutory period. *ITT Rayonier, Inc. v. Bell*, 112 Wn.2d 754, 757, 774 P.2d 6 (1989); *Chaplin v. Sanders*, 100 Wn.2d 853, 857, 676 P.2d 431 (1984).[1]

When the issue is governed by a statute, you will cite to the statute for the rules set out in the statute but to the cases for the rules that the courts have created in applying that statute. For example, if the courts have defined a word that is used in the statute, you will set out that definition and then cite a case as authority. Likewise, if the courts have set out rules or tests for determining whether a particular element is met, you will set out those rules or tests and cite a case or cases as authority.

EXAMPLE 2   **Author Sets Out Definition Developed by Florida Courts in Interpreting and Applying Florida's Service of Process Statute**

The Florida courts have defined "usual place of abode" as "the fixed place of residence for the time being when the service is made." *Shurman v. A. Mortg. & Inv. Corp.*, 795 So. 2d 952, 953-54 (Fla. 2001). "If a person has more than one residence, a summons must be served at the residence at which the defendant is actually living at the time of service." *Id.* at 954.

---

1. Because the issue would be decided by a Washington court, the author has used the Washington Style Sheet. See Appendix 2 in the *ALWD Guide to Legal Citation*, 5th ed.

If there are only one or two cases that have set out a common law, or court-made rule, cite those one or two cases as authority. If, however, there are a number of cases that have set out the same rules, do not cite all of the cases. Instead, select the one or two "best" cases. Begin by identifying the cases that are mandatory authority. From this group, you will usually want to select cases from higher courts over cases from lower courts and more recent cases over older cases. The exception is when all of the decisions from the higher courts are quite old. In this situation, you will usually want to cite one of the older higher court cases to show that the rule was established by the jurisdiction's highest court and then cite to one of the newer lower court decisions to show that the rule is still good law.

Selecting Cases to Cite as Authority for a Common Law or Court-Made Rule

1. Select cases that are mandatory authority over cases that are persuasive authority.
2. Of those cases that are mandatory authority, select cases that are from higher courts over cases from lower courts.
3. Of those cases that are from higher courts, select more recent cases over older cases.

Exception:

If all of the cases from higher courts are old, also cite to a more recent lower court decision to show that the rule is still being applied by the courts.

For more on setting out the general and specific rules, see Chapters 7 and 8.

§ 4.2.2   Using Analogous Cases to Illustrate How the Courts Have Applied a Statute or Common Law Rule

In addition to citing cases as authority for a common law, or court-made, rule, attorneys also use cases to illustrate how the courts have applied a particular rule. For example, attorneys will use cases to illustrate the types of situations in which the courts have held that a particular element of a statute or common law rule was met or not met. In selecting these analogous cases, most attorneys try to select cases that illustrate the types of situations in which the courts have held that the element was met and cases that illustrate the types of situations in which the courts have held that the element was not met. The attorneys then place those cases and their client's case along a continuum, arguing either that their client's case is more like the cases in which the element was met or more like the cases in which the element was not met.

| Element Met | Client's Case | Element Not Met |

The criteria for selecting analogous cases are a bit different from the criteria for selecting cases to cite as authority for a rule. Although you want to select cases that are mandatory authority over cases that are only persuasive authority, you will not always choose cases from higher courts over cases from lower courts or more recent cases over older cases. Instead, the cases that will be the "best" cases will be those that are most factually analogous to your case. Thus, you might select an intermediate court of appeals decision over a case from the jurisdiction's highest appellate court if the facts in the intermediate court of appeals decision are more similar to the facts in your case. Similarly, you might select an older case over a more recent one if the facts in the older case are more analogous to the facts in your case.

Selecting Analogous Cases

1. Select cases that are mandatory authority over cases that are persuasive authority.
2. Select cases that are more factually analogous over cases that are less factually analogous.
3. When possible, select representative cases in which the element was met and representative cases in which the element was not met.

§ 4.3   Reading and Analyzing Cases

Just as some statutes are hard to read and analyze, so too are some cases. Sometimes, a case is difficult to read and analyze because it has a complicated set of facts and a complicated procedural history. In these cases, just figuring out who the parties are and who did what may take effort. At other times, the case is difficult to read and analyze because it involves a complicated area of law and a complicated issue or set of issues. Unless you already understand the area of law, you will have a difficult time understanding the court's opinion. At still other times, the judge simply did a bad job writing the opinion: The opinion is poorly organized, the sentences are hard to read, or the writing is wordy or imprecise.

In the end, though, it does not matter whether a case is easy or difficult to read and analyze or why that might be the case. To do your job, you need to figure out what the case says and does not say and how the case might be applied.

§ 4.3.1   Finding Cases Using the Citation

Just as you can use the citation to a statute to find a copy of the statute (see section 3.4.1), you can use the case citation to find a copy of the case in the book form of a reporter, which is the name that is given to the sets of books that contain copies of judicial opinions. For more on state reporters, see section 4.2.4 in *Just Research*; for more on federal reporters, see section 5.2.3 in *Just Research*. You can also use the citation to find copies of cases on fee-based services — for example, on Lexis Advance, WestlawNext, or Bloomberg Law — or on free websites.

Most case citations contain three parts: the name of the case; references to the reporter or reporters in which the case can be found; and a parenthetical that includes, at a minimum, the year in which the opinion was issued. A case citation may also include a subsequent history section that provides information about what happened after the court issued its opinion and a parenthetical that provides the reader with additional information about the case. The following citation is a typical case citation.

Thompson v. State, Dept. of Revenue, 867 So. 2d 603 (Fla. App. 1 Dist., 2004).

In this citation, the first piece of information is the name of the case: *Thompson v. State, Dept. of Revenue*. In the second slot is set out the information that you will need to find a copy of the case. The first number, "867," is the volume number; the letters "So. 2d" are the abbreviation for the reporter; and the second number, "603," is the page on which the case begins. Thus, you can find a copy of *Thompson v. State, Dept. of Revenue* in volume 867 of the *Southern Reporter, Second Series*, beginning on page 603. The parenthetical gives you the information you need to determine whether the case is mandatory or persuasive authority: the name of the court that decided the case and the year of the decision.

Thompson v. State, Dept. of Revenue, 867　So. 2d　603　(Fla. App. 1 Dist.,　2004).

Case Name　　　　　　　　　　　Vol. Reporter Page　　　Court　　　　　Year

PRACTICE POINTER	For more on case citations, see Rule 12 in *ALWD Guide to Legal Citation, Fifth Edition*; Rule 10 in *The Bluebook, Nineteenth Edition*; or your jurisdiction's citation rules.

To find a copy of a case in the book form of a reporter, locate the appropriate set of reporters in the library, locate the correct volume, and then turn to the correct page. To find a copy of a case on a fee-based or free website, type the citation in the search text box.

PRACTICE POINTER	The following websites are free websites that contain the text of court opinions.

A. Federal Cases

1. United States Supreme Court

http://www.supremecourtus.gov/opinions/opinions.html
http://www.gpoaccess.gov/judicial.html
http://supct.law.cornell.edu/supct/

(continues)

2. United States Courts of Appeal, United States District Courts, and Special-ized Courts

http://www.uscourts.gov/links.html
http://www.gpoaccess.gov/judicial.html
http://www.law.cornell.edu/federal/opinions.html
http://www.law.emory.edu/FEDCTS/

B. State Cases

http://www.law.cornell.edu/opinions.html
state court websites

§ 4.3.2   Distinguishing Between the Text of an Opinion and Material Added by the Publisher

What you see when you locate a copy of a case depends on the source in which you have looked up that case. If you have found a copy of the case on a free website, more likely than not all that you will see is the text of the court's opinion. If, however, you have looked up the case in the book form of a reporter or on a fee-based website such as Lexis Advance, WestlawNext, or Bloomberg Law, you will find not only the text of the court's opinion but also editorial enhancements, for example, a syllabus and headnotes. Although these editorial enhancements are not part of the court's opinion and cannot, therefore, be cited as authority, they are useful tools for obtaining an overview of the opinion and for locating those parts of the opinion that are most relevant to the issue you have been asked to research.

Chart 4.3 walks you through the WestlawNext version of *Thompson v. State, Dept. of Revenue*.

Chart 4.3	**Thompson v. State, Dept. of Revenue, as It Appears on WestlawNext**

Original Image of 867 So.2d 603 (PDF)	This is a link to the PDF version of the case.
867 So.2d 603 District Court of Appeal of Florida, First District.	Caption: • Citation • Court
Calvin THOMPSON, Appellant, v. STATE of Florida, DEPARTMENT OF REVENUE, Appellee.	• Parties
No. 1D03-2975. March 5, 2004.	Case number Date of decision

Synopsis

Background: Department of Revenue filed action against father to
establish and enforce child support for daughter. The Circuit Court,
Duval County, E. McRae Mathis, J., denied father's motion to quash
service of process. Father appealed.

Holding: The District Court of Appeal, Van Nortwick, J., held that father
made prima facie showing that Department's petition was not served on
him at his usual place of abode.

Reversed and remanded.

West Headnotes (5)Collapse West Headnotes

Change View

1 Child Support
Father's affidavit stating that he was separated from wife and had not
resided with her for over three years was sufficient to make a prima
facie showing that Department of Revenue's petition to establish and
enforce child support, which was left with wife at her residence, was
not served on father at his usual place of abode, for purposes of Department's attempt to establish valid substituted service. West's F.S.A.
§ 48.031.
0 Case that cites this headnote
⌖

76EChild Support
76EVProceedings
76EV(A)In General
76Ek180Process

2 Process
The requirement that substituted service of process be at a defendant's
"usual place of abode" means the place where the defendant is actually
living at the time of service. West's F.S.A. § 48.031.
3 Cases that cite this headnote
⌖

313Process
313IIService
313II(B)Substituted Service
313k76Mode and Sufficiency of Service
313k78Leaving copy at residence or other place

This is the publisher's
(West's) synopsis of the
court's decision

West headnotes are
written by attorneys
employed by Thomson
Publishing Company, the
company that oper-
ates Westlaw Classic
and WestlawNext. The
attorney who is assigned
case reads the case and,
for each rule of law
set out by the court,
prepares a one-sentence
statement. These state-
ments are then placed
at the beginning of the
case as headnotes, in
West's digests, and if the
case involves a statute,
in the notes of decision
following the statute in
the West version of the
code.

To find the place in the
court's opinion from
which the attorney drew
the statement, click on
the number that is next
to the headnote or scroll
through the opinion
until you find the num-
ber. For example, to find
the place from which the
attorney drew the "rule"
set out in headnote 2,
click on the "2."

(continues)

3 Process

The burden of proof to sustain the validity of service of process is upon the person who seeks to invoke the jurisdiction of the court and, without proper service of process, the court lacks personal jurisdiction over the defendant. West's F.S.A. § 48.031.

2 Cases that cite this headnote

☞

313Process
313IIService
313II(A)Personal Service in General
313k48Nature and necessity in general

☞

313Process
313IIService
313II(E)Return and Proof of Service
313k144Evidence as to Service
313k145Presumptions and burden of proof

> To find cases that have cited *Thompson* click "Cases that cite this headnote."
>
> To find cases that have been indexed under the same key number, click on the applicable key number.

4 Process

A process server's return of service on a defendant which is regular on its face is presumed to be valid absent clear and convincing evidence presented to the contrary.

3 Cases that cite this headnote

☞

313Process
313IIService
313II(E)Return and Proof of Service
313k144Evidence as to Service
313k145Presumptions and burden of proof
(Formerly 313k149)

5 Process

A simple denial of having received service is not sufficient to contradict a process server's return of service that is regular on its face.

2 Cases that cite this headnote

☞

313Process
313IIService
313II(E)Return and Proof of Service
313k144Evidence as to Service
313k148Evidence to impeach or contradict return, certificate, or affidavit of service

Attorneys and Law Firms

*604 Esther A. Zaretsky, West Palm Beach, for Appellant.
Charles J. Crist, Jr., Attorney General and Toni C. Bernstein and William H. Branch, Assistant Attorneys General, Tallahassee, for Appellee.

> These are the attorneys of record in the case
>
> The *604 tells you that the text following the *604 is at the top of page 604 in the official reporter.

Opinion

VAN NORTWICK, J.

Calvin Thompson appeals a non-final order denying his motion to quash service of process in this support-administrative paternity action filed by the Department of Revenue. We reverse and remand for an evidentiary hearing pursuant to *Venetian Salami Co. v. Parthenais*, 554 So.2d 499, 502-03 (Fla.1989).

Pursuant to section 409.2564, Florida Statutes (2002), the Department filed an action to establish and enforce child support for Thompson's four year-old daughter. The petition was served at 625 F Covenant Drive, Belle Glade, Florida 33430, and accepted by Thompson's wife. Thompson filed a motion to dismiss/quash for lack of service of process stating that he was not present at the Belle Glade address and was not personally served. In his attached affidavit, Thompson stated that he has been separated from his wife, that he has not resided at that address for over three years, and that he did not authorize anyone to accept service of process on his behalf.

The trial court entered an order ruling that any jurisdictional defect could be cured by mailing a copy of the petition and accompanying documents to Thompson's attorney, "who has made a general appearance." The Department correctly concedes that the jurisdictional defect cannot *605 be cured in the manner suggested by the trial court and that Thompson's argument that the trial court lacked personal jurisdiction was not waived because Thompson neither took affirmative action nor sought affirmative relief prior to raising the alleged defect. *See Coto-Ojeda v. Samuel*, 642 So.2d 587, 588 (Fla. 3d DCA 1994)(Cope, J., specially concurring).

| 1 | 2 | 3 | Turning to the merits, "[s]ection 48.031 expressly requires that substituted service be at the person's usual place of abode." *Shurman v. Atlantic Mortgage & Investment Corp.*, 795 So.2d 952, 954 (Fla.2001). The requirement "usual place of abode" means "the place where the defendant is actually living at the time of service." *Id., citing State ex rel. Merritt v. Heffernan*, 142 Fla. 496, 195 So. 145, 147 (1940). The burden of proof to sustain the validity of service of process is upon the person who seeks to invoke the jurisdiction of the court and, without proper service of process, the court lacks personal jurisdiction over the defendant. *M.J.W. v. Department of Children and Families*, 825 So.2d 1038, 1041 (Fla. 1st DCA 2002).

| 4 | 5 | "[A] process server's return of service on a defendant which is regular on its face is presumed to be valid absent clear and convincing evidence presented to the contrary." *Telf Corp. v. Gomez*, 671 So.2d 818 (Fla. 3d DCA 1996). Although simple denial of service is not sufficient, *id.* at 819, Thompson's motion and affidavit are based on the fact that the service did not comply with section 48.031 and was therefore legally deficient. *National Safety Associates, Inc. v. Allstate Insurance Co.*, 799 So.2d 316, 317 (Fla. 2d DCA 2001). Thompson's affidavit makes a prima facie showing that he was not served at his usual

This is where the court's opinion begins.

In this case, Judge Van Nortwick wrote the opinion. (The "J" stands for judge or justice.)

*The *605 tells you that this is where page 604 ends and page 605 begins.*

The numbers 1, 2, and 3 tell you that this is the portion of the opinion from which the West attorney drew headnotes 1, 2, and 3.

The numbers 4 and 5 tell you that this is the portion of the opinion from which the West attorney drew headnotes 4 and 5.

(continues)

place of abode by valid substituted service. *See, e.g., S.H. v. Department of Children and Families*, 837 So.2d 1117, 1118 (Fla. 4th DCA 2003) (invalidating substituted service on father at mother's address, where mother's residence was not father's "usual place of abode" at the time of service); *Gonzalez v. Totalbank*, 472 So.2d 861 (Fla. 3d DCA 1985) (invalidating substituted service when wife was separated from husband and not living at address where service was attempted). Having raised the issue of personal jurisdiction, Thompson's motion and accompanying affidavit placed the burden on the Department to establish the validity of service of process. *M.J.W.*, 825 So.2d at 1041. Accordingly, the cause is reversed and remanded for an evidentiary hearing to determine whether the attempted service of Thompson pursuant to section 48.031, Florida Statutes (2003), was valid. *See Venetian Salami*, 554 So.2d at 502-03; *Mowrey Elevator of Florida, Inc. v. Automated Integration*, 745 So.2d 1046, 1047-48 (Fla. 1st DCA 1999).

REVERSED and REMANDED.   This is the end of the
                                                          court's opinion.
KAHN and BENTON, JJ., concur.

Parallel Citations   These are the names
                                                          of the judges who
29 Fla. L. Weekly D566   concurred in the court's
                                                          decision. (JJ means
                                                          judges or justices.)

§ 4.3.3   Reading the Opinion

If the opinion is relatively short, for example, only two or three pages long, you will usually want to begin by reading quickly through the entire case. If, however, the case is longer, you will want to make sure that the case is on point or relevant to the issue you have been asked to research before you invest too much time reading and analyzing it. Therefore, if the case is more than a few pages long, begin by reading any introductory material, for example, the background section or the syllabus and the headnotes. If the introductory material or headnotes indicate that the case deals with the statute, common law doctrine, or issue that you have been asked to research, use the headnote numbers to locate those portions of the opinion from which the headnotes were drawn, and read those portions of the opinion. If those portions of the opinion appear to be on point, go back and read the entire opinion.

PRACTICE POINTER While the time saved by reading just the headnotes may seem to outweigh the cost of taking the time to read the entire case, you cannot cite headnotes. Because the headnotes are written by an attorney working for a publishing company and not by the court, they are not authority.

When you read the full opinion, look for specific types of information. First, identify the issue. If the opinion is a trial court opinion, was the issue a procedural issue, for example, whether the plaintiff was entitled to summary judgment, or did the court decide the case on its merits? In contrast, if the opinion is from an appellate court, was the issue (1) whether the statute is constitutional, (2) whether the regulations are valid, (3) whether the trial court set out the law correctly or correctly instructed the jury, (4) whether the trial court judge abused his or her discretion in granting or denying a motion or granting or denying an objection, or (5) whether there is sufficient evidence to support the trial court judge's or the jury's findings of fact?

Second, if the opinion is from an appellate court, determine what standard of review the appellate court applied. If the issue involves an issue of law, the standard of review is usually *de novo*. Under this standard of review, the appellate court does not defer to the trial court. Instead, it makes its own independent determination of what law applies or what the law is. In contrast, if the issue involves an issue of fact or an exercise of judgment, the standard of review is usually more deferential. For example, in reviewing most factual determinations, the standard of review is a sufficiency of the evidence standard. The appellate court looks to see only if there is sufficient evidence to support the trial court's findings of fact or the jury's verdict. Similarly, in reviewing a trial court's decision to admit evidence, the appellate courts usually defer to the trial court, reversing the trial court only when the appellate court determines that the trial court judge abused his or her discretion.

Third, determine what rule or test the court applied in deciding the issue. Begin by determining whether the parties agreed about what the rule was. If the parties agreed on the rule, the issue is not what the rule is but how that rule should be applied in a particular fact situation. If the parties did not agree about what the rule was, what rule did the plaintiff ask the court to apply? What rule did the defendant ask the court to apply? What rule did the court choose?

Fourth, evaluate the court's reasoning. If the parties agreed about what the rule was, what facts did the court consider in applying that rule to the facts of the case? If the parties disagreed about what the rule was, why did the court pick one rule over another? For example, in deciding how to interpret a statute, did the court rely on the plain language of the statute, on the canons of statutory construction, or on the statute's legislative history?

Fifth, look carefully at the court's disposition of the case. Did the court affirm the trial court? Reverse the trial court? Remand the case back to the trial court for further action?

Last, think about how you might be able to the use the case. Can you use the case as authority for a rule? To illustrate how the courts have applied a particular rule? Similarly, think about how the other side might use the case, about how a trial court might use the case, and how the appellate court might use the case.

As the preceding paragraphs indicate, in reading and analyzing a case, your role is anything but that of a passive reader. Instead, you are reading the case as a lawyer, looking not only for the rules and how those rules have been applied, but also for how you and any other parties might be able to use the case.

Chart 4.4 demonstrates how an attorney would approach the reading of an opinion on Westlaw. In this "think aloud," the attorney who is reading the case represents Ms. Olsen, a woman who wants to overturn a decision terminating her parental rights on the grounds that she was not properly served. At the time of service, Ms. Olsen was spending four nights each week at a halfway house for recovering addicts and three nights each week at her sister's house. The summons was left with her sister at her sister's house on a day on which Ms. Olsen was not at her sister's house. The text of the opinion is in the left-hand column and what the defense attorney thought as she read the opinion is in the right-hand column. Because the case is short, the attorney read the entire case.

Chart 4.4	**Defense Attorney's Thoughts While Reading** *Thompson v. State, Dept. of Revenue*

Original Image of 867 So.2d 603 (PDF)

What Attorney Thought as She Read Opinion

867 So.2d 603
District Court of Appeal of Florida,
First District.

Calvin THOMPSON, Appellant,

v.

STATE of Florida, DEPARTMENT OF REVENUE, Appellee.
No. 1D03-2975.
March 5, 2004.

Okay, because this is a Florida case, it is mandatory authority. I need to remember to cite check it to make sure that it is still good law.

Synopsis

Background: Department of Revenue filed action against father to establish and enforce child support for daughter. The Circuit Court, Duval County, E. McRae Mathis, J., denied father's motion to quash service of process. Father appealed.

Holding: The District Court of Appeal, Van Nortwick, J., held that father made prima facie showing that Department's petition was not served on him at his usual place of abode.

Reversed and remanded.

West Headnotes

[1] KeyCite Notes

I am going to read the synopsis to see if the case is on point.

The father wanted the same thing that I want: to quash service.

Good. The issue in this case seems to be the same as the issue in my case. I want to establish that the sister's house was not my client's usual place of abode.

☞ 76E Child Support
  ☞ 76EV Proceedings
   ☞ 76EV(A) In General
    ☞ 76Ek180 k. Process. Most Cited Cases

Father's affidavit stating that he was separated from wife and had not resided with her for over three years was sufficient to make a prima facie showing that Department of Revenue's petition to establish and enforce child support, which was left with wife at her residence, was not served on father at his usual place of abode, for purposes of Department's attempt to establish valid substituted service. West's F.S.A. § 48.031.

> The facts in this case seem to be pretty different from the facts in my case. My client was staying with her sister a couple of nights a week. I may not be able to use this case as an analogous case.

[2] KeyCite Notes 🔲

☞ 313 Process
  ☞ 313II Service
   ☞ 313II(B) Substituted Service
    ☞ 313k76 Mode and Sufficiency of Service
     ☞ 313k78 k. Leaving Copy at Residence or Other Place. Most Cited Cases

The requirement that substituted service of process be at a defendant's "usual place of abode" means the place where the defendant is actually living at the time of service. West's F.S.A. § 48.031.

> This looks like the rule. It also looks like a rule that I can use to support our argument. I need to look at this part of the opinion.

[3] KeyCite Notes 🔲

☞ 313 Process
  ☞ 313II Service
   ☞ 313II(A) Personal Service in General
    ☞ 313k48 k. Nature and Necessity in General. Most Cited Cases

☞ 313 Process KeyCite Notes 🔲
  ☞ 313II Service
   ☞ 313II(E) Return and Proof of Service
    ☞ 313k144 Evidence as to Service
     ☞ 313k145 k. Presumptions and Burden of Proof. Most Cited Cases

The burden of proof to sustain the validity of service of process is upon the person who seeks to invoke the jurisdiction of the court and, without proper service of process, the court lacks personal jurisdiction over the defendant. West's F.S.A. § 48.031.

> Good. Here is the rule about burden of proof. It looks like the state has the burden. I need to look at this part of the opinion.

[4] KeyCite Notes 🔲

☞ 313 Process
  ☞ 313II Service
   ☞ 313II(E) Return and Proof of Service

☞ 313k144 Evidence as to Service
   ☞ 313k145 k. Presumptions and Burden of Proof. Most Cited
Cases

☞ 313 Process KeyCite Notes
  ☞ 313II Service
   ☞ 313II(E) Return and Proof of Service
    ☞ 313k144 Evidence as to Service
     ☞ 313k149 k. Weight and Sufficiency. Most Cited Cases

A process server's return of service on a defendant which is regular on
its face is presumed to be valid absent clear and convincing evidence
presented to the contrary.

[5] KeyCite Notes

☞ 313 Process
  ☞ 313II Service
   ☞ 313II(E) Return and Proof of Service
    ☞ 313k144 Evidence as to Service
     ☞ 313k148 k. Evidence to Impeach or Contradict Return, Certifi-
cate, or Affidavit of Service. Most Cited Cases

A simple denial of having received service is not sufficient to contradict
a process server's return of service that is regular on its face.

*604 Esther A. Zaretsky, West Palm Beach, for Appellant. Charles J. Crist,
Jr., Attorney General and Toni C. Bernstein and William H. Branch, Assistant Attorneys General, Tallahassee, for Appellee.

VAN NORTWICK, J.

Calvin Thompson appeals a non-final order denying his motion to quash
service of process in this support-administrative paternity action filed
by the Department of Revenue. We reverse and remand for an evidentiary hearing pursuant to *Venetian Salami Co. v. Parthenais*, 554 So.2d
499, 502-03 (Fla.1989).

Pursuant to section 409.2564, Florida Statutes (2002), the Department
filed an action to establish and enforce child support for Thompson's
four year-old daughter. The petition was served at 625 F Covenant Drive,
Belle Glade, Florida 33430, and accepted by Thompson's wife. Thompson
filed a motion to dismiss/quash for lack of service of process stating
that he was not present at the Belle Glade address and was not personally served. In his attached affidavit, Thompson stated that he has been
separated from his wife, that he has not resided at that address for over
three years, and that he did not authorize anyone to accept service of
process on his behalf. The trial court entered an order ruling that any
jurisdictional defect could be cured by mailing a copy of the petition
and accompanying documents to Thompson's attorney, "who has made
a general appearance." The Department correctly concedes that the jurisdictional defect cannot

---

This rule may hurt
us. If the phrase
"return of service"
means what I think
it does, then there
will be a presump-
tion that the service
is valid, and we will
have to present clear
and convincing evi-
dence. I need to read
this part of the opin-
ion, make sure that
I know what return
of service means,
and check the file to
see if in our case the
return of service was
regular.

This is just the
procedural history.
This was a paternity
action. Thompson,
who seems to be
the father, moved to
quash service.

Okay, the court is
setting out the facts.

The petition was
served at his wife's
house, and his wife
accepted service.

Thompson filed an
affidavit stating

*605 be cured in the manner suggested by the trial court and that Thompson's argument that the trial court lacked personal jurisdiction was not waived because Thompson neither took affirmative action nor sought affirmative relief prior to raising the alleged defect. *See Coto-Ojeda v. Samuel*, 642 So.2d 587, 588 (Fla. 3d DCA 1994)(Cope, J., specially concurring).

> that he had been separated from his wife and had not resided at her house for three years.
>
> Given our facts, most of this does not seem relevant.

[1] 🗒️ [2] 🗒️ [3] 🗒️ Turning to the merits, "[s]ection 48.031 expressly requires that substituted service be at the person's usual place of abode." *Shurman v. A. Mortg. & Investment Corp.*, 795 So.2d 952, 954 *(Fla.2001)*. The requirement "usual place of abode" means "the place where the defendant is actually living at the time of service." *Id., citing State ex rel. Merritt v. Heffernan*, 142 Fla. 496, 195 So. 145, 147 (1940).

> Although the court does not set out the issue on appeal, the issue seems to be whether the service was at the defendant's usual place of abode.
>
> Good. Here is a definition of usual place of abode. Court cites an old Florida Supreme Court decision as authority.

The burden of proof to sustain the validity of service of process is upon the person who seeks to invoke the jurisdiction of the court and, without proper service of process, the court lacks personal jurisdiction over the defendant. *M.J.W. v. Department of Children and Families*, 825 So.2d 1038, 1041 (Fla. 1st DCA 2002).

> Here are the rules about the burden of proof.

[4] 🗒️ [5] 🗒️ "[A] process server's return of service on a defendant which is regular on its face is presumed to be valid absent clear and convincing evidence presented to the contrary." *Telf Corp. v. Gomez*, 671 So.2d 818 (Fla. 3d DCA 1996). Although simple denial of service is not sufficient, *id.* at 819, Thompson's motion and affidavit are based on the fact that the service did not comply with section 48.031 and was therefore legally deficient. *National Safety Associates, Inc. v. Allstate Insurance Co.*, 799 So.2d 316, 317 (Fla. 2d DCA 2001). Thompson's affidavit makes a *prima facie* showing that he was not served at his usual place of abode by valid substituted service. *See, e.g., S.H. v. Department of Children and Families*, 837 So.2d 1117, 1118 (Fla. 4th DCA 2003) (invalidating substituted service on father at mother's address, where mother's residence was not father's "usual place of abode" at the time of service); *Gonzalez v. Totalbank*, 472 So.2d 861 (Fla. 3d DCA 1985) (invalidating substituted service when wife was separated from husband and not living at address where service was attempted). Having raised the issue of personal jurisdiction, Thompson's motion and accompanying

> Okay, we are going to have to do more than just allege that the sister's house is not our client's usual place of abode. We are going to have to submit an affidavit establishing that her residence was somewhere else.
>
> These cases look like they are on point. I need to look at them once I finish reading this case.

affidavit placed the burden on the Department to establish the validity of service of process. *M.J.W.*, 825 So.2d at 1041. Accordingly, the cause is reversed and remanded for an evidentiary hearing to determine whether the attempted service of Thompson pursuant to section 48.031, Florida Statutes (2003), was valid. *See Venetian Salami*, 554 So.2d at 502-03; *Mowrey Elevator of Florida, Inc. v. Automated Integration*, 745 So.2d 1046, 1047-48 (Fla. 1st DCA 1999).
REVERSED and REMANDED.

KAHN and BENTON, JJ., concur.

I don't know whether Mr. Thompson won. However, the affidavit was enough to get the case back to the trial court for an evidentiary hearing.

We can use this case for the rules relating to what is and is not a person's usual place of abode and for the rules relating to the burden of proof. The State is going to say that our case is much weaker than this case. While Ms. Olsen was staying with her sister three nights a week, Mr. Thompson hadn't (or says he hadn't) lived with his wife for three years. We are going to have to focus on the language—"actually living at the time of service" to argue that at the time of service Ms. Olsen was not actually living with her sister.

§ 4.4   Exercise

As you read the following case, write in the right-hand margin what you are thinking as you read. After you have finished doing your own "think aloud," compare what you wrote to what one of your classmates wrote.

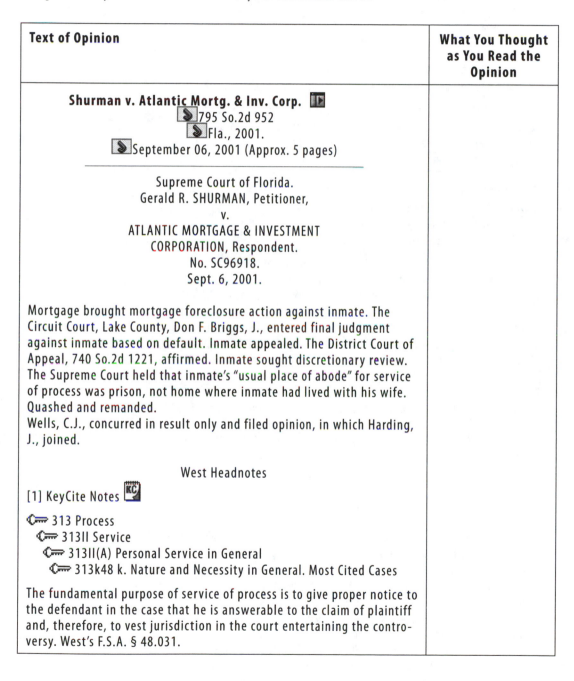

Text of Opinion	What You Thought as You Read the Opinion

Shurman v. Atlantic Mortg. & Inv. Corp.
795 So.2d 952
Fla., 2001.
September 06, 2001 (Approx. 5 pages)
 	
Supreme Court of Florida.
Gerald R. SHURMAN, Petitioner,
v.
ATLANTIC MORTGAGE & INVESTMENT
CORPORATION, Respondent.
No. SC96918.
Sept. 6, 2001.
 	
Mortgage brought mortgage foreclosure action against inmate. The Circuit Court, Lake County, Don F. Briggs, J., entered final judgment against inmate based on default. Inmate appealed. The District Court of Appeal, 740 So.2d 1221, affirmed. Inmate sought discretionary review. The Supreme Court held that inmate's "usual place of abode" for service of process was prison, not home where inmate had lived with his wife. Quashed and remanded.
Wells, C.J., concurred in result only and filed opinion, in which Harding, J., joined.
 	
West Headnotes
 	
[1] KeyCite Notes
 	
313 Process
  313II Service
    313II(A) Personal Service in General
      313k48 k. Nature and Necessity in General. Most Cited Cases
 	
The fundamental purpose of service of process is to give proper notice to the defendant in the case that he is answerable to the claim of plaintiff and, therefore, to vest jurisdiction in the court entertaining the controversy. West's F.S.A. § 48.031.	

[2] KeyCite Notes 🔲

⟜ 313 Process
  ⟜ 313II Service
    ⟜ 313II(A) Personal Service in General
    ⟜ 313k49 k. Statutory Provisions. Most Cited Cases
⟜ 313 Process KeyCite Notes 🔲
  ⟜ 313II Service
    ⟜ 313II(A) Personal Service in General
    ⟜ 313k64 k. Mode and Sufficiency of Service. Most Cited Cases

Because of the importance of litigants receiving notice of actions against them, statutes governing service of process are to be strictly construed and enforced. West's F.S.A. § 48.031.

[3] KeyCite Notes 🔲

⟜ 266 Mortgage
  ⟜ 266X Foreclosure by Action
    ⟜ 266X(E) Parties and Process
    ⟜ 266k440 k. Process in General. Most Cited Cases

Inmate's "usual place of abode" for service of process in foreclosure action was prison, not house where prisoner formerly lived with his wife, where inmate actually lived in prison. West's F.S.A. § 48.031.

*952 Gerald R. Shurman, pro se, Orlando, FL, for Petitioner. Anne S. Mason and Jennifer S. Ebanks of Mason & Associates, P.A., Clearwater, FL, for Respondent.

PER CURIAM.
We have for review *Shurman v. Atlantic Mortgage & Investment*, 740 So.2d 1221 (Fla. 5th DCA 1999), which expressly and directly conflicts with *953 *State ex rel. Merritt v. Heffernan*, 142 Fla. 496, 195 So. 145 (1940). We have jurisdiction. *See* art. V, § 3(b)(3), Fla. Const. For the reasons set forth below, we quash the decision of the district court.

FACTS

The record reflects that Gerald Shurman was criminally prosecuted, convicted, and incarcerated in state prison in May of 1997. Subsequently, Shurman was named as a defendant in a mortgage foreclosure action commenced in March of 1998 by Atlantic Mortgage & Investment Corporation (Atlantic). Service of process was effected on Shurman by substituted service on his wife, Emily, at their home where they had resided together before Shurman's incarceration. At the time of service of process Shurman was incarcerated in state prison. Because no responsive pleadings were filed by Shurman a default was entered against him in May of 1998. Thereafter, the trial court granted Atlantic's motion for final summary judgment of foreclosure and the property was sold at a foreclosure sale on June 25, 1998, to the second mortgagee.

On January 11, 1999, Shurman filed a motion to set aside the judgment alleging that he was not properly served process in the action and, therefore, the judgment as to his interest in the property was void. Following an evidentiary hearing on Shurman's motion, the trial court concluded that Shurman's "usual place of abode" for purposes of serving process under section 48.031, Florida Statutes (1997), was the residence where he lived with his wife prior to his incarceration and where his wife continued to reside afterward. As such, the trial court found that service was perfected when a copy of the process and complaint was left with Shurman's wife at their marital residence. In light of its finding that service was valid and that Shurman had not demonstrated any meritorious defense to the foreclosure action, the trial court denied Shurman's motion to set aside the judgment.

On appeal, the Fifth District affirmed the trial court's denial of Shurman's motion to set aside the judgment. *See Shurman v. Atlantic Mortgage & Inv.*, 740 So.2d 1221 (Fla. 5th DCA 1999). Relying on *Bull v. Kistner*, 257 Iowa 968, 135 N.W.2d 545 (1965), and *Montes v. Seda*, 157 Misc.2d 895, 599 N.Y.S.2d 401, 403 (Sup.Ct.1993), *aff'd*, 208 A.D.2d 388, 626 N.Y.S.2d 61 (1994), the district court agreed with the trial court's conclusion that service was made at Shurman's "usual place of abode." *Shurman*, 740 So.2d at 1222. The district court noted that Shurman and his wife had resided at the subject property for years prior to his incarceration and his family continued to reside there afterward. *See id.* at 1223. Accordingly, the court held that service was valid. *See id.* Shurman subsequently sought discretionary review in this Court.

ANALYSIS

The issue presented in this case is whether Shurman was properly served at his "usual place of abode" as required under section 48.031, Florida Statutes (1997). Shurman argues that since he was incarcerated at the time of service his "usual place of abode" was prison and, as such, he should have been served there in order to be afforded due process. By contrast, Atlantic asserts that an incarcerated party's "usual place of abode" is where the party resided prior to incarceration if the party's family continues to reside there.

[1] It is well settled that the fundamental purpose of service is "to give proper notice to the defendant in the case that he is answerable to the claim of plaintiff and, therefore, to vest jurisdiction in the court entertaining the controversy." *State ex rel. Merritt v. Heffernan*,

142 Fla. 496, 195 So. 145, 147 (1940); *see also* *954 *Klosenski v. Flaherty*, 116 So.2d 767, 768 (Fla.1959) (quoting *Heffernan*); *Clark v. Clark*, 158 Fla. 731, 30 So.2d 170, 171 (1947) ("The purpose of constructive or substituted service is to bring knowledge of the pending litigation to the defendant in order that he may appear and guard his interests."); *Gribbel v. Henderson*, 151 Fla. 712, 10 So.2d 734, 739 (1942); *Arcadia Citrus Growers Ass'n v. Hollingsworth*, 135 Fla. 322, 185 So. 431, 434 (1938). In other words, the purpose of this jurisdictional scheme is to give the person affected notice of the proceedings and an opportunity to defend his rights.

[2] 🖳 Section 48.031, Florida Statutes (1997), provides in pertinent part:

> (1)(a) Service of original process is made by delivering a copy of it to the person to be served with a copy of the complaint, petition, or other initial pleading or paper or by leaving the copies at his or her usual place of abode with any person residing therein who is 15 years of age or older and informing the person of their contents.

§ 48.031(1)(a), Fla. Stat. (1997). Section 48.031 expressly requires that substituted service be at the person's "usual place of abode." *Id.* Further, because of the importance of litigants receiving notice of actions against them, statutes governing service of process are to be strictly construed and enforced. *See Schupak v. Sutton Hill Assocs.*, 710 So.2d 707, 708 (Fla. 4th DCA 1998); *Aero Costa Rica, Inc. v. Dispatch Servs., Inc.*, 710 So.2d 218, 219 (Fla. 3d DCA 1998); *Hauser v. Schiff*, 341 So.2d 531, 531 (Fla. 3d DCA 1977).

In *Heffernan*, this Court defined the term "usual place of abode" as meaning the place where the defendant is actually living at the time of service. *See Heffernan*, 195 So. at 147. In so doing, we quoted favorably from *Eckman v. Grear*, 14 N.J. Misc. 807, 187 A. 556 (Com. Pl.1936), and *Mygatt v. Coe*, 63 N.J.L. 510, 44 A. 198 (Sup.Ct.1899):

We quote further from the case of *Eckman v. Grear*, 187 A. 556, 558, 14 N.J.Misc. 807:

> "Going one step further, 'usual place of abode' is the place where the defendant is actually living at the time of the service. The word abode means one's fixed place of residence for the time being when the service is made. Thus, if a person have several residences, he must be served at the residence in which he is actually living at the time service is made."

And in *Mygatt v. Coe*, 63 N.J.L. 510, 512, 44 A. 198, 199, the following pertinent statement appears:

> "The statute does not direct service to be made at the 'residence' of the defendant, but at his 'dwelling house' or 'usual place of

abode,' which is a much more restricted term. As was said in *Stout v. Leonard*, 37 N.J.L. 492, many persons have several residences, which they permanently maintain, occupying one at one period of the year and another at another period. Where such conditions exist, a summons must be served at the dwelling house in which the defendant is living at the time when the service is made."

Heffernan, 195 So. at 147. *See also Milanes v. Colonial Penn Ins. Co.*, 507 So.2d 777, 778 (Fla. 3d DCA 1987); *Panter v. Werbel-Roth Securities, Inc.*, 406 So.2d 1267, 1268 (Fla. 4th DCA 1981); *Hauser*, 341 So.2d at 532.

Not surprisingly, in applying the definition of the term "usual place of abode" set forth in *Heffernan*, courts have frequently invalidated substituted service of process in cases where the defendant was not actually living at the place where service was made. *See, e.g.,* *955 *Alvarez v. State Farm Mutual Auto Ins. Co.*, 635 So.2d 131, 132 (Fla. 3d DCA 1994) (invalidating substituted service on defendant's cousin where affidavits and supporting documentation, including a telephone bill and marriage license, established defendant was not living at that address on the date of service); *Milanes*, 507 So.2d at 778 (noting that service of process on the residence of defendant's ex-wife did not satisfy section 48.031); *Stern v. Gad*, 505 So.2d 531, 532 (Fla. 3d DCA 1987) (holding mere ownership of a condominium and service upon the wife of an owner will not suffice to establish "usual place of abode," when defendant submitted affidavit that he was not in the jurisdiction on the date of purported service and did not reside in the United States); *Gonzalez v. Totalbank*, 472 So.2d 861, 864 (Fla. 3d DCA 1985) (invalidating substituted service where wife was separated from husband and no longer living at address where service was attempted); *Panter*, 406 So.2d at 1268 (finding substituted service at home of appellant's father invalid where uncontradicted affidavits stated appellant was living in Michigan when service was made). Notably, several of these cases involved familial relationships where presumably the defendant would be more likely to receive notice, yet the courts still invalidated the service of process because the defendant was not actually living at the place where service was made. *See Alvarez*, 635 So.2d at 132 (substituted service on defendant's cousin); *Stern*, 505 So.2d at 532 (substituted service on wife); *Panter*, 406 So.2d at 1268 (substituted service on appellant's father).

[3] 🎞️ In this case it is uncontradicted that Shurman had been incarcerated in prison in May of 1997 and had not been living with his wife for at least nine months prior to the time substituted service was effected. Although Atlantic argues that Shurman's "usual place of abode" was where he lived with his family before being incarcerated, Shurman was "actually living" in prison at the time of service. Thus, under our obligation to strictly construe the statutory notice provisions and our analysis in *Heffernan*, it is apparent that Shurman's

"usual place of abode" was prison, not his prior residence. *See Heffernan*, 195 So. at 147.

We find additional support for our decision in *Heffernan* and our conclusion that prison was Shurman's "usual place of abode" in *Fidelity & Deposit Co. v. Abagnale*, 97 N.J.Super. 132, 234 A.2d 511 (1967), and *Saienni v. Oveide*, 355 A.2d 707 (Del.Super.Ct.1976).[FN1] In *Abagnale*, the court rejected the defendant's argument that he could be reached by substituted service in New Jersey while he was incarcerated out-of-state. The court explained:

> FN1. We recognize that the majority of jurisdictions have reached a different conclusion. *See Blue Cross & Blue Shield v. Chang*, 109 F.R.D. 669 (E.D.Mich.1986); *Bohland v. Smith*, 7 F.R.D. 364 (E.D.Ill.1947); *Grant v. Dalliber*, 11 Conn. 234 (1836); *Bull v. Kistner*, 257 Iowa 968, 135 N.W.2d 545 (1965); *Fidelity & Deposit Co. v. Boundy*, 236 Mo.App. 656, 158 S.W.2d 243 (1942); *Walker v. Stevens*, 52 Neb. 653, 72 N.W. 1038 (1897); *Montes v. Seda*, 157 Misc.2d 895, 599 N.Y.S.2d 401 (Sup.Ct.1993), *aff'd,* 208 A.D.2d 388, 626 N.Y.S.2d 61 (1994); *Smith v. Hooton*, 3 Pa.D. 250 (1894). *See generally* Allen E. Korpela, Annotation, *Construction of Phrase "Usual Place of Abode," or Similar Terms Referring to Abode, Residence, or Domicil, as Used in Statutes Relating to Service of Process,* 32 A.L.R.3d 112, § 16 (1970). However, we believe that the better view is that one's "usual place of abode" is where the person is actually living at the time of service, even in cases involving prisoners.

The law in this State has developed in somewhat rigid conformity to the principle that provisions for substituted service, being in derogation of the common law, must be strictly construed. Hence, the rule has been consistently applied *956 that one's "dwelling house or usual place of abode" is limited in its meaning to the place where one is "actually living" at the time when service is made. The expectation that a defendant will normally receive notice of process served through a competent member of his household living at the same place of abode as he, does not, it seems to me, prevail in the setting of familial disorganization frequently ensuing where the head of the household is committed to prison. *Abagnale*, 234 A.2d at 519 (citations omitted). While the court recognized some jurisdictions had concluded that an incarcerated party's usual place of abode continues to be where his family resides, it distinguished those cases on the basis that they were "largely influenced, if not governed, by a hybrid of residence and domicile." *Id.* The Delaware court in *Saienni* followed *Abagnale* and held that the defendant, who was incarcerated in Pennsylvania, was not properly served at his usual place of abode by substituted service on his wife in Delaware. The court noted that in Delaware a person's usual place of abode is not the equivalent of his domicile. *See Saienni*, 355 A.2d at 708. Rather, for purposes of substituted service, a defendant must be served at the place where he is

actually living at the time service is made. *See id.* (citing *Whetsel v. Gosnell*, 181 A.2d 91 (Del.1962)). Relying on *Abagnale* and *Whetsel*, the court concluded that the defendant's usual place of abode was the Pennsylvania State Correctional Institution since that was where the defendant was physically living at the time of service. *See id.* We find the reasoning of the courts in *Abagnale* and *Saienni* persuasive in this case. As stated previously, the object of all process is to impart to the person affected notice of the proceeding and an opportunity to defend his rights. *See Klosenski*, 116 So.2d at 768; *Clark*, 30 So.2d at 171; *Gribbel*, 10 So.2d at 739; *Heffernan*, 195 So. at 147; *Arcadia Citrus Growers Ass'n*, 185 So. at 434. By applying the definition of "usual place of abode" set forth in *Heffernan* to the facts in this case, we are adhering to this underlying principle. Further, it is clear that the Legislature contemplated that people in prison would be sued and served with process. Section 48.051, Florida Statutes (1997), provides that "[p]rocess against a state prisoner shall be served on the prisoner." *Id. Cf. State ex rel. Page v. Hollingsworth*, 117 Fla. 288, 157 So. 887 (1934). Had the Legislature intended the term "usual place of abode" to apply differently to prisoners, it could have so stated. Hence, we see no need to depart from *Heffernan* in cases involving prisoners. In sum, we adhere to *Heffernan* and reaffirm that for purposes of substituted service one's "usual place of abode" is where the person is actually living at the time of service. In this case, it is uncontroverted that Shurman was actually living in prison at the time substituted service was made on his wife at their marital residence. Thus, Shurman was not properly served at his usual place of abode as required under section 48.031(1)(a), Florida Statutes (1997). Accordingly, we quash the decision of the district court of appeal and remand for further proceedings consistent herewith.
It is so ordered.

SHAW, HARDING, ANSTEAD, PARIENTE, LEWIS, and QUINCE, JJ., concur.

WELLS, C.J., concurs with an opinion, in which HARDING, J., concurs.

WELLS, C.J., concurring.
I concur in result only in this case. I conclude that this decision should be controlled by the plain meaning of *957 section 48.051, Florida Statutes, which states: "Process against a state prisoner shall be served on the prisoner." I would read this to mean that process should be served on the prisoner at the prison. I do not believe reliance on section 48.031(1)(a), Florida Statutes, is appropriate.

HARDING, J., concurs.

Reprinted with permission.

Reading Like a Lawyer

U ntil a few years ago, most law professors and experienced attorneys assumed that law students and new attorneys read statutes and cases in the same way that they read them. While some individuals come to law school reading as experienced attorneys read, most do not. As a consequence, during their first year of law school, many law students have to "unlearn" the reading strategies that they used as undergraduates or in their home countries and learn a new way of reading. For example, many first-year law students have to change their focus from passively reading for information to a much more engaged and critical form of reading.

   This chapter tries to speed up the process of learning how to read as lawyers read by identifying both the characteristics of good legal readers and the strategies that good legal readers use. Although you may be tempted to skip this chapter, don't. While the research on legal reading is limited, the research that does exist suggests that there is a strong correlation between reading like a lawyer and doing well on law school exams.

§ 5.1   Good Lawyers Are Good Readers

   Good lawyers are good readers. When they read a document, statute, or case, they read exactly what is on the page. They do not skip words, read in words, or misread words. In addition, they have good vocabularies. They recognize and understand most of the words that they read, and the ones that they do not recognize or understand they look up either in a book or an online dictionary.

> **PRACTICE POINTER**
>
> There are a number of good, free online dictionaries. For example, *Merriam-Webster's Online Dictionary* is at *http://www.m-w.com;* the *Cambridge Dictionaries Online* is at *http://dictionary .cambridge.org;* JURIST's *Legal Dictionaries* are at *http://jurist.law.pitt .edu/dictionary.htm;* and FindLaw's *Legal Dictionary* is at *http://dictionary .lp.findlaw.com.*

Poor reading skills can significantly affect your ability to understand what you are reading. For instance, in the following example, which is taken from the transcript of a law student reading a case aloud, Jackie, a first-year student, mispronounced and apparently did not recognize the word "palatial."[1]

EXAMPLE   **Transcript of Jackie's Think Aloud**

Some months prior to the alleged imprisonment, the plaintiff, while in Jaffa, announced her intention to leave the sect. The defendant, with the help of the plaintiff's husband, persuaded the plaintiff to return to the United States aboard the sect's [platial] yacht, the Kingdom.

James, another student who read the same case, misread the following sentence. The first example shows how the sentence appears in the casebook. The second sentence shows how James read it when he read the sentence aloud.

EXAMPLE   **Sentence as It Appears in the Casebook**

According to the uncontradicted evidence, at no time did any one physically restrain the plaintiff except for the defendant's refusal, once the plaintiff announced her decision to quit the yacht, to let the plaintiff use a small boat to take herself, her children, and belongings ashore.

EXAMPLE   **Sentence as James Read It**

According to the uncontradicted evidence, at no time did any one physically restrain the plaintiff except for the defendant's (pause) defendant's refusal once (pause) defendant's refusal once (pause) the plaintiff announced her decision to quit the yacht to let the plaintiff use a small boat to take herself, her children, and belongings ashore.

When questioned about what the court was saying in this sentence, James stated that the defendant had, on one occasion, refused to let the plaintiff take the boat. In fact, the court says that the refusal came once the defendant announced her decision to quit the yacht.

Although at first these errors may seem insignificant, in each instance they resulted in the student misunderstanding the case and, thus, the rules and the

---

1. The examples in this section come from Laurel Currie Oates, *Beating the Odds, Reading Strategies of Law Students Admitted Through Special Admissions Programs,* 83 Iowa L. Rev. 139 (1997). See also Laurel Currie Oates, *Leveling the Playing Field: Helping Students Succeed by Helping Them Learn to Read as Expert Lawyers,* 80 St. John's L. Rev. 227 (2006).

court's reasoning. In addition, in both instances, the errors were a harbinger of things to come. Both students ended up doing poorly on their exams. At the end of the first year, Jackie was in the bottom 20 percent of her class, and James had flunked out.

To determine whether you may be misreading cases, make two copies of one of the cases in your casebook. Keep one copy for yourself, and give the other to a trusted classmate or teaching assistant. Then read aloud from your copy while your partner follows along on his or her copy, highlighting any words or phrases that you misread and any words that you mispronounce or do not appear to understand. After you have finished your reading of the case, compare your understanding of the case with your partner's. Did you both read the case in essentially the same way? If your partner noted more than one or two problems or if your understanding of the case is substantially different from your partner's, try the following. First, try reading more slowly. You may be trying to read the material too quickly. Second, take the time to look up any words that you are not sure that you understand. Third, if the problems appear to be serious, ask your school's learning center if it can provide you with a more thorough evaluation of your reading skills.

§ 5.2   Good Legal Readers Read and Reread Material Until They Are Sure that They Understand It

While in some types of reading you can skip sections that you do not completely understand, such a strategy does not work when you are doing legal reading. If the document, statute, or case is one that is relevant to your problem, you need to read and reread it until you are sure that you understand it.

The following example shows how a first-year student, William, read and reread a case until he was sure that he understood it. The material in the regular typeface is the text of the case. The material in italics is what William said after he had read that section of the text.

EXAMPLE	**Excerpt from William's Think Aloud**

Whittaker v. Sanford
110 Me. 77, 88 S. 399 (1912)

Savage, J. Action for false imprisonment. The plaintiff recovered a verdict for $1100. The case comes up on defendant's exceptions and a motion for a new trial.

So the defendant is the appellant and is appealing the verdict of $1100.

The plaintiff had been a member of a religious sect, which had colonies in Maine and in Jaffa, Syria, and of which the defendant was a leader. Some months prior to the alleged imprisonment, the plaintiff, while in Jaffa, announced her intention to leave the sect.

I need to reread this again [rereads sentence]. So just prior to the alleged imprisonment the plaintiff was in Jaffa and expressed an intention to leave the sect. At this point, I am a bit confused about who the parties are. I need to reread this to make sure that I have the facts straight. [rereads from the beginning.]

OK. This is an action for false imprisonment. The plaintiff recovered a verdict for $1100. The case came up on the defendant's exceptions. The plaintiff is a member of the sect and the defendant is the head of the sect so Whittaker is the member of the sect and Sanford is its leader.

Although it took William more time to read the case than it took some of the other students, the payoff was substantial. Although his undergraduate GPA and LSAT placed William in the bottom 10 percent of his entering law school class, at the end of his first year, his law school GPA placed him in the top 10 percent.

There are several things you can do to make sure that you understand the cases that you are reading. First, see if you can diagram the action. At the trial court level, who sued whom and what was the cause of action? Who "won" at trial, who filed the appeal, and what is the issue on appeal?

> **PRACTICE POINTER**   In some instances, you may be able to compare your chart showing the case's prior and subsequent history with the chart that is on KeyCite under Direct History, Graphical View.

Second, do not underestimate the value of preparing your own case briefs. While it may be faster and easier to highlight sections of a statute or case, highlighting does not ensure that you understand the material you are reading. In fact, there is some evidence that students who highlight remember less than students who do not highlight. (In highlighting a section, some students focus their attention on the process of highlighting and not on the material that they are highlighting. As a result, when they are asked to recall what it is that they just highlighted, they are unable to do so.)

Finally, after reading a statute or case, test yourself to make sure you understand what you just read. After reading a statute, diagram that statute. See section 3.4.4. After reading a case, answer the following questions: (1) What issue was before the court? (2) What was the standard of review? (3) What rule did the court apply? (4) In applying the rule, what facts did the court consider? (5) What did the court decide, and why did it decide the case that way? (6) What was the disposition: Did the appellate court affirm, reverse, or remand? See section 3.4.4. If you cannot diagram the statute or answer these questions about the case, keep reading until you can.

§ 5.3   Good Legal Readers Synthesize the Statutes and Cases that They Read

In addition to reading accurately and until they understand the statutes and cases, good legal readers synthesize the statutes and cases that they read.

Synthesis is the process of putting the pieces together. You take each of the statutory sections and cases you have read and try to make sense of them. Are they consistent? What are the steps in the analysis? How do they fit into your existing conceptual frameworks?

The following example shows the type of synthesis that a law professor did in reading a restatement section and a case. The text is set out in regular type and the professor's comments in italics.

| **EXAMPLE** | **Excerpt from Law Professor's Think Aloud** |

There was evidence that the plaintiff had been ashore a number of times, had been on numerous outings and had been treated as a guest during her stay aboard the yacht. According to the uncontradicted evidence, at no time did anyone physically restrain the plaintiff except for the defendant's refusal, once the plaintiff announced her decision to quit the yacht, to let the plaintiff use a small boat to take herself, her children, and her belongings ashore.

I'm sort of getting a visual image of the boat that she was in and out of . . . uhm . . . the plaintiff had been ashore. I'm thinking about the elements that I just read [a reference to the *Restatement* section that had been set out immediately before the case] *and I'm trying to see how, I guess, frankly how I would decide the case on a certain level before I even want to know what Judge Savage thought.* [pause] *I need to look at the Restatement section* [looks back at the *Restatement* section]. *Is the defendant acting to or with intent to confine the plaintiff? She got off the boat. That kind of bothers me. That results directly or indirectly in confinement. Maybe that's relevant here. The other is conscious of the confinement or is harmed by it. Given the facts, that bothers me too.*

Doing synthesis is time consuming and hard work. You are no longer reading just for information. Instead, as you are reading, you are either placing new information into existing conceptual frameworks or constructing completely new frameworks.

If you are like most law students, at some point you will argue that law school would be a lot easier if your professors put the pieces together for you, if they just gave you their conceptual frameworks. If you had come to law school just to learn the law, you would be right. It would be easier for both you and your professors if they just gave you the law. However, there is a lot more to law school than just learning the law. Although you will learn some law while you are in law school, the real reason that you came to law school was to learn to think like a lawyer. Thus, the primary skills you will need to teach yourself while you are in law school are how to do legal analysis and synthesis. You need to be able to look at a statute and a group of cases and determine what the law is and how it might be applied in a particular situation.

§ 5.4   Good Legal Readers Place Statutes and Cases that They Read into Their Historical, Social, Economic, Political, and Legal Contexts

Good legal readers understand that statutes are usually enacted to solve a problem or to promote certain interests and that judicial decisions reflect, at least in part, the time and place in which they were written. As a consequence, in reading statutes and cases, good legal readers place those statutes and cases in their historical, social, economic, political, and legal contexts. They note the date that the statute was enacted and amended (if applicable) and the year in which the case was decided. They think about the social and economic conditions during those periods and about the political issues that were in the headlines when the statute was enacted or amended or the case was decided. Finally, they place the case in its larger legal context. They determine how the particular issue fits into the broader area of law, they note whether the decision is from an intermediate court of appeals or from the highest court in the jurisdiction, and they read the court's decision in light of the standard of review that the court applied. Was the court deciding the issue *de novo*, or was it simply looking to see whether there was sufficient evidence to support the jury's verdict?

> ### PRACTICE POINTER
>
> If you do not know what the phrase *de novo* means, look it up in a print or online dictionary. When you use the online link on FindLaw, you retrieve the following information:
>
> [de-'no-vo, da-]
> Medieval Latin, literally, from (the) new
> : over again: as if for the first time: as
> a: allowing independent appellate determination of issues (as of fact or law)
> Example: a de novo review
> b: allowing complete retrial upon new evidence
> (compare abuse of discretion clearly erroneous)
>
> Note: A *de novo* review is an in-depth review. Decisions of federal administrative agencies are generally subject to *de novo* review in the United States District Courts, and some lower state court decisions are subject to *de novo* review at the next level.
>
> Reprinted with permission.

In reading the case that is set out in the examples in this chapter, the professor placed the case in its historical, social, and political context. First, she noted that the case was an old one. It was decided by the Maine Supreme Judicial Court in 1912. Second, she noted that, in 1912, $1,100 would have been a substantial amount of money. Third, she considered the social climate in 1912: the role of women and their rights and the public's attitudes about "religious cults." She knew that in 1912 women had far fewer rights than they do today. For instance, it was often the husband who determined where the couple lived and what religion they practiced. What she did not know was how religious cults were viewed. In 1912 did people view religious cults in the same way that most people view them today? Were cults seen as a problem? How did these factors influence the court's decision and the way it wrote its opinion?

You need to think about the cases that you read in similar ways. When you are reading cases, pay close attention to the dates of the decisions and the courts that issued them. If you read the cases in chronological order, can you discern a trend? Over the last five, twenty-five, or fifty years have the rules or the way the courts apply those rules changed? If the answer is yes, what social, economic, or political events might account for those changes? In contrast, if you arrange the decisions by jurisdiction, does a pattern appear? For example, do industrial states tend to take one approach and more rural states another? Are some jurisdictions more conservative while others more liberal? If you read between the lines, what do you think motivated the judges and persuaded them to decide the case in one way rather than another?

§ 5.5   Good Legal Readers "Judge" the Statutes and Cases that They Read

As a beginning law student, you may be tempted to "accept" everything you read. You may be thinking, who am I to judge the soundness of a Supreme Court Justice's analysis or Congress's choice of a particular word or phrase? Do not give in to this temptation. If you are going to be a good legal reader, you need to question and evaluate everything you read.

In judging the cases that you read, make sure you do more than evaluate the facts. Although in the following example William engages in some evaluation, it is the evaluation of a non-lawyer. He evaluates the witness's testimony but not the court's choice of rule, application of the rules to the facts, or reasoning. Once again, the text of the case is set out using a regular typeface and William's thoughts are in italics.

| **EXAMPLE** | **Excerpt from William's Think Aloud** |

There was evidence that the plaintiff had been ashore a number of times, had been on numerous outings and had been treated as a guest during her stay aboard the yacht.

So at this point I'm getting a picture of what happened . . . I'm not sure though. There is evidence that the plaintiff had been ashore so at this point I'm thinking was she really held against her will. So I have doubts . . . doubts about the plaintiff's story at this point.

According to the uncontradicted evidence, at no time did anyone physically restrain the plaintiff except for the defendant's refusal, once the plaintiff announced her decision to quit the yacht, to let the plaintiff use a small boat to take herself, her children, and her belongings ashore.

Well . . . the defendant by this point isn't really stopping the plaintiff from leaving.

Throughout the entire episode the plaintiff's husband was with her and repeatedly tried to persuade her to change her mind and remain with the sect.

At this point, mentally, I think . . . I don't think the plaintiff's story holds water . . . that's what I am thinking. Because her husband was there so maybe you, there's in my mind that her story doesn't hold water. So I am thinking at this point that the court might end up reversing her position.

In contrast, the professor evaluated the court's conclusion and reasoning. After she finished reading the case, the professor made the following comments. (Note how the professor talks about the elements of the tort and how she poses a hypothetical.)

> **EXAMPLE**   **Excerpt from Professor's Think Aloud**

> *I'm not sure that the plaintiff proved all of the elements of false imprisonment. For example, I'm not sure that the plaintiff proved that the defendant intended to confine the plaintiff. If I remember correctly, [pause] on a number of occasions he allowed her to go ashore. He just wouldn't let her use the small boat to take her children and their things ashore. It would have been interesting to know what would have happened if a boat had come to get the plaintiff. Would the defendant have let her go? If he would have, there wouldn't have been false imprisonment [pause]. The facts may, however, support a finding that the defendant's actions resulted in confinement. In those days, the plaintiff may not have had a way to contact anyone on shore to ask them to come get her. Although the court may have reached the right result, I wish Judge Savage had done more analysis [pause]. I get the feeling that he had made up his mind, maybe he didn't like cults, and then just tried to justify his conclusion.*

---

§ 5.6   Good Legal Readers Read for a Specific Purpose

The reading you do for your law school classes is very different from the reading you will do in practice. In law school, you read so you will be prepared for class. Consider the following comment made by James.

> When I read cases, I usually read them not for briefing cases per se, but more out of fear of being called on in class. I don't want to look like a fool so I just want to know the basic principles.

In contrast, in practice, you will read for a specific purpose. For example, you will read to keep up to date in an area of law, to find the answer to a question a client has posed, to find statutes or cases to support your client's position, or to find holes in your opponent's arguments.

In reading the statutes and cases for your legal writing assignments, read not as a student, but as a lawyer. Initially, read to find out what the law is. Analyze the statutes and cases that you have found, and then put the pieces together. Then read the cases as the parties and the court would read them. Begin by putting yourself in your client's position. How can your client use the statutes and cases to support its position? Put yourself in the other side's shoes. How could the other side use the same statutes and cases to support its position? Finally, put yourself in the court's position. If you were the judge, how would you read the statutes and cases?

§ 5.7   Good Legal Readers Understand that Statutes and Cases Can Be Read in More than One Way

Different people have different beliefs about text. While some people believe that there is a right way to read each statute or case, others believe that most statutes and cases can be read in more than one way. For those in the first group, the meaning of a particular text is fixed. For those in the second group, the meaning of a particular text is "constructed" by juries and judges and the attorneys who practice before them.

As a general rule, the students who seem to have the easiest time in their first year of law school are those students who believe that statutes and cases can be read in more than one way, that the meaning of a particular text is socially constructed. These students have an easier time seeing how each side might interpret a particular statute and in stating a rule so it favors their client's position. When they talk about a court's holding, they refer to it as "a holding" and not "the holding."

If you are a student who believes that meaning is fixed, be aware of how your belief system is affecting the way you read statutes and cases and the way you make arguments. In reading cases, can you see how both the plaintiff and the defendant might be able to use the same case to support its argument? In making arguments, are you able to see what the other side might argue and how you might be able to respond to those arguments? Are you spending too much time looking for the correct answer and not enough time creating that answer? In contrast, if you are a student who believes that meaning is socially constructed, be careful that you do not become cynical or only a hired gun. Although there may be many ways of reading a particular statute or case, not all of those readings will lead to a "just" result.

In closing, keep in mind that learning to read, think, and write like a lawyer takes time. There are no crash courses, shortcuts, or magic wands. Instead, you will learn to read and think like a lawyer through trial and error and by observing how real lawyers — not T.V. lawyers — read and think about statutes and cases.

§ 5.8   Exercise

Using the think aloud that you did as an exercise at the end of Chapter 4 (see section 4.4), diagnose your own strengths and weaknesses as a legal reader.

1. Did you read what was on the page? Did you skip words, read in words, or misread words? Did you look up words that you did not know?
2. If you did not understand the opinion, or a part of it, did you read and reread until you did?
3. Did you engage in synthesis? For example, did you compare the court's decision in *Shurman* (the case set out in section 4.4) with the court's decision in *Thompson* (the case set out in Chart 4.3)? Did both cases involve the same issue? Are the decisions consistent? Did both courts rely on the same authorities? Did both courts employ the same reasoning?
4. Did you put *Shurman* in its historical, political, social, economic, and legal context? Is *Shurman* a relatively old or a relatively new case? Was there anything going on at the time that *Shurman* was decided that might have influenced the court? Have political, social, or economic conditions changed since *Shurman* was decided? How are the issues that were raised in *Shurman* related to other legal issues?

5. Did you evaluate the court's decision? Did the majority apply the rule or rules that it set out? Is the majority's reasoning sound? Is the approach that is set out in the concurring opinion better or worse than the approach set out in the majority opinion? Is the result "just"?

6. In reading the opinion, what role did you assume? Did you think about how you might use the case if you were representing a client who wanted to challenge service of process? If you were representing a client who wanted to argue that service was proper? If you were a trial court judge?

7. Is there more than one way to read the court's opinion? What would be a narrow reading of the court's holding? A broad reading of the court's holding?

Objective Memoranda — Memos, Opinion Letters, and Email and Text Messages

Drafting Memos

More likely than not, one of your first assignments as an intern, extern, or associate will be to research a legal issue and prepare a memo for your supervising attorney. Sometimes, your supervising attorney will give you several days to complete the assignment and will want you to prepare a formal memo; at other times, the attorney needs the answer "now," and wants not a formal memo but just an email in which you set out your analysis and conclusion.

So that you are ready for practice, this chapter and the following four chapters walk you through the process of writing both formal memos and shorter memos, which we call e-memos. Because they are an effective tool for teaching you to think like a lawyer, we begin by showing you how to write a formal memo: In Chapter 7, we show you how to write a formal memo using a "script" format, in Chapter 8 we show you how to write a formal memo using an "integrated" format, and in Chapter 9 we talk about other types of formal memos. Then, in Chapter 10, we explain how you can use what you have learned to write shorter, less formal e-memos.

PRACTICE POINTER So how difficult can it be to write a memo? Unfortunately, if the memo is a legal memo, it can be very difficult. To write an effective memo, you need to know how to do legal research; how to analyze and synthesize statutes, regulations, and cases; how to construct arguments; how to evaluate the relative merits of different arguments; and how to write about complex issues clearly and concisely.

§ 6.1   Audience

For an objective, or office, memo, your primary audience is other attorneys in your office. In most instances, a more experienced attorney asks a law student or newer attorney to research an issue and write a memo setting out not only the law but also how that law applies to a particular situation, for example, how the law might apply in a particular client's case. While sometimes a copy of the memo will be sent to the client, memos are, if appropriate precautions are taken, attorney work product and are not, therefore, discoverable. Consequently, neither an opposing party nor the courts have a right to see these memos.

§ 6.2   Purpose

Your primary purpose in writing an office memo is to give the attorneys in your law office the information they need to evaluate a case, advise a client, or draft another document, for example, a complaint, brief, or contract. Thus, your memo needs to be objective. In drafting the statement of facts, include both the facts that favor your client and the facts that favor the other side. In addition, make sure that your issue statement, your summaries of the general and specific rules, and your descriptions of the analogous cases are neutral. Most importantly, in setting out the arguments, give appropriate weight to each side's arguments and, in setting out your conclusions, be candid.

§ 6.3   Conventions

Because objective memos are in-house documents, there are no rules governing their format. As a result, the format used for a memo varies from office to office and even from lawyer to lawyer. In addition, the practice of law is changing. While historically lawyers wanted longer, more formal memos, today many lawyers prefer shorter memos that are either imbedded in or attached to an email. These less formal memos save supervising lawyers time and save clients money, both important efficiencies in today's law firm.

Therefore, before writing a memo, ask the attorney who is assigning the project the following questions:

1. Should I prepare a formal memo or a less formal, shorter "e-memo"?
2. About how much time should I spend on this project?
3. What research resources may I use (e.g., can I use Lexis Advance® and WestlawNext™)?

> **PRACTICE POINTER** As an intern or clerk, you also need to know what types of questions you should not ask. Do not, for example, ask how many cases you should include in the memo. Writing a memo is not a school assignment. If the attorney knew how many cases were relevant, he or she would not have asked you to do the research and write the memo.

§ 6.4   Sample Memos

In the first two examples set out below, we show the final drafts of the memos that we discuss in Chapters 7 and 8. While both examples involve a single issue that requires an elements analysis, the examples differ in two ways. In the first example, the writer sets out the facts before the issue statement and brief answer and organizes the discussion section using what we call a script format. In contrast, in the second example, the writer sets out the issue statement first, does not include a brief answer, and organizes the discussion section using an integrated format. (For more on organizing the discussion section using a script format, see Chapter 9. For more on organizing the discussion section using an integrated format, see Chapter 9. For a discussion of memos requiring other types of analysis, see Chapter 9.)

The third, fourth, and fifth examples are e-memos that provide the attorney with a "quick" answer to his or her question. Once again, the format varies: Because e-memos are in-house memos, there are no rules governing the format. You do, however, want to present the information in the order in which the attorney expects to see it: rules before examples of how those rules have been applied in analogous cases and rules and analogous cases before your analysis and conclusion.

The first time that you read the examples, focus on the content. What is the issue? What is the law? How does that law apply in the client's situation? The second time that you read the examples, focus on organization. How is the memo organized? How is each subsection organized? The last time that you read the examples, focus on the writing. Have the writers used what is commonly known as legalese? If they haven't, how would you describe the tone and the writing style?

PRACTICE POINTER	More likely than not, once you begin applying for jobs, you will need a writing sample. Because some employers allow first-year students to use a memo that they prepared as part of a class, you may be

able to use one of your legal writing memos as a writing sample. Accordingly, make sure that you understand what information needs to go into a memo and why that information needs to be presented in a particular order and in particular ways. In addition, make sure that your analysis is sophisticated and that your writing is clear, concise, and correct.

§ 6.4.1   Sample Formal Memo 1

For a description of the process involved in writing this memo,[1] see Chapter 7.

---

1. Because this memo was written for a Florida attorney and involves an issue of Florida law, it uses the Florida citation rules. See Fla. R. Civ. P. 9.800, *available at* http://www.floridasupreme court.org/decisions/barrules.shtml.

To: Christina Galeano

From: Legal Intern

Date: September 9, 2013

Re: Elaine Olsen, Case No. 13-478
           Service of Process, Usual Place of Abode; Notification of
           Contents

Statement of Facts

Elaine Olsen has contacted our office asking for assistance in overturning an order terminating her parental rights. You have asked me to determine whether the service of process was valid.

On February 1, 2013, Ms. Olsen entered an inpatient drug treatment program in Miami, Florida. She remained in the program until March 27, 2013, when she moved into a residential treatment house for recovering addicts.

During April, May, and June 2013, Ms. Olsen was a full-time resident at the residential treatment house. She had a bedroom in the house, ate her meals there, and had some of her possessions there. In addition, when she applied for jobs, she listed the treatment house address as her address.

Beginning in July 2013, Ms. Olsen began spending less time at the treatment house and more time with her sister, Elizabeth Webster, who is 32. Both Ms. Olsen's sister and the manager of the halfway house will testify that, during July and August 2013, Ms. Olsen spent weeknights at the treatment house and Friday, Saturday, and Sunday nights at her sister's house. Because she was spending time at her sister's house, Ms. Olsen moved some of her clothing and personal effects into her sister's house.

On Wednesday, July 24, 2013, a process server went to Ms. Webster's house and asked for Elaine Olsen. When Ms. Webster told the process server that "Elaine isn't here today," the process server handed the summons to Ms. Webster and told her that Ms. Olsen "needed to go to court."

Ms. Webster will testify that she never gave the summons to her sister. Because she thought that the papers related to some of Ms. Olsen's unpaid bills, she simply put the summons in a shoebox in the kitchen with a stack of Ms. Olsen's other mail. Ms. Olsen says she never received the summons and, as a result, did not respond. The return of service is regular on its face.

Ms. Olsen has been employed since August 1, 2013, and she has lived in her own apartment since September 1, 2013. She has her sister's address on her driver's license.

There is nothing in the record that indicates whether the State tried to personally serve Ms. Olsen or whether it tried to serve her at the halfway house.

Issue

Under Florida's service of process statute, was Ms. Olsen properly served when (1) during the month when service was made, Ms. Olsen spent weeknights at a residential treatment house where she had a room, ate meals, and kept belongings, and spent Friday, Saturday, and Sunday nights at her sister's house, where she had some belongings; (2) Ms. Olsen listed the treatment house address on job applications but her sister's address on her driver's license; (3) service was made on Ms. Olsen's 32-year-old sister on a Wednesday at Ms. Olsen's sister's house; (4) the process server told Ms. Olsen's sister that Ms. Olsen needed to go to court; and (5) Ms. Olsen's sister did not give the summons and petition to Ms. Olsen, and Ms. Olsen states that she did not receive notice?

Brief Answer

Probably not. Because the return is regular on its face, Ms. Olsen has the burden of proving that she was not properly served. Because the petition was left with Ms. Olsen's 32-year-old sister at the sister's house, Ms. Olsen will have to concede that service was made on a person 15 years or older who was living at the house at which the service was made. In addition, because the process server told Ms. Olsen's sister that Ms. Olsen needed to go to court, more likely than not the court will decide that the person served was informed of the contents of the documents. However, because Ms. Olsen can present evidence that establishes that she was staying at the residential treatment house on the day that service was made, the court may decide that the petition was not left at Ms. Olsen's usual place of abode.

Discussion

The Florida courts have repeatedly stated that the fundamental purpose of service of process is to give defendants notice of claims that have been filed against them and to provide them with an opportunity to defend their rights. *E.g., Shurman v. Atl. Mortg. & Inv. Corp.*, 795 So. 2d 952, 953-54 (Fla. 2001). Because these rights are so important, the courts strictly construe and enforce statutes governing service of process. *Id.* at 954.

In the present case, the relevant portion of the statute reads as follows:

> (1)(a) Service of original process is made by delivering a copy of it to the person to be served with a copy of the complaint, petition, or other initial pleading or paper or by leaving the copies at his or her usual place of abode with any person residing therein who is 15 years of age or older and informing the person of their contents. . . .

§ 48.031(1)(a), Fla. Stat. (2013).

Although the party seeking to invoke the jurisdiction of the court has the burden of proving that service was proper, if the return is regular on its face, the courts presume that the service was valid. *Busman v. State, Dep't of Revenue*, 905 So. 2d 956, 958 (Fla. 3d DCA 2005); *Thompson v. State*,

Dep't of Revenue, 867 So. 2d 603, 605 (Fla. 1st DCA 2004). In such instances, the party challenging the service has the burden of presenting clear and convincing evidence that the service was invalid. *Id.*

In this case, Ms. Olsen may be able to present clear and convincing evidence that the petition was not left at her usual place of abode. However, if the court decides that the petition was left at her usual place of abode, Ms. Olsen will have to concede that the summons was left with a person 15 years or older who was residing at the house where service was made. In addition, although Ms. Olsen can argue that her sister was not informed of the contents of the documents, it is unlikely that she can meet her burden of proof.

A. Usual Place of Abode

Although the statute does not define the phrase "usual place of abode," the courts have said that a defendant's usual place of abode is the place "where the defendant was actually living at the time of service." *E.g., Shurman v. Atl. Mortg. & Inv. Corp.*, 795 So. 2d 952, 953-54 (Fla. 2001); *Busman v. State, Dep't of Revenue*, 905 So. 2d 956, 957 (Fla. 3d DCA 2005).

In an early case, and one of the few published decisions in which the court concluded that the defendant had been served at his usual place of abode, the court emphasizes that, at the time of service, defendant's wife and children were living at the apartment where service was made. *State ex rel. Merritt v. Heffernan*, 195 So. 145, 146-47 (Fla. 1940). In that case, the defendant had relocated his family to Florida two months before service was made and had twice visited them while they were in Florida, the second time leaving the apartment to return to Minnesota just an hour before service was made. *Id.* Although the defendant argued that his usual place of abode was Minnesota, where he had an office, paid taxes, and voted, the court disagreed, stating that "[w]e do not hold the view that Florida was the permanent residence of the defendant, but we do feel that in the circumstance reflected in the record, it was his usual place of abode . . . ." *Id.* at 148.

In contrast, in the more recent cases, the courts have emphasized that it is not enough that the complaint or petition is left with a relative. *See, e.g., Busman*, 905 So. 2d at 947; *Torres v. Arnco Const., Inc.*, 867 So. 2d 583 (Fla. 5th DCA 2004). For example, in *Busman*, the court concluded that service of process was not valid even though the summons and complaint had been left with the defendant's half brother. *Id.* at 958. Similarly, in *Torres*, the court concluded that service had not been made at the defendant's usual place of abode when, after trying unsuccessfully to serve the defendant at his New York apartment, the plaintiff served the defendant's mother at her home in Florida. *Id.* at 585, 587. Although the defendant's mother told the process server that her son "would be home soon," the court decided that this statement was, at best, ambiguous. *Id.* at 585; *accord Portfolio Recovery Assocs., LLC v. Gonzalez*, 951 So. 2d 1037, 1038 (Fla. 3d DCA 2007) (service was not made at the defendants' usual place of abode when the summons and complaint were left with a woman who was the mother of one defendant and the mother-in-law of the other defendant, but the defendants had not lived at the residence for five years).

Ms. Olsen can make three arguments to support her assertion that her sister's house was not her usual place of abode. First, Ms. Olsen will argue that, under the plain language of the statute, her sister's house was not her usual place of abode. As the courts have stated, service must be made at the place where the defendant was actually living at the time the summons and complaint were served. In this case, the summons and complaint were served on a weekday, and on weekdays Ms. Olsen was actually living at the residential treatment house.

Second, Ms. Olsen will argue that the facts in her case are more like the facts in *Busman* and *Torres* than the facts in *Heffernan*. Like Mr. Busman, who produced a lease that corroborated his testimony that he was not living with his half brother on the day that the summons and complaint were served, Ms. Olsen can produce evidence that establishes that on the day she was served she was living at the residential treatment house. Both Ms. Olsen's sister and the manager of the residential treatment house have said they will testify that during June and July Ms. Olsen lived at the treatment house during the week and stayed with her sister only on weekends. In the alternative, Ms. Olsen can argue that the facts in her case are even stronger than the facts in *Torres*. While Mr. Torres's mother's statement that Mr. Torres "would be home soon" suggested that Mr. Torres would be returning to his mother's house that day, Ms. Olsen's sister told the process server that Ms. Olsen "isn't here today." In addition, Ms. Olsen can distinguish *Heffernan*: Although Mr. Heffernan had been at his family's apartment only an hour before the summons and complaint were served, Ms. Olsen had not been at her sister's house for several days.

Finally, Ms. Olsen can argue that, as a matter of public policy, the court should decide that the summons and petition were not left at her usual place of abode. The courts have stated that the statute should be narrowly construed, and this policy is particularly important in cases in which the State is seeking to terminate a mother's parental rights. In addition, this is not a case in which the State tried but could not locate Ms. Olsen: There is no evidence that the State tried to serve Ms. Olsen at the residential treatment house.

In response, the State will argue that Ms. Olsen was served at one of her usual places of abode. The courts have not required that the plaintiff be living at the house where the summons and complaint are served on the day on which the service is made. Therefore, while Ms. Olsen may not have been at her sister's house on the day that the summons and complaint were served, she had been there the previous weekend, and she was there the following weekend. In addition, Ms. Olsen had possessions at her sister's house.

Thus, the State will argue that the facts in this case are much stronger than the facts in *Heffernan*. While in *Heffernan*, Mr. Heffernan visited his family only "twice during the season," Ms. Olsen lived at her sister's house on weekends. In addition, while Mr. Heffernan had another permanent residence, Ms. Olsen was staying at a halfway house, which, by definition, is only a temporary residence. Finally, while in *Heffernan* there was no indication that Mr. Heffernan listed the Florida address on any documents, Ms. Olsen listed her sister's address on her driver's license, and there is evidence indicating that Ms. Olsen received other types of mail at her sister's house.

The State will use these same facts to distinguish *Torres*. While in *Torres*, Mr. Torres presented evidence establishing that his permanent residence was in New York, in the present case, Ms. Olsen did not have a permanent residence. In the five months before service, she had been an inpatient in a treatment facility, she had lived at the halfway house, and she had lived with her sister. The plaintiff can also distinguish *Shurman* and *Busman*. While in *Shurman* and *Busman* the record indicated that the defendants had not lived at the house where service had been made for months or years, in this case, Ms. Olsen admits that she stayed at her sister's house on the weekend before her sister was served.

Finally, the State will argue that, because the return was regular on its face, Ms. Olsen has the burden of proving, by clear and convincing evidence, that her sister's house was not her usual place of abode. In this instance, Ms. Olsen has not met that burden. When there is evidence that the defendant was in fact living at the house where service was made, the courts should not require plaintiffs to determine which house the defendant was living at on any particular day.

While both sides have strong arguments, the court will probably conclude that the summons and petition were not left at Ms. Olsen's usual place of abode. In the more recent cases, the courts have emphasized that it is not enough that service is made on a relative and concluded that the service was invalid when the defendant presented evidence establishing that he or she was not actually living at the place where the summons and complaint were left. Therefore, we can argue that it is not enough that the summons and petition were left with Ms. Olsen's sister: Service was invalid because, on the day that service was made, Ms. Olsen was not actually living with her sister. The problem, of course, is that Ms. Olsen stayed with her sister the weekend preceding and following service. Although these facts make this case weaker than the analogous cases, the court may be persuaded by the fact that this case involves termination of parental rights, that there is no evidence that the State tried to serve Ms. Olsen personally or at the treatment house, and that Ms. Olsen did not have actual notice.

B. Person 15 Years Old or Older Residing Therein

In addition to leaving the summons at the defendant's usual place of abode, the process server must leave the summons with a person 15 years old or older residing therein. Because Ms. Webster is 32 and lives at the house where the summons and complaint were left, Ms. Olsen will have to concede that the summons was left with a person residing therein who is at least 15 years old.

C. Informed of Contents

[Not shown]

Conclusion

Because of the strong public policy in favor of ensuring that defendants receive notice of actions that have been filed against them, the court will probably decide that the substituted service of process was not valid and vacate the judgment terminating Ms. Olsen's parental rights.

Ms. Olsen will have to concede that her sister, Ms. Webster, is a person of suitable age and that Ms. Webster was residing at the house where the service was made. In addition, because the process server told Ms. Webster that Ms. Olsen needed to go to court, it seems unlikely that Ms. Olsen will be able to prove that Ms. Webster was not informed of the contents.

Ms. Olsen may, however, be able to prove that the summons and complaint were not served at her usual place of abode. In the more recent cases, the courts have concluded that service made on a relative was invalid when the defendants produced evidence establishing that they were not actually living with that relative on the day that service was made. While in most of these cases the defendants had not lived at the house where service was made for several months or several years, in the present case the court may be swayed by three facts: This case involves the termination of Ms. Olsen's parental rights; there is no evidence that the State tried to personally serve Ms. Olsen or that it tried to serve Ms. Olsen at the treatment house; and Ms. Olsen states that she did not receive notice.

§ 6.4.2   Sample Formal Memo 2

For a description of the process involved in writing this memo,[2] see Chapter 8.

To:	Julia Fishler
From:	Legal Intern
Date:	November 1, 2013
Re:	Michael Garcia Adverse possession; Washington law

Issue

Whether Doctors and Nurses Who Care (DNWC) has obtained a right to Mr. Garcia's land through adverse possession when (1) it has used Mr.

---

2. Because this memo was written for a Washington attorney and involves an issue of Washington law, it uses the Washington citation rules. *See* Wash. Courts, Style Sheet (Dec. 28, 2010), *available at* http://www.courts.wa.gov/appellate_trial_courts/supreme/?fa=atc_supreme.style.

Garcia's land for campouts several nights a week for eight weeks each summer since 1997; (2) to facilitate these campouts, DNWC has maintained the campsites, fire area, outhouse, and dock; (3) in 2001, DNWC sent a letter to Mr. Garcia asking him whether it could continue using the land for campouts, but Mr. Garcia did not respond to the letter; and (4) Mr. Garcia has paid the taxes but did not visit the land from 1999 until August 2013.

Statement of Facts

Michael Garcia has contacted our office regarding property that he owns in Washington State. Mr. Garcia is concerned that the organization that owns the property next to his, Doctors and Nurses Who Care (DNWC), may be able to claim title to his property through adverse possession.

Mr. Garcia's property is on Lake Chelan, which is in the eastern part of Washington State. Mr. Garcia's grandfather, Eduardo Montoya, purchased the two-acre waterfront parcel in 1958, and the Montoya family used the land every summer from 1958 until Eduardo Montoya became ill in the early 1990s. When it used the land, the family would camp on the site and use a small dock for swimming, fishing, and boating. In 1999, Mr. Garcia's grandfather died and left the property to Mr. Garcia. Although Mr. Garcia spent one weekend at the property in fall of 1999, he moved to California in 2000 and did not visit the property until last August. He has, however, continued to pay all of the taxes and assessments.

In 1996, DNWC purchased the five-acre parcel that adjoins Mr. Garcia's property. Since 1997, DNWC has used its land as a summer camp for children with serious illnesses or disabilities. In a typical summer, the DNWC runs two one-week camps for children with cancer, two one-week camps for children who are blind, two one-week camps for children with autism, and two one-week camps for children with diabetes.

Most of the time the children stay in cabins located on the DNWC property. However, DNWC uses Mr. Garcia's property for "campouts." On one night, one group of about 10 children will camp out in tents on Mr. Garcia's property, the next night another group of 10 will camp out on the property, and so on. Thus, DNWC has been using the Garcia property four or five nights a week for eight weeks each summer since 1997. During these campouts, the children pitch and stay in tents, cook over a fire, and use the dock. To facilitate these campouts, DNWC has maintained the campsite, the fire area, the outhouse, and the dock.

In February 2001, DNWC sent Mr. Garcia a letter asking him whether it could continue using his land for campouts. Mr. Garcia was busy and did not respond to the letter. Sometime during the summer of 2001, DNWC posted a no trespassing sign on the dock, and the sign is still there.

Last August, Mr. Garcia visited the property with the intent of spending a few days camping on the lake. When he got there, he discovered the children and their counselors on the property.

After discovering the children on his land, Mr. Garcia went to the DNWC camp headquarters and talked to the director, Dr. Liu, who told Mr. Garcia that it was his understanding that the land belonged to DNWC. Although Mr. Garcia did not spend that night at the property, he did spend the next night there after the children left. DNWC did not ask him to leave.

Although over the years the land around the lake has become more and more developed, the area in which the camp is located is still relatively undeveloped. Most of the property owners use their land only during the summer.

Discussion

The doctrine of adverse possession was developed to assure maximum use of the land, to encourage the rejection of stale claims, and to quiet titles. *Chaplin v. Sanders*, 100 Wn.2d 853, 859-60, 676 P.2d 431 (1984); *see also* William B. Stoebuck, *The Law of Adverse Possession in Washington,* 35 Wash. L. Rev. 53, 53 (1960).

To establish title through adverse possession, the claimant must prove that its possession was (1) exclusive, (2) actual and uninterrupted, (3) open and notorious, and (4) hostile for the statutory period. *ITT Rayonier, Inc. v. Bell*, 112 Wn.2d 754, 757, 774 P.2d 6 (1989); *Chaplin v. Sanders*, 100 Wn.2d 853, 857, 676 P.2d 431 (1984). In this case, the statutory period is 10 years. RCW 4.16.020(1).

Adverse possession is a mixed question of law and fact. *Chaplin*, 100 Wn.2d at 863. Whether the essential facts exist is for the trier of fact to decide; but whether the facts, as found, constitute adverse possession is for the court to determine as a matter of law. *Id.*

In this case, DNWC can easily prove that its possession was open and notorious and exclusive. In addition, it can probably prove that its possession is actual and uninterrupted. The only element that it may not be able to prove is that its possession was hostile.

A. Open and Notorious

A claimant can satisfy the open and notorious element by showing either (1) that the title owner had actual notice of the adverse use throughout the statutory period or (2) that the claimant used the land such that any reasonable person would have thought that the claimant owned it. *Riley v. Andres*, 107 Wn.2d 391, 396, 27 P.3d 618 (2001).

In this case, DNWC can prove both that Mr. Garcia had actual notice of its adverse use and that any reasonable person would have thought that DNWC owned the land. To prove that Mr. Garcia had actual knowledge of DNWC's use of the land, DNWC can offer the letter that it sent to Mr. Garcia in 2001 asking for continuing permission to use his land for campouts. To prove that a reasonable person would have thought that DNWC owned the land, DNWC will point out that it not only used the land for campouts but also maintained the campsites, fire area, outhouse, and dock and posted a no trespassing sign.

B. Actual and Uninterrupted

Although the Washington courts have not set out a test for actual possession, the cases illustrate the types of acts that are needed to establish actual possession. 17 *Wash. Prac., Real Estate: Property Law* § 8.10 (2d ed.).

The courts have held that the claimants had actual possession of rural land when the claimants built a fence and cultivated or pastured up to it, *Faubion v. Elder*, 49 Wn.2d 300, 301 P.2d 153 (1956); cleared the land, constructed and occupied buildings, and planted orchards, *Metro. Bldg. Co. v. Fitzgerald*, 122 Wash. 514, 210 P. 770 (1922); or cleared and fenced the land, planted an orchard, and built a road, *Davies v. Wickstrom*, 56 Wash. 154, 105 P. 454 (1909). In contrast, the courts have held that the claimants did not have actual possession of rural land when they maintained a fence intended to be a cattle fence and not a line fence, *Roy v. Goerz*, 26 Wn. App. 807, 614 P.2d 1308 (1980); erected two signboards and a mailbox and ploughed weeds, *Slater v. Murphy*, 55 Wn.2d 892, 339 P.2d 457 (1959); or occasionally used the land for gardening, piling wood, and mowing hay, *Smith v. Chambers*, 112 Wash. 600, 192 P. 891 (1920). *See generally* 17 *Wash. Prac., Real Estate: Property Law* § 8.10 (2d ed.).

If DNWC had used the land only for occasional campouts, it would have been difficult for it to prove that it had actual possession. However, in addition to using the land for campouts, DNWC maintained the campsites, the fire area, the outhouse, and the dock, and it posted a no trespassing sign. Because DNWC maintained permanent structures and posted the no trespassing sign, more likely than not a court will hold that it had actual possession.

In addition, DNWC's use and maintenance of the campsites, fire area, outhouse, and dock are probably enough to establish that its possession was uninterrupted. In all of the cases in which the claimants maintained and used permanent structures, the courts have held that the use was uninterrupted. For instance, in *Howard v. Kunto*, 3 Wn. App. 393, 477 P.2d 210 (1970), the court held that the claimants' use was continuous even though the claimants used the property only during the summer. As the court noted in that case, "the requisite possession requires such possession and dominion 'as ordinarily marks the conduct of owners in general in holding, managing, and caring for property of like nature and condition.'" *Id.* at 397. Consequently, while Mr. Garcia might be able to argue that DNWC's use of the land was not uninterrupted because it used the land only during the summer months, this argument is a weak one. Because the land is recreational land, DNWC's use of the land only in summer is consistent with how the owners of similar land hold, manage, and care for their property.

C. Exclusive

To establish that its possession was exclusive, the claimant must show that its possession was "of a type that would be expected of an owner . . . ." *ITT Rayonier*, 112 Wn.2d 754, 758, 774 P.2d 6 (1989). Therefore, while sharing possession of the land with the true owner will prevent a claimant from establishing that its possession was exclusive, sharing possession with a tenant or allowing occasional use by a neighbor does not. *Id.*

In this case, Mr. Garcia has stated that he did not visit the property between 1999 and 2013. Thus, during that period, DNWC did not share the property with the true owner. Although DNWC "shared" its use of Mr. Garcia's land with its campers, this fact should not prevent a court from finding that its possession was exclusive. Because the campers used the Garcia land under the supervision of DNWC, they are analogous to tenants.

D. Hostile

While before 1984 the Washington courts considered the claimant's subjective intent in determining whether its use of the land was hostile, since 1984 the claimant's subjective intent has been irrelevant. *Chaplin*, 100 Wn.2d at 860-61 (overruling cases in which the courts had considered the claimant's subjective intent). Accordingly, under current Washington law, the claimant must prove only that it used the land as if it were its own for the statutory period. *Id.*; *Miller v. Anderson*, 91 Wn. App. 822, 828, 964 P.2d 365 (1998). If the claimant proves that it used the land as if it were its own, the use was hostile unless the true owner can prove that it gave the claimant permission to use the land. *Id.*

Permission can be express or implied. *Miller*, 91 Wn. App. at 829 (case dealt with a prescriptive easement and not adverse possession). The courts infer that the use was permissive if, under the circumstances, it is reasonable to assume that the use was permitted. *Id.* If there was permission, the party claiming adverse possession bears the burden of proving that permission terminated because either (1) the servient estate changed hands through death or alienation or (2) the claimant has asserted a hostile right. *Id.*

In deciding whether a claimant was using the land as if it were its own, the courts consider whether the claimant made improvements to the land, whether the claimant maintained the property, and whether the claimant used the land on a regular basis. *See, e.g., Chaplin*, 100 Wn.2d at 855-56; *Timberlane Homeowners Ass'n, Inc. v. Brame*, 79 Wn. App, 303, 310-11, 901 P.2d 1074 (1995). For example, in *Chaplin*, the court held that the claimants were using the land as if it were their own when the claimants built a road across the disputed land, cleared and maintained the disputed land, installed utility lines, and used the area for recreational activities. *Id.* at 855-56. Similarly, in *Timberlane*, the court held that claimants had used land belonging to the homeowners' association as if it was their own when they built and maintained a fence and a concrete patio and the claimants' children played on the land. *Id.* at 310-11.

In deciding whether the claimants' use was permissive, the courts consider whether the parties are related or have a friendly relationship, whether the improvements benefited both the claimants' and the title owners' property, and whether the title owners allowed the claimants to use the land as a neighborly accommodation. *See, e.g., Granston v. Callahan*, 52 Wn. App. 288, 294-95, 759 P.2d 462 (1988); *Miller v. Jarman*, 2 Wn. App.

994, 471 P.2d 704 (1970). For instance, in *Granston*, the court held that the claimants' use was permissive because the original owners of the two parcels were brothers who worked together to build driveways, walkways, and other improvements that benefited both properties. *Id.* at 294-95. Likewise, in *Miller*, the court held that the use was permissive because the title owners had allowed the claimants, who were their neighbors, to use their driveway as a neighborly accommodation. *Id.* at 998. In contrast, in *Lingvall v. Bartmess*, 97 Wn. App. 245, 256, 982 P.2d 690 (1999), the court held that the antagonistic relationship between two brothers negated a finding that the claimant's use of the land was permissive.

In the Garcia case, the court will probably conclude that DNWC's use of Mr. Garcia's land was hostile.

First, the court will probably conclude that DNWC used Mr. Garcia's land as if it were the true owner. Although DNWC did not build any new structures on Mr. Garcia's land, it maintained the campsites, the fire area, the outhouse, and the dock. In addition, although DNWC did not use the property year-round, it did use the property during the summer, which is how a typical owner would have used the land. As a result, this case is similar to *Chaplin* and *Timberlane,* in which the claimants maintained and used the disputed land as a true owner would have used the land. While in *Chaplin* and *Timberlane* the claimants built new structures (in *Chaplin*, the claimants built a road, and in *Timberlane*, they built a fence and a patio), the courts have held that the claimant does not have to do everything that a title owner might do.

Second, the court will probably conclude that DNWC's use of Mr. Garcia's land was not permissive. Unlike *Granston*, in which the parties were related and had a close relationship, there is no evidence that the members of DNWC are related to Mr. Garcia. In addition, unlike *Miller*, in which the title owners allowed their neighbors to use their driveway as a neighborly accommodation, the typical owner of recreational land does not allow a neighboring property owner to use its land several days a week during the peak season.

While Mr. Garcia can argue that the letter that DNWC sent to him establishes that DNWC's use of the land was permissive, the court will probably reject this argument. More likely than not, the court will conclude that, if Mr. Garcia's grandfather gave DNWC permission to use his land, that permission terminated when his grandfather died. In addition, the court will probably conclude that even if DNWC used Mr. Garcia's land with Mr. Garcia's implied permission from the time of his grandfather's death until it sent the letter in February of 2001, that permission terminated in the summer of 2001 when DNWC posted the no trespassing sign and continued to use the property as its own.

Conclusion

More likely than not, DNWC will be able to establish title to Mr. Garcia's land through adverse possession.

To prove that its possession was open and notorious, DNWC needs to show only that Mr. Garcia had actual notice of its use of his land throughout the statutory period or that it used his land in such a way that any reasonable person would have thought that it owned this land. In this case, DNWC can use the letter that it sent to Mr. Garcia to prove that he had actual notice, and it can show that its use of the land for campouts was such that any reasonable person would have thought that DNWC owned the land.

To prove that its possession was actual and uninterrupted, DNWC needs to show only that it actually used the land and that its use was consistent with how the true owner might have used the land. The case law suggests that DNWC's maintenance of the campsites, fire area, outhouse, and dock were sufficient to establish actual possession. In addition, although DNWC used the land only during the summer months, the court is likely to find that such use was uninterrupted because most owners of recreational land use their land only during certain seasons.

To prove that its use of the land was exclusive, DNWC will have to show that it did not share the land with anyone else. Although we could try to argue that DNWC's use was not exclusive because it allowed campers to use the land, this argument is weak because the campers used the land under DNWC's supervision.

Finally, to prove that its use was hostile, DNWC will have to prove that it used the land as if it were its own and that it did not do so with Mr. Garcia's permission. DNWC's maintenance and use of the property is probably sufficient to establish that it used Mr. Garcia's land as if it were its own. In addition, DNWC will be able to prove that its use was not permissive. Even if DNWC's initial use of the property was with Mr. Garcia's grandfather's permission, that permission terminated when Mr. Garcia's grandfather died. In addition, although in its 2001 letter DNWC asked Mr. Garcia for permission to continue using the land, DNWC has a strong argument that it did a hostile act that terminated permission when, even after Mr. Garcia did not respond, it continued maintaining and using the property and it posted the no trespassing sign.

Because all of these elements have been met for the statutory period, which is 10 years, it is likely that a court will decide that DNWC has established a right to title to the land through adverse possession.

§ 6.4.3   Sample E-Memo (For more on e-memos, see Chapter 10)

You asked me to research Illinois law and determine what the statute of limitations is on actions to recover damages to personal property. The applicable statute is 735 ILCS 5/13-205, which states that the statute of limitations is five years:

> [A]ctions on unwritten contracts, expressed or implied, or on awards of arbitration, or *to recover damages for an injury done to property, real or personal,* or to recover the possession of personal property or damages for the detention

or conversion thereof, and all civil actions not otherwise provided for, shall be commenced within 5 years next after the cause of action accrued.

(Emphasis added.)

If you need additional research, please let me know.

§ 6.4.4   Sample E-Memo (For more on e-memos, see Chapter 10)

You have asked me to determine whether KOSLaw LLP, must provide one of its employees, Melissa Karimi, with parental leave under the Family and Medical Leave Act (FMLA.) Specifically, the issue is whether Ms. Karimi's worksite is the firm's Des Moines insourcing office,[3] which has 12 employees, or the firm's Chicago office, which has approximately 175 employees. If Ms. Karimi's worksite is Des Moines, she would not be entitled to leave under the FMLA; if her worksite is Chicago, she is entitled to FMLA leave.

To be entitled to leave under the FMLA, an employee must work for an employer that has 50 or more employees working at worksites that are within a 75-mile radius of one another (50/75 rule). 29 U.S.C. § 2611(2)(B)(ii) (2012) According to the Act's legislative history, Congress included the 50/75 rule to protect employers who might not have enough employees within a particular geographic area to cover FMLA leaves. *See Harbert v. Healthcare Serv. Grp., Inc.*, 391 F.3d 1140, 1149 (10th Cir. 2004).

As a general rule, an employee's worksite is the site to which the employee reports to *or*, if the employee does not report to a particular site, the site from which the employee's work is assigned. 29 C.F.R. § 825.111(a) (2013). However, the regulations set out a different test for employees who work from home or who telecommute. In those situations, the employee's worksite is the office where the employee reports *and* from which assignments are given. *Id.* § 825.111(a)(2).

In our case, it is not clear which test applies. Although Ms. Karimi works from home the majority of the time, she does go into the Des Moines office once or twice a week to use the Des Moines office's conferencing technology, to review sensitive documents, or to receive assistance from the IT staff. However, her supervising attorney is in the Chicago office, and she receives her assignment from that attorney and sends her completed work to that attorney, usually via email.

In other cases in which the employee had a connection to more than one worksite, the courts have held that the location of the employee's worksite was a question of fact. *See, e.g., Podkovich v. Glazer's Distrib. of Iowa, Inc.*, 446 F. Supp. 2d 982, 1000-02 (N.D. Iowa 2006) (concluding that there was an issue of fact when a traveling saleswoman physically

---

3. Insourcing is similar to outsourcing. However, instead of sending work to individuals in a different country, the work is sent to individuals who live in another part of the United States.

reported to one worksite but received her assignments from another site); *Collinsworth v. Earthlink/Onemain, Inc.*, CIV.A. 03-2299GTV, 2003 WL 22916461, at *4 (D. Kan. Dec. 4, 2003) (concluding that there was an issue of fact when the plaintiff worked from home, sometimes used a branch office with fewer than 50 people within 75 miles, yet received and delivered her work product to the main office with more than 50 people within 75 miles).

Given the courts' decision in the above cases, if Ms. Karimi files a lawsuit, it is unlikely that a court would grant KOSLaw summary judgment. Instead, the case would have to go to trial, and a jury would have to decide whether the Des Moines or the Chicago office is Ms. Karimi's worksite. If the jury decides that Ms. Karimi reports to the Des Moines office because that is the office that she sometimes uses, that office would be her worksite, and she would not be entitled to FMLA leave. If, however, the jury decides that Ms. Karimi reports to the Chicago office because that it is the office from which she receives her assignments, then she would be entitled to FMLA leave. The result is more uncertain if the jury decides that Ms. Karimi works from home. In that situation, Ms. Karimi's worksite would be the place where she reports to *and* from which she receives her assignments.

Although a jury might find that the Des Moines office is Ms. Karimi's worksite because she "reports" to that office once or twice a week, I recommend that the firm grant Ms. Karimi the leave she has requested. Litigation is expensive, the type of leave that Ms. Karimi is requesting is unpaid leave, and the policy underlying the rule does not apply in this case. Because the Des Moines office is an insourcing office, the work does not need to be done by someone in Des Moines. It can be done by someone in the Chicago office or in any of the firm's other offices.

Please let me know whether you have any more questions or need additional research.

§ 6.4.5   Sample E-Memo (For more on e-memos, see Chapter 10)

TO: Supervising Attorney

FROM: Jessica Burns, Intern

RE: Amanda Nickerson, Admissibility of Prior Convictions for Purpose of Impeachment

You have asked me to determine whether any of Ms. Nickerson's prior convictions can be used to impeach her credibility as a witness in our upcoming products liability trial. I have determined that Ms. Nickerson's conviction for the possession of stolen property is admissible for purposes of impeachment.

The Washington Rules of Evidence state that, for the purpose of attacking the credibility of a witness in a civil case, evidence of a prior criminal conviction can be used to impeach the credibility of a witness if the information is elicited from the witness or established by public record during examination of the witness. ER 609(a). However, evidence of a prior conviction can be used for the purpose of impeachment *only if*

> the crime (1) was punishable by death or imprisonment in excess of 1 year under the law under which the witness was convicted, and the court determines that the probative value of admitting this evidence outweighs the prejudice to the party against whom the evidence is offered, or (2) involved dishonesty or false statement, regardless of the punishment.

ER 609(a)(1)-(2).

The Washington Rules of Evidence have also imposed a time limit on the admissibility of criminal convictions for the purposes of impeachment of a witness:

> [E]vidence of a conviction under this rule is not admissible if a period of more than 10 years has elapsed since the date of the conviction or of the release of the witness from the confinement imposed for that conviction, whichever is the later date, unless the court determines, in the interests of justice, that the probative value of the conviction supported by specific facts and circumstances substantially outweighs its prejudicial effect.

ER 609(b).

1. Assault Charge

Ms. Nickerson's assault charge was an offense punishable by more than one year: Assault in the second degree is punishable by no more than 10 years in prison, RCW 9A.36.021. However, because Ms. Nickerson's assault conviction is more than 10 years old, evidence of the conviction is not admissible unless the court determines that the probative value of the conviction *substantially* outweighs the prejudicial effect of admitting the evidence.

In this case, a products liability case, the prior conviction has no probative value. The fact that Ms. Nickerson committed an assault is not relevant to whether she was injured by a defective product. In addition, the admission of the conviction could be prejudicial because if the jury hears about the conviction, it may view Ms. Nickerson in a less favorable light. Consequently, because the probative value does not outweigh the prejudicial effect, the court is unlikely to admit evidence of the assault conviction.

2. DUI Conviction

The courts have held that a DUI conviction is not admissible for the purposes of impeachment. *State v. Kilgore*, 107 Wn. App. 160, 186, 26 P.3d 308 (2001), *aff'd*, 147 Wn.2d 288 (2002).

3. Possession of Stolen Property

Ms. Nickerson's conviction for possession of stolen property in 2009 could be used to impeach her credibility. Although Ms. Nickerson's conviction for possession of stolen property was not punishable by more than one year in jail, the courts have held that possession of stolen property is admissible because it is a crime of dishonesty. *State v. McKinsey*, 116 Wn.2d 911, 912, 801 P.2d 908 (1991).

In conclusion, it is unlikely that a court would allow the defendant to use either Ms. Nickerson's assault charge or DUI charge to impeach Ms. Nickerson. However, the court could admit Ms. Nickerson's conviction for possession of stolen property.

Please let me know whether you have any additional questions or concerns.

Drafting Memo 1

lthough you are still a first-year law student, you have just gotten a part-time job at a local law firm. On your first day, your supervising attorney stops by your desk and asks you to help her with one of her cases.

§ 7.1   The Assignment

Assignments come in different shapes and sizes. While sometimes the attorney will give you the facts orally, at other times you may need to find the facts, pulling them from documents in the client's file or from other sources. In this instance, however, the attorney has set out the facts, and the issue that she wants you to research, in the following memo.

To: Legal Intern

From: Christina Galeano

Date: September 9, 2013

Re: Elaine Olsen, Case No. 13-478

Elaine Olsen has requested our help in overturning an order terminating her parental rights.

- Ms. Olsen says she never received the summons and, as a result, did not respond.
- On Wednesday, July 24, 2013, a process server went to Ms. Webster's house and asked for Elaine Olsen. (Ms. Webster is Ms. Olsen's sister.) When Ms. Webster told the process server that "Elaine isn't here today," the process server handed what was probably a summons and complaint to Ms. Webster and told Ms. Webster that Ms. Olsen "needed to go to court."
- On February 1, 2013, Ms. Olsen entered an inpatient drug treatment program in Miami, Florida. She remained in the program until March 27, 2013, when she moved into a "halfway" house. The residential treatment house was a four-bedroom house in a residential neighborhood. Up to eight women live in the house for three to twelve months while they make the transition from inpatient treatment to living on their own. The house is staffed 24/7; staff members provide counseling; enforce house rules, including no drug or alcohol use; and handle administrative duties.
- During April, May, and June, Ms. Olsen was a full-time resident at the residential treatment house. She had a bedroom in the house, ate her meals there, and had some of her possessions there.
- Beginning in July 2013, Ms. Olsen began spending less time at the residential treatment house and more time with her sister, Elizabeth Webster. During July and August 2013, Ms. Olsen usually spent weeknights at the residential treatment house and Friday, Saturday, and Sunday nights at her sister's house. Because she was spending time at her sister's house, Ms. Olsen moved some of her clothing and personal effects into her sister's house.
- Ms. Webster is 32. She will testify that she never gave the summons to her sister. Because she thought that the papers related to some of Ms. Olsen's unpaid bills, she simply put them in a shoebox in the kitchen with a stack of Ms. Olsen's other mail.
- During April and May 2013, Ms. Olsen put the residential treatment house address on employment applications. However, her driver's license showed her sister's address as her address.
- On September 1, 2013, Ms. Olsen moved into her own apartment. Since August 1, 2013, she has worked part-time.
- I looked at the return on the service of process and everything appears to be in order. Thus, please assume that the return of service is regular on its face.
- There is nothing in the record that indicates whether the State tried to personally serve Ms. Olsen or whether it tried to serve her at the residential treatment house.

As the first step, I need to determine whether the service of process is valid under the applicable Florida statute or statutes. Therefore, please research the rules relating to substituted service of process in Florida, and prepare an objective memo in which you set out the applicable rules and apply those rules to the facts of this case.

§ 7.2   Researching the Law

After reading, and rereading, the assignment, your next step is to do the research. See the electronic supplement for step-by-step instructions on how to research an issue governed by a state statute using free sources, Lexis Advance®, WestlawNext™, Bloomberg Law, Lexis.com®, and Westlaw® Classic. You can access the electronic supplement by going to *http://www.aspenlawschool.com/ books/oates_legalwritinghandbook/* and typing in the access code that is on the card that came with this book. One you are on the website, click on the links to Sections 4.3.1-4.3.7.

> **PRACTICE POINTER** You can often research an issue governed by a state statute using free sources: You can find a copy of the applicable statutory sections on the state legislature's website, and you can find copies of cases on Google® Scholar. You will, however, need to cite check using *Shepard's*®, KeyCite®, or BCite. Before doing other research on a fee-based service, get permission from your supervising attorney.

Do not, however, treat research as a separate stage in the process. As you research, read and analyze the statutes and cases that you find, determining whether they help answer the question or questions that you were asked to research. In addition, as soon as possible, begin creating a research log in which you record and organize the information that you find during your research. This log will help guide your research, reminding you of what types of information you need to find, and will serve as an outline for the discussion section of your memo. See the sample set out in Example 1 below.

> **PRACTICE POINTER** In your log, be clear about what material is quoted directly and what is paraphrased. Record cites, including pinpoint cites. Finally, come up with a system that tells you when you have cited checked a case.

EXAMPLE 1   ## Research Log

I. General Rules

A. What are the policies underlying the statute?

■ *Torres v. Arnco Constr., Inc.*, **867 So. 2d 583, 586 (Fla. 5th DCA 2004). (Cite checked; still good law.)**

The purpose of service of process is to advise the defendant that an action has been commenced and to warn the defendant that he or she must appear in a timely manner to state such defenses as are available.

■ *Shurman v. Atl. Mortg. & Inv. Corp.*, **795 So. 2d 952, 953-54 (Fla. 2001) (citing *State ex rel. Merritt v. Heffernan*, 142 Fla. 496, 195 So. 145, 147 (1940)). (Cite checked; still good law.)**

It is well settled that the fundamental purpose of service is "to give proper notice to the defendant in the case that he is answerable to the claim of plaintiff and, therefore, to vest jurisdiction in the court entertaining the controversy.

B. What is the applicable statute?

■ **§ 48.031(1)(a), Fla. Stat. (2013). (Cite checked; this is the applicable version of the statute.)**

Service of original process is made by delivering a copy of it to the person to be served with a copy of the complaint, petition, or other initial pleading or paper or by leaving the copies at his or her usual place of abode with any person residing therein who is 15 years of age or older and informing the person of their contents. . . .

C. What are the elements?

a. the usual place of abode of the person being served
b. with any person residing therein
c. who is 15 years of age or older and
d. informing the person of their contents.

D. Who has the burden of proof?

■ *Thompson v. State, Dep't of Revenue*, **867 So. 2d 603 (Fla. 1st DCA 2004). (Cite checked; still good law.)**

Quote from page 605:
    "The burden of proof to sustain the validity of service of process is upon the person who seeks to invoke the jurisdiction of the court and, without proper service of process, the court lacks personal jurisdiction over the defendant." *M.J.W. v. Department of Children and Families*, 825 So. 2d 1038, 1041 (Fla. 1st DCA 2002).
    [4] [5] "[A] process server's return of service on a defendant which is regular on its face is presumed to be valid absent clear and convincing evidence presented to the contrary." *Telf Corp. v. Gomez*, 671 So. 2d 818 (Fla. 3d DCA 1996). Although simple denial of service is not sufficient, *id.* at 819, Thompson's motion and affidavit are based on the fact that the service did not comply with section 48.031 and was therefore legally deficient. *National Safety Associates, Inc. v. Allstate Insurance Co.*, 799 So. 2d 316, 317 (Fla. 2d DCA 2001). Thompson's affidavit makes a *prima facie* showing that he was not served at his usual place of abode by valid substituted service. . . . Having raised the issue of personal jurisdiction, Thompson's motion and accompanying affidavit placed the burden on the Department to establish the validity of service of process. M.J.W., 825 So. 2d at 1041.

■ *Busman v. State, Dep't of Revenue*, **905 So. 2d 956, 958 (Fla. 3d DCA 2005). (Cite checked; still good law.)**

Quote from page 958:
Although the sheriff's return of service, which is regular on its face, is presumptively valid, [footnote omitted] see *Department of Revenue v. Wright*, 813 So. 2d 989, 992 (Fla. 2d DCA 2002); *Fla. Natl. Bank v. Halphen*, 641 So. 2d 495, 496 (Fla. 3d

DCA 1994), Busman presented clear, convincing and uncontradicted evidence that the 327 N.W. 4th Avenue address was not his "usual place of abode."

E. Other general rules

"The statutes regulating service of process are to be strictly construed to assure that a defendant is notified of the proceedings." Torres, 867 So. 2d at 586. "Indeed, because statutes authorizing substituted service are exceptions to the general rule requiring a defendant to be served personally, due process requires strict compliance with their statutory requirements." *Id.*

II. Elements

A. Usual place of abode (in dispute)

1. Specific rules (what test do the courts use in determining whether a particular place is a person's usual place of abode?)

■ *Thompson v. State, Dep't of Revenue*, 867 So. 2d 603 (Fla. 1st DCA 2004). (Cite checked; still good law.)

Quote from page 605:
Turning to the merits, "[s]ection 48.031 expressly requires that substituted service be at the person's usual place of abode." *Shurman v. Atl. Mortg. & Inv. Corp.*, 795 So. 2d 952, 954 (Fla. 2001). The requirement "usual place of abode" means "the place where the defendant is actually living at the time of service." *Id., citing State ex rel. Merritt v. Heffernan*, 142 Fla. 496, 195 So. 145, 147 (1940).

■ *Torres v. Arnco Const., Inc.*, 867 So. 2d 583 (Fla. 5th DCA 2004). (Cite checked; still good law.)

Quote from page 586:
In *State ex rel. Merritt v. Heffernan*, 142 Fla. 496, 195 So. 145, 147 (1940), the Florida Supreme Court defined the term "usual place of abode" as the place where the defendant "is actually living at the time of service." The word "abode" means "one's fixed place of residence for the time being when service is made." *Id.* If a person has more than one residence, he must be served at the residence in which he is actually living at the time of service. *Id.*

■ *Shurman v. Atl. Mortg. & Inv. Corp.*, 795 So. 2d 952 (Fla. 2001). (Cite checked; still good law.)

Quote from page 954:
Going one step further, "usual place of abode" is the place where the defendant is actually living at the time of the service. The word abode means one's fixed place of residence for the time being when the service is made. Thus, if a person has several residences, he must be served at the residence in which he is actually living at the time service is made.

2. Analogous cases

■ *State ex rel. Merritt v. Heffernan*, 142 Fla. 496, 195 So. 145, 147 (1940). (Cite checked; still good law.)

Quote from pages 147-48.
The summons was left with the defendant's wife at the family's apartment in Florida an hour after the defendant boarded a train to Minnesota. Although the defendant argued that his usual place of abode was Minnesota, where he had an office, paid taxes, and voted, the court disagreed, noting that the defendant had moved his family to the Florida apartment two months before his wife was served, that the defendant had visited his family at the apartment twice "during the season," and that the defendant's family had remained in Florida for some time after he was served. As the court stated, "We do not hold the view that Florida was the permanent residence of the defendant, but we do feel that in the circumstance reflected in the record, it was his usual place of abode . . . ." *Id.* at 148.

■ *Busman v. State, Dep't of Revenue*, 905 So. 2d 956 (Fla. 3d DCA 2005). (Cite checked; still good law.)

Quote from page 958:
In a paternity action, service was made on the defendant' half-brother on July 16, 2003. Defendant testified that he had moved out of his half-brother's house on July 1, 2002, and presented lease and landlord's testimony. Although the return of service was regular on its face, the court held that Busman had presented clear, convincing, and uncontradicted evidence that service was not made at his usual place of abode. The court stated that the statute must be strictly construed.

■ *Thompson v. State, Dep't of Revenue*, 867 So. 2d 603 (Fla. 1st DCA 2004). (Cite checked; still good law.)

Quote from page 605:
In a child support case service was made with the defendant's wife. The defendant filed an affidavit stating that he had been separated from his wife for three years and that he not lived at the address where service was made. The court reversed and remanded for an evidentiary hearing.

■ *Torres v. Arnco Const., Inc.*, 867 So. 2d 583 (Fla. 5th DCA 2004). (Cite checked; still good law.)

Quote from page 587:
NY process server tried to serve the defendant at his NY address, where he had lived for 12 years. Although NY neighbors told process server that the defendant lived at the house, they also said that he traveled a lot. Service was then made on the defendant's mother, who lived in Florida. When process server left the papers with defendant's mother, mother said that the defendant "would be home soon, and she would see to it that he received the papers." Majority concluded that the plaintiff had not met its burden of proof and that the mother's statement was ambiguous. The dissent argued that if the defendant spent substantial amounts of time visiting family in Florida the Florida house was his usual place of abode at the time service was made.

3. Ms. Olsen's arguments:

■ On the day that service was made, Ms. Olsen was living not at her sister's house but at the residential treatment house.
■ Service on a relative is not sufficient.
■ Her more permanent address was the residential treatment house address. She had a room, etc., at the residential treatment house.
■ *Heffernan* is an old case.
■ In *Torres*, the court held that the defendant's mother's house was not the defendant's usual place of abode even though the mother indicated that the defendant would be home later.

4. The State's arguments:

■ Ms. Olsen stayed at her sister's house three nights a week.
■ Ms. Olsen apparently received mail at her sister's house—the shoebox.
■ Ms. Olsen listed her sister's address on her driver's license.
■ In *Heffernan*, the court held that the apartment was the defendant's usual place of abode even though the defendant had left the apartment and was on a train back to his permanent residence.
■ In *Torres*, the defendant had a permanent residence where he had lived for 12 years. He was just visiting his mother.

B. Any person residing therein (not in dispute)

■ Service was left with Ms. Webster, who is a person, at Ms. Webster's house.

C. 15 years old or older (not in dispute)

◼ Ms. Webster is 32.

D. Informing the person of their contents (in dispute)

1. Specific rules (what test do the courts use in determining whether the process server informed the person being served of the contents of the documents?)
2. Analogous cases
3. Ms. Olsen's arguments
4. State's arguments

§ 7.3   Understanding What You Have Found

§ 7.3.1   Make Sure You Understand the Big Picture

Your first step should be a step back. Can you place the issue that you were asked to research into the bigger picture? For instance, in the Olsen case, do you understand how service of process relates to jurisdiction and how jurisdiction relates to whether the court had the power to enter a default judgment? If you don't, don't panic. The law is complicated, and neither professors nor employers expect first-, second-, or even third-year students to have a complete understanding of how the system works. However, both professors and employers expect students to look for answers and, if they can't find them, to ask questions.

§ 7.3.2   Make Sure You Understand the Statute

Once you understand the big picture, make sure you understand the statute. In particular, make sure you understand the requirements, or elements, and that you have looked for statutory sections that explain the statute's purpose and that define terms used in the statute. In addition, if the statute is a complicated one, take the time to diagram the statute.

In the example problem, the applicable statute is Fla. Stat. § 48.031(a)(1) (2013), which reads as follows:

> Service of original process is made by delivering a copy of it to the person to be served with a copy of the complaint, petition, or other initial pleading or paper or by leaving the copies at his or her usual place of abode with any person residing therein who is 15 years of age or older and informing the person of their contents. . . .

A close reading of the statute reveals that service can be accomplished in either of two ways: (1) by delivering a copy of the summons, complaint, petition, or other initial pleading or paper to the person to be served or (2) by leaving a copy of those documents at the person's usual place of abode with a person who resides there who is 15 years old or older and by informing the person with whom the documents are left of their contents.

Note that in this instance there is an "or" between the (1) and the (2) but that there is an "and" between the "c" and the "d." While you can accomplish service of process either by delivering the summons to the person being served or by leaving it at his or her usual place of abode, if you leave it at the person's usual place of abode, you must leave the summons with a person who is residing therein, that person must be 15 years old or older, and you must inform the person with whom you leave the documents of their contents.

Also note that, in some instances, the statutory language will be ambiguous. Some of these ambiguities are the result of poor drafting; some may, however, be intentional. To get enough votes to enact the legislation, the drafters may have intentionally used vague language. Don't despair. You will often be able to use these ambiguities to make an argument on behalf of your client.

> **PRACTICE POINTER**
>
> There is often more than one way to list the elements. For example, you can list "any person residing therein" and "who is 15 years of age or older" as separate elements, or you can combine these two elements and treat them as one: "any person residing therein who is 15 years of age or older." In deciding whether to combine elements, look at how the cases have listed the elements (do they separate or combine them?) and think about whether, in your memo, it make more sense to treat the requirements as separate elements or one element.

§ 7.3.3 Make Sure You Understand the General and Specific Rules

In addition to reading the statute carefully, read carefully those portions of the cases that are relevant to the issue you were asked to research.

Begin by focusing on the cases that have set out general rules, that is, the cases that have listed the elements, the cases that have set out the rules relating to the burden of proof, and the cases that have explained the policies underlying the statute. For example, in researching the sample problem, we found several cases that set out the rules relating to the burden of proof.

If all of the cases set out the same rule, all you need to do is make sure that you understand that rule. If, however, different cases set out different rules, you need to determine which of those rules governs. To do this, begin by cite checking the cases. If one or more of the cases have been reversed or overruled on the point of law for which you are looking at the case, do not use those cases. They are no longer good law.

If the remaining cases, that is, the cases that are still good law, set out the same rule, use that rule. If, though, there is still a discrepancy, try to resolve that discrepancy by looking to see if different rules apply in different types of cases (for example, is there a different rule in child custody cases than there is in contract cases?); whether different divisions apply different rules (for example, does the 1st DCA apply one rule and the 3d DCA apply a different rule?); or whether the rule seems to be evolving.

In our example case, all of the cases seem to set out the same rule of law. Although it takes some careful reading to determine what that rule is, the rule seems to be as follows:

1. The party who is seeking to invoke the jurisdiction of the court (the plaintiff) has the burden of proving that the service was valid.
2. If, however, the "return of service" is regular on its face, service is presumed to be valid.
3. Thus, if the "return of service" is regular on its face, the party challenging the validity of the service (the defendant) must present clear and convincing evidence that the service is invalid.

> **PRACTICE POINTER**   When you are not sure what a particular word or phrase means, take a few minutes to look up the definition. For example, if you are not sure what the phrase "return of service" means, look up that phrase. If you are online, the easiest way to find a definition is to go to Bing or Google and type in the word "definition" and the phrase "return of service." When you do, you will be taken to a site like thefreedictionary.com, which provides plain English definitions for legal terms. In this instance, the website sets out the following definition for "return of service": "n. Written confirmation from a process server under oath that declares that the legal documents were served (such as a summons and complaint)." Although you should not cite to this type of dictionary in a memo or brief, you can use this type of dictionary to help you understand terms used in a statute or case.

Accordingly, in our example problem, because the return is regular on its face, Ms. Olsen would have to present clear and convincing evidence that the service was not valid.

> **PRACTICE POINTER**   If several cases set out the same rule, you will usually want to cite a recent case from the jurisdiction's highest court as authority for that rule. For instance, in our sample case, you would want to cite to a recent Florida Supreme Court case. If there is not a recent case from the jurisdiction's highest court, you can cite to an older case from the jurisdiction's highest court and then to a more recent decision from an intermediate court of appeals. The exception to this "rule" is when the rule is known by the name of the case that announced it. For example, if you are setting out the *Miranda* rule, cite to *Miranda v. Arizona*, 384 U.S. 436 (1966), and not to a more recent United States Supreme Court case.

Once you understand the general rules, turn your attention to the specific rules, that is, the rules that the courts apply in determining whether a particular element, or requirement, is met. For instance, in the Olsen case, look at the rules that the courts apply in determining whether the service was made at the defendant's usual place of abode. Do all of the cases set out the same rule? If they do not set out the same rule, are some of the cases no longer good law?

If all of the cases are still good law, is there a way of reconciling the various rules?

Once you understand the big picture and have a good understanding of both the general and specific rules, it is time to start writing. As you do this writing, keep two things in mind. First, writing a memo is usually a multi-step process. If you want to do a good job, you will need to do a first draft, a second draft, and maybe even a third or fourth draft. As a consequence, do not put off writing the first draft until the night before the final draft is due. Second, most of the time drafting a memo involves more than recording completely formed ideas and arguments. Most law students and attorneys find that they rethink their analysis and synthesis as they write. Consequently, do not be surprised if, part way through writing the first draft, you have one of those "aha!" moments in which you see the issue, the law, or an argument in a different light.

The rest of this chapter walks you through the process of writing the memo. Although we discuss the sections in the order in which they appear in a formal memo, you do not have to write the sections in order. For example, many law students and attorneys find that it works better to write the first draft of the discussion section before they write the first draft of the statement of facts, issue statement, and brief answer.

Chapter 7 Quiz No. 1

Draft answers for each of the following questions. Make your points clearly and concisely, and write sentences that are easy to read and that are grammatical and correctly punctuated.

1. How will keeping a research log like the one set out in Example 1 help you research and write a memo?
2. What is an element?
3. What is the difference between burden of proof and standard of review?
4. What is the difference between a general rule and a specific rule?
5. If more than one case sets out the applicable rule, what factors should you consider in deciding which case or cases to cite as authority for that rule?

§ 7.4   Drafting the Heading

The heading is the easiest section to write. It consists of only four entries: the name of the person to whom the memo is addressed, the name of the person who wrote the memo, the date, and an entry identifying the client and the issue or issues discussed in the memo. Although the first three entries are self-explanatory, the fourth needs some explanation.

In some firms, the memo is filed only in the client's file. For such firms, the "Re:" entry can be quite general.

EXAMPLE 1   **Sample Heading**

To: Christina Galeano

From: Legal Intern

Date: September 9, 2013

Re: Elaine Olsen, Case No. 13-478

In other firms, the memo is filed not only in the client's file but also in a "memo bank"—that is, a computer or paper file in which all memos are filed by topic. In these offices, the "Re:" section serves two purposes: (1) within the client's file, it distinguishes the memo from other memos that have been or will be written, and (2) in the memo bank, it provides either the database for a word search or topic categories under which the memo will be filed. To serve this last purpose, the heading should include the key terms.

EXAMPLE 2   **Sample Heading**

To: Christina Galeano

From: Legal Intern

Date: September 9, 2013

Re: Elaine Olsen, Case No. 13-478
          Service of Process, Usual Place of Abode; Notification of Contents

---

§ 7.5   Drafting the Statement of Facts

Just as every case starts with a story, so does every memo. Therefore, in most instances, begin your memo by telling your supervising attorney who did what when.

§ 7.5.1   Decide What Facts to Include

In a typical statement of facts, there are three types of facts: the legally significant facts, the emotionally significant facts, and the background facts. In addition, in some instances you will want to identify the facts that are not yet known.

a.   Legally Significant Facts

A legally significant fact is a fact that a court would consider in deciding whether a statute or rule is applicable or that a court would use in applying that statute or rule. For instance, in the Olsen case, the legally significant facts are those facts that the court would consider in determining whether service of process was valid. More specifically, the legally significant facts are the facts that the court would consider in determining (1) whether the summons was left at the defendant's usual place of abode, (2) whether the summons was left with a person residing therein who is 15 years old or older, and (3) whether the process server notified the person being served of the contents of the documents. Because a change in one of the legally significant facts could change your analysis and prediction, you should include all of the legally significant facts in your statement of facts.

You can use either of two techniques to determine whether a fact is legally significant. Before you write the discussion section, you can prepare a two-column chart in which you list the elements in the first column and the facts that relate to those elements in the second column. See Exhibit 7.1.

Exhibit 7.1	**Determining Which Facts Are Legally Significant**
Element	**Facts Related to Element**
Usual Place of Abode	Ms. Webster told the process server that "Elaine isn't here today."
	On February 1, 2013, Ms. Olsen entered an inpatient drug treatment program in Miami. She remained in the program until March 27, 2013, when she moved into a residential treatment house for recovering addicts.
	During April, May, and June 2013, Ms. Olsen was a full-time resident at the residential treatment house. She had a bedroom in the house, ate her meals there, and had some of her possessions there.
	Beginning in July 2013, Ms. Olsen began spending less time at the residential treatment house and more time with her sister, Elizabeth Webster.
	During July and August 2013, Ms. Olsen spent weeknights at the residential treatment house and Friday, Saturday, and Sunday nights at her sister's house. Because she was spending time at her sister's house, she moved some of her clothing and personal effects into her sister's house.
	During April and May 2013, Ms. Olsen put the residential treatment house address on employment applications. However, her driver's license showed her sister's address as her address.
	On September 1, 2013, Ms. Olsen moved into her own apartment.

Element	Facts Related to Element
	The return on the service of process appears to be in order.
	The service was made on Wednesday, July 24, 2013.
	At this point there is no evidence indicating that the state tried to serve Ms. Olsen at the treatment house.
Person Residing Therein Who Is 15 Years Old or Older	Ms. Webster lives in the house where the summons was left.
	Ms. Webster is 32.
Element	Facts Related to Element
Informing Person of Contents	The process server handed what was probably a summons and complaint to Ms. Webster and told Ms. Webster that Ms. Olsen "needed to go to court."

The second technique is used after the discussion section has been completed. To ensure that you have included all of the legally significant facts in your statement of facts, go through your discussion section, checking to make sure that each of the facts that you used in setting out the arguments is in your statement of facts. If you used a fact in the analysis, that fact is legally significant and should be included in the statement of facts.

PRACTICE POINTER   Remember, writing a memo is a recursive process. Even though you may write the statement of facts first, you may need to revise it after you have completed the discussion section.

b. Emotionally Significant Facts

An emotionally significant fact is one that, while not legally significant, may affect the way the judge or jury decides the case.

For example, in the Olsen case, while it is not legally significant that Ms. Olsen was in a drug treatment program, that fact may color the way the judge views her. Therefore, this fact is an emotionally significant fact and should be included in the statement of facts. In addition, while it is not legally significant that Ms. Olsen got a job, that fact may also color the way in which the judge views her and should, therefore, be included in the statement of facts.

c. Background Facts

In addition to including the legally and emotionally significant facts, also include those facts that are needed to tell the story and that provide the context for the legally and emotionally significant facts.

d.   Unknown Facts

Sometimes you are not given all of the facts needed to analyze an issue. For instance, because the attorney did not know the law, he or she may not have asked the right questions, or the documents containing the unknown facts are in the possession of the opposing party. If the unknown facts are legally significant and you can obtain them, try to do so before writing the memo. If, however, the unknown facts are not legally significant or if you cannot obtain them, write the memo, but tell the attorney, either in the statement of facts, the discussion section, or the conclusion what facts are unknown.

> **PRACTICE POINTER**   You may not realize a fact is unknown until you have read the cases. For instance, in the example problem, at the time that she interviewed Ms. Olsen, the attorney did not ask Ms. Olsen whether the process server had tried to serve her at the residential treatment house or on any other occasions. However, after doing the research, you know that these facts may be legally significant.

§ 7.5.2   Select an Organizational Scheme

As a general rule, begin your statement of facts with an introductory sentence or paragraph that identifies the parties and the issue. Then present the facts using one of three organizational schemes: a chronological organizational scheme, a topical organizational scheme, or a combination of the two, for example, a scheme in which you organize the facts by topic and then, within each topic, you set out the facts in chronological order.

Most of the time, the facts dictate which organizational scheme will work best. If the case involves a series of events related by date, then the facts should be presented chronologically. If, however, there are a number of facts that are not related by date (for example, the description of several different pieces of property) or a number of unrelated events that occurred during the same time period (for example, four unrelated crimes committed by the defendant over the same two-day period), the facts should be organized by topic.

Sometimes, though, the facts can be presented in more than one way. For example, in the Olsen case, the facts can be presented using either a scheme that is primarily chronological or a scheme that is primarily topical. See Examples 1 and 2.

EXAMPLE 1   **Statement of Facts with Facts Presented in Chronological Order**

Elaine Olsen has contacted our office asking for assistance in overturning a judgment terminating her parental rights. You have asked me to determine whether the service of process was valid.

On February 1, 2013, Ms. Olsen entered an inpatient drug treatment program in Miami, Florida. She remained in the program until March 27, 2013, when she moved into a residential treatment house for recovering addicts.

During April, May, and June 2013, Ms. Olsen was a full-time resident at the treatment house. She had a bedroom in the house, ate her meals there, and had some of her possessions there. In addition, when she applied for jobs, she listed the treatment house address as her address.

Beginning in July 2013, Ms. Olsen began spending less time at the treatment house and more time with her sister, Elizabeth Webster, who is 32. Both Ms. Olsen's sister and the manager of the residential treatment house will testify that, during July and August 2013, Ms. Olsen spent weeknights at the residential treatment house and Friday, Saturday, and Sunday nights at her sister's house. Because she was spending time at her sister's house, Ms. Olsen moved some of her clothing and personal effects into her sister's house.

On Wednesday, July 24, 2013, a process server went to Ms. Webster's house and asked for Elaine Olsen. When Ms. Webster told the process server that "Elaine isn't here today," the process server handed the summons to Ms. Webster and told her that Ms. Olsen "needed to go to court."

Ms. Webster will testify that she never gave the summons to her sister. Because she thought that the papers related to some of Ms. Olsen's unpaid bills, she simply put the summons in a shoebox in the kitchen with a stack of Ms. Olsen's other mail. Ms. Olsen says she never received the summons and, as a result, did not respond. The return of service is regular on its face.

Ms. Olsen has been employed since August 1, 2013, and she has lived in her own apartment since September 1, 2013. She has her sister's address on her driver's license.

There is nothing in the record that indicates whether the State tried to personally serve Ms. Olsen or whether it tried to serve her at the residential treatment house.

EXAMPLE 2   **Statement of Facts with Facts Organized by Topic**

You have asked me to determine whether the service of process on one of our clients, Elaine Olsen, is valid.

During the past six months, Ms. Olsen has lived in three places. From February 1, 2013, until March 27, 2013, Ms. Olsen was a patient in an in-patient drug treatment program in Miami, Florida. On March 27, 2013, she moved into a residential treatment house for recovering addicts. During April, May, and June, Ms. Olsen was a full-time resident at the treatment house. She had a bedroom in the house, ate her meals there, and had some of her possessions there. In addition, Ms. Olsen listed the treatment house address on job applications. Beginning in July 2013, Ms. Olsen began spending more time at her sister's house. During July and August 2013, Ms. Olsen spent weeknights at the treatment house and Friday, Saturday, and Sunday nights at her sister's house. Because she was spending time at her sister's house, Ms. Olsen moved some of her clothing and personal effects into her sister's house. Ms. Olsen has her sister's address on her driver's license.

On Wednesday, July 24, 2013, a process server went to Ms. Olsen's sister's house and asked for Elaine Olsen. When Ms. Olsen's sister, Ms. Webster, told the process server that "Elaine isn't here today," the process server handed the summons to Ms. Webster and told her that Ms. Olsen "needed to go to court."

Ms. Webster, who is 32, will testify that she never gave the summons to her sister. Because she thought that the papers related to some of Ms. Olsen's unpaid bills, she simply put the summons in a shoebox in the kitchen with a stack of Ms. Olsen's other mail. Ms. Olsen says she never received the summons and complaint, and as a result, she did not respond.

You have asked me to presume that the return of service is regular on its face. There is nothing in the record that indicates whether the State tried to personally serve Ms. Olsen or whether it tried to serve her at the residential treatment house.

PRACTICE POINTER	If you are using a chronological organizational scheme, you can signal that fact to your readers by starting the sentence that follows your introduction with a date. In contrast, if you are using a topical organizational scheme, try to use topic sentences that identify the topics. Do not, however, include law or argue the facts in the statement of facts; save that material for the discussion section.

§ 7.5.3   Present the Facts Clearly and Concisely

Most attorneys prefer statements of facts that are short and to the point. This does not, however, mean that they want the facts set out using bullet points. While bullet points are common in some types of business writing, most attorneys want the facts presented in easy-to-read sentences in well-constructed paragraphs.

Well-written sentences and paragraphs have several advantages over bullet points. First, most readers have an easier time understanding what happened when the facts are presented in the form of a "story." The narrative quality of a story helps readers understand who the actors are and the sequence of events. Second, setting out the facts in story form makes it easier to use the statement of facts in the memo to write the summary of facts for a letter to the client or the statement of the case for a brief.

§ 7.5.4   Present the Facts Accurately and Objectively

In writing the statement of facts for an objective memorandum, present the facts accurately and objectively. Do not include facts that are not in your file, and do not set out legal conclusions, misstate facts, leave out facts that are legally significant, or present the facts so that they favor one side over the other. In Example 3, the writer has violated all of these "rules."

PRACTICE POINTER	You set out a legal conclusion when you set out as a fact that one of the elements or rules is met or is not met. Whether an element or rule is or is not met is a legal conclusion and not a fact.

EXAMPLE 3	**Writer Has Not Presented the Facts Accurately and Objectively**

Hoping to obtain a default judgment against Ms. Olsen, the plaintiff had the sheriff serve the summons and petition at Ms. Olsen's sister's house and not at the residential treatment house where Ms. Olsen was actually living. Although Ms. Olsen occasionally visited her sister at her sister's house, she did not keep any of her personal belongings at her sister's house.

In the first sentence, the writer violates the first two rules. First, she sets out facts that are not in the record when she states that the plaintiff hoped to get a default judgment and when she states that the plaintiff had a sheriff serve Ms. Olsen at her sister's house and not at the residential treatment house. Second, she sets out legal conclusions when she states that the defendant was actually living at the residential treatment house. Because a person's usual place of abode is the place where the defendant is actually living, in the context of this case, the statement that the defendant was actually living in the residential treatment house is a legal conclusion.

In the second sentence, the writer violates the last three rules. The writer misstates the facts when she states that Ms. Olsen did not keep any personal belongings at her sister's house; she leaves out legally significant facts when she does not include the fact that Ms. Olsen had her sister's address on her driver's license; and she presents the facts in a light favorable to her client when she states that Ms. Olsen visited her sister only occasionally.

PRACTICE POINTER	As a general rule, do not refer to individuals by their first names only. Instead, use the appropriate title and family name. For instance, instead of referring to Elaine Olsen as "Elaine," use "Elaine Olsen" or "Ms. Olsen."

§ 7.5.5   Checklist for Critiquing the Statement of Facts

a.   Content

- The writer has included all of the legally significant facts.
- When appropriate, the writer included emotionally significant facts.
- The writer included enough background facts that a person not familiar with the case can understand what happened.
- The writer has identified the unknown facts.
- The writer presented the facts accurately.
- The writer presented the facts objectively.
- The writer has not included legal conclusions in the statement of facts.

b.   Organization

- The writer has included an introductory sentence or paragraph that identifies the parties and the nature of the dispute.
- The writer has used one of the conventional organizational schemes: chronological, topical, or a combination of chronological and topical.

c.   Writing

- The attorney can understand the facts of the case after reading the statement of facts once.
- The paragraph divisions are logical, and the paragraphs are neither too long nor too short.

- Transitions and dovetailing have been used to make the connection between ideas clear.
- In most sentences, the writer has used the actor as the subject of the sentence, and the subject and verb are close together.
- The writer has varied the length of the sentences and the sentence patterns so that each sentence flows smoothly from the prior sentence.
- The writing is concise and precise.
- The writing is grammatically correct and correctly punctuated.
- The statement of facts has been proofread.

§ 7.6   Drafting the Issue Statement

It is not unusual for students to ask whether they really need to include an issue statement in their memo. Doesn't the attorney know the issue? The answer to both questions is yes. However, even though your supervising attorney told you what issue to research, you should include an issue statement.

You should include an issue statement, or question presented, because, by convention, formal memos have an issue statement. While at first it may seem as if writing a formal statement of the issue is a waste of time, the opposite is often true. Writing an issue statement provides you the opportunity to do more sophisticated analysis: Given your research, what is the applicable law? What is the legal question? What are the most important facts?

As a general rule, you should have the same number of issue statements as you have "parts" to the discussion section. Accordingly, if you have three issue statements — (1) whether service of process was valid, (2) whether the statute of limitations has run, and (3) whether the defendant is entitled to judgment as a matter of law — you should also have three parts to the discussion section, one corresponding to each of the three issues. If, however, you have only one issue statement, for example, whether service of process is valid, your discussion section will have only one part.

| **PRACTICE POINTER** | As a general rule, do not treat each element as a separate issue. For example, if the issue is whether the service of process was valid, do not treat the first element, usual place of abode, as |

one issue; the second element, person residing therein who is 15 or older, as a second issue; and the third element, informing about the contents, as a third issue.

Convention also dictates that in a multi-issue memo you list the issues in the same order in which you discuss those issues in the discussion section. The first issue statement will correspond to the first part of the discussion section, the second will correspond to the second part, and so on.

In this chapter we describe how to write an issue statement using the "under-does-when" format. In the next chapter, we describe the "whether" format.

§ 7.6.1   Select a Format: The "Under-Does-When" Format

The under-does-when format is easy to use because the format forces you to include all of the essential information. After the "under," insert a reference to the applicable law; after the verb (for example, "does," "is," or "may"), insert the legal question; and after "when," insert the most important of the legally significant facts. Because the format is written as a question, place a question mark at the end.

> Under [insert reference to applicable law]
> does/is/may [insert legal question]
> when [insert the key facts]?

a.   Reference to the Applicable Law

To be useful to the reader, the reference to the rule of law cannot be too specific or too general. For example, a reference to "Florida law" is too broad; hundreds of cases are filed each year in which the issue is governed by Florida law.

EXAMPLE 1   **Reference to the Rule of Law Too General**

Under Florida law, . . .

EXAMPLE 2   **Appropriate References**

Under Florida's service of process statute, . . .
Under Florida's service of process statute, § 48.031 Fla. Stat. (2013), . . .

If you identify the statute in your statement of the legal question, you can refer to the statute by number in your reference to the rule of law. For example, in some instances, the following format works well: "Under § 48.031 Fla. Stat. (2013), was service of process valid when . . . ."

b.   Statement of the Legal Question

After identifying the applicable law, set out the legal question. In doing so, make sure that your statement of the legal question is neither too narrow nor too broad. If stated too narrowly, your statement of the legal question will not cover all of the issues and subissues; if stated too broadly, the question does not serve its function of focusing the reader's attention on the real issue.

PRACTICE POINTER	Although we refer to this format as the "under-does-when" format, you do not need to use "does" as the verb. As the following examples illustrate, a number of different verbs can work.

| **EXAMPLE 3** | **Legal Questions that Are Too Narrow** |

- ■ Was the summons left at Ms. Olsen's usual place of abode when . . . ?
- ■ Was the summons left at the place where Ms. Olsen was actually living when . . . ?
- ■ Did the process server inform Ms. Webster about the contents of the summons when . . . ?

| **EXAMPLE 4** | **Legal Questions that Are Too Broad** |

- ■ Did the court properly terminate Ms. Olsen's parental rights when . . . ?
- ■ Were Ms. Olsen's rights violated when . . . ?

| **EXAMPLE 5** | **Legal Questions that Are Properly Framed** |

- ■ Was service valid when . . . ?
- ■ Was Ms. Olsen properly served when . . . ?
- ■ Was service at Ms. Olsen's sister's house valid when . . . ?
- ■ Was the substituted service on the defendant's sister at the sister's house valid when . . . ?

c.   The Key Facts

Unless the issue that you have been asked to research involves only a question of law, end your issue statement by setting out the key facts. How will the court apply the rule of law to the facts in your client's case?

How many facts you include depends on how many facts are legally significant. If there are only a few legally significant facts, you will usually want to include all of them. If, however, there are a large number of legally significant facts, be selective. Either list only the most important of the legally significant facts, or list only the facts that relate to the disputed element or elements.

In Example 6, the writer has not included enough facts: While he has included the facts that the court would consider in deciding whether the process server informed the person served of the contents of the documents, he has not included facts that the court would consider in deciding whether the summons was left at Ms. Olsen's usual place of abode with a person 15 years or older residing therein.

| **EXAMPLE 6** | **Writer Has Not Included Enough Facts** |

Under Florida's service of process statute, § 48.031, Fla. Stat. (2013), was the service valid when the process server told Ms. Webster that Ms. Olsen "needed to go to court"?

In contrast, in Example 7, the writer has included too many facts. As a result, the issue statement is so long that some attorneys would not read it.

| EXAMPLE 7 | **Writer Has Included Too Many Facts** |

Under Florida's service of process statute, was substituted service on Ms. Olsen's sister at the sister's house valid when (1) Ms. Olsen was a patient in an inpatient drug treatment program in Miami from February 1, 2013, until March 27, 2013; (2) Ms. Olsen moved into a residential treatment house for recovering addicts on March 27, 2013; (3) during April, May, and June 2013, Ms. Olsen was a full-time resident at the residential treatment house, where she had a bedroom, where she ate her meals, and where she had some possessions; (4) during April and May 2013, Ms. Olsen listed the residential treatment house address on job applications; (5) beginning in July 2013, Ms. Olsen began spending less time at the residential treatment house and more time with her sister, Ms. Webster; (6) during July and August 2013, Ms. Olsen usually spent weeknights at the residential treatment house and Friday, Saturday, and Sunday nights at her sister's house; (7) on July 24, 2013, a process server went to Ms. Webster's house and asked for Elaine Olsen; (8) when Ms. Webster told the process server that "Elaine isn't here today," the process server handed the summons to Ms. Webster and told her that Ms. Olsen "needed to go to court"; and (9) Ms. Webster is 32 years old and lives at the house where she received the summons?

Examples 8 and 9 are better: They include the key facts without going into too much detail.

| EXAMPLE 8 | **Better Example** |

Under Florida's service of process statute, was Ms. Olsen properly served when (1) during the month when service was made, Ms. Olsen spent weeknights at a residential treatment house and spent Friday, Saturday, and Sunday nights at her sister's house; (2) Ms. Olsen listed the address of the residential treatment house on job applications but her sister's address on her driver's license; (3) service was made on Ms. Olsen's 32-year-old sister on a Wednesday at Ms. Olsen's sister's house; (4) the process server told Ms. Olsen's sister that Ms. Olsen needed to go to court; and (5) Ms. Olsen's sister did not give the summons to Ms. Olsen, and Ms. Olsen states that she did not receive notice?

| EXAMPLE 9 | **Better Example** |

Under Florida's statute authorizing substituted service of process, was service on the defendant's adult sister at the sister's house valid when the defendant spent weeknights at a residential treatment house and weekends at her sister's house; when the service was made on a weekday; when the process server told the defendant's sister that the defendant "needed to go to court"; and when the defendant states that she did not receive notice?

| **PRACTICE POINTER** | While some attorneys will want you to "personalize" your issue statements by using the parties' names, other attorneys will want you to write issue statements that are more generic. Compare |

Example 8 in which the writer used Ms. Olsen's name with Example 9 in which the writer uses the words, "the defendant."

In setting out the facts, make sure you set out facts and not legal conclusions. While what is a fact and what is a legal conclusion will vary from case to case, saying or implying that an element is or is not met will always be a legal conclusion. In Example 10, the writer has set out legal conclusions. Instead of setting out the facts that the court would consider in deciding whether an element is met, she has simply listed the elements.

| **EXAMPLE 10** | **Writer Has Incorrectly Set Out Legal Conclusions Rather Than Facts** |

Under Florida's statute authorizing substituted service of process, was the service valid when the process server left the summons with a person of suitable age and discretion at one of the defendant's usual places of abode and told the person about the contents of the notice?

Finally, make sure that you set out the facts accurately and objectively. Do not misstate a fact, and do not include only those facts that favor your client. While in a brief to a court you will want to present the facts in the light most favorable to your client, in an office memo you need to be objective.

| **EXAMPLE 11** | **Writer Has Not Set Out Facts Accurately and Objectively** |

Under Florida's service of process statute, was the service invalid when (1) at the time that service was made, Ms. Olsen's permanent residence was a residential treatment house where she had a room, ate meals, and kept belongings; (2) Ms. Olsen listed the residential treatment house address on job applications; (3) the process server did not tell Ms. Olsen's sister that the State was planning to terminate Ms. Olsen's parental rights; and (4) Ms. Olsen's sister did not give the summons to Ms. Olsen, and Ms. Olsen states that she did not receive notice?

---

§ 7.6.2   Make Sure that Your Issue Statement Is Easy to Read

It is not enough to include the right information in your issue statement. You must also present that information in such a way that your issue statement is easy to read.

The "under-does-when" format helps you write a readable issue statement by forcing you to use the three slots in a sentence: the reference to the rule of law goes into the introductory phrase or clause, the legal question goes into the main clause, and the key facts go into a list of "when" clauses at the end of the sentence.

_____, _____ _____?

introductory phrase or clause,   main clause   "when" clauses

You can also make your issue statement easier to read by using the active voice and concrete subjects and action verbs. Finally, in listing the key facts, use parallel constructions for each item in the list and, when appropriate, use enumeration.

> **PRACTICE POINTER**　End issue statements written using the "under-does-when" format with a question mark. End issue statements written using the "whether" format, which is discussed in Chapter 8, with a period.

§ 7.6.3　Checklist for Critiquing the Issue Statement

a.　Content

- The reference to the rule of law is neither too broad nor too narrow.
- The legal question is properly focused.
- The most significant of the legally significant facts have been included.
- Legal conclusions have not been set out as facts.

b.　Format

- The writer has used one of the conventional formats, for example, the "under-does-when" format or the "whether" format.

c.　Writing

- The issue statement is easy to read and understand.
- In setting out the legal question, the writer has used a concrete subject and an action verb.
- In listing the facts, the writer has used parallel constructions for all of the items in the list.
- If the list of facts is long, the writer has used enumeration or has repeated key structural cues, for example, words like "when" and "that."

§ 7.7　Drafting the Brief Answer

The brief answer serves a purpose similar to that served by the formal conclusion: it tells the attorney how you think a court will decide an issue and why. The brief answer is not, however, as detailed as the formal conclusion.

§ 7.7.1　Select a Format

Convention dictates that, in a formal memo, you should include a separate brief answer for each issue statement. In addition, convention dictates that you should start each of your brief answers with a one- or two-word short answer. The words that are typically used are "probably," and "probably not." After this one- or two-word answer, briefly explain your answer.

§ 7.7.2   Set Out Your Conclusion and Reasoning

In writing your brief answers, keep a couple of things in mind. First, remember your audience and purpose. You are writing to an attorney who needs an objective evaluation of the client's case. Second, make sure that you answer the question you set out in your issue statement and that you match the style you used in your issue statement. For example, if you used the parties' names in your issue statement, also use them in your brief answer. Third, be specific. Tell the attorney which elements you or the other side will or will not be able to prove. Finally, make sure that you get the burden of proof right. If you have personalized your issue statement and your client has the burden of proof, talk about what your client can and cannot prove. If, however, the other side has the burden of proof, talk about what it can and cannot prove. In contrast, if you wrote a more generic issue statement, talk about what the court will do.

EXAMPLE 1	Issue Statement and Brief Answer in Which the Writer Uses the Parties' Names

Issue

Under Florida's service of process statute, was Ms. Olsen properly served when (1) during the month when service was made, Ms. Olsen spent weeknights at a residential treatment house and spent Friday, Saturday, and Sunday nights at her sister's house; (2) Ms. Olsen listed the address of the residential treatment house on job applications but her sister's address on her driver's license; (3) service was made on Ms. Olsen's 32-year-old sister on a Wednesday at Ms. Olsen's sister's house; (4) the process server told Ms. Olsen's sister that Ms. Olsen needed to go to court; and (5) Ms. Olsen's sister did not give the summons to Ms. Olsen, and Ms. Olsen states that she did not receive notice?

Brief Answer

Probably not. Because the return is regular on its face, Ms. Olsen has the burden of proving that she was not properly served. Because the summons and petition were left with Ms. Olsen's 32-year-old sister at the sister's house, Ms. Olsen will have to concede that service was made on a person 15 years or older who was living at the house at which the service was made. In addition, because the process server told Ms. Olsen's sister that Ms. Olsen needed to go to court, more likely than not the court will decide that the person served was informed of the contents of the documents. However, because Ms. Olsen can present evidence that establishes that she was staying at the residential treatment house on the day that service was made, the court may decide that the summons and petition were not left at Ms. Olsen's usual place of abode.

EXAMPLE 2	Issue Statement and Brief Answer in Which the Writer Does Not Use the Parties' Names

Issue

Under Florida's statute authorizing substituted service of process, was service at the defendant's adult sister's house valid when the defendant spent weeknights at a residential treatment house and weekends at her sister's house; the service was made on a Wednesday; the process server told the defendant's sister that the defendant "needed to go to court"; and the defendant states that she did not receive notice?

Brief Answer

Probably not. The court will conclude that the service was made on a person 15 years old or older living at the place where service was made and that the process server informed the person served of the contents of the documents. However, the court will probably conclude that the service was not made at the defendant's usual place of abode because the defendant was not actually living at her sister's house on the day service was made.

§ 7.7.3   Checklist for Critiquing the Brief Answer

a.   Content

- The writer has predicted but not guaranteed how the issue will be decided.
- The writer has briefly explained his or her prediction, for example, the writer has explained which elements will be easy to prove and which will be more difficult and why.

b.   Format

- The writer has included a separate brief answer for each issue statement.
- The answer begins with a one- or two-word short answer. This one- or two-word short answer is then followed by a short explanation.

c.   Writing

- The brief answer is easy to read and understand.
- Most of the sentences have concrete subjects and action verbs.
- There are no grammatical or punctuation errors.

Chapter 7 Quiz No. 2

Draft answers for each of the following questions. Make your points clearly and concisely, and write sentences that are easy to read and that are grammatical and correctly punctuated.

1. What is a legally significant fact?
2. Why should you include all of the legally significant facts in a statement of facts?
3. How can you determine whether a fact is legally significant?
4. What is a legal conclusion? Why is there a "rule" against including legal conclusions in your statement of facts?
5. Given that your supervising attorney gave you the issue, why should you include an issue statement in a formal memo?

§ 7.8   Drafting the Discussion Section Using a Script Format

Expectations. We all have them, and we have them about a variety of things. If we go to the symphony, we expect to be handed a program, have an usher show us to our seats, wait until the hall is darkened, hear the orchestra members tuning their instruments, and then applaud the conductor as he or she takes the podium. We expect these things to be in a certain order, and there is a sense of satisfaction when our expectations are met.

We even have expectations about the organization of the most mundane things in our lives. If you walk into a house, you expect to see certain types of rooms (kitchen, bedrooms, bathroom, living or family room), and you expect those rooms to be in specific places. Dining rooms should be near kitchens; bathrooms should be near bedrooms, and so on. We even expect certain things to be in each room. Stoves should be in kitchens, not in dining rooms, and desks are usually in bedrooms, offices, or studies, not in bathrooms.

The same is true of discussion sections. When attorneys read a discussion section, they expect to see specific types of information. For example, in a formal memo, the attorney expects to see the applicable rules, examples of how those rules have been applied in analogous cases, each side's arguments, and a conclusion. In addition, the attorney expects to see each of those types of information in specific places. In most instances, the rules should be before, and not after, the descriptions of the analogous cases, and the descriptions of analogous cases should be before, and not after, the arguments. Finally, the attorney expects to see specific things in each section. Just as you would be surprised to see a dining table in a bedroom, an attorney would be surprised to see arguments in the rules section.

These expectations are not born of whim. Instead, they reflect the way attorneys in the United States think about legal questions. In most instances, attorneys begin their analysis by identifying the applicable statute or common law rule and by determining who has the burden of proof and what that burden is. If this "general rule" sets out a list of elements, most attorneys then go through those elements one by one, determining which elements the party with the burden of proof can easily prove and which elements will be more difficult to prove.

In most situations, the attorney gives relatively little space to the elements that the party with the burden of proof can easily prove: For these "undisputed elements," the attorney simply applies the law to the facts. Instead, the attorney focuses on the elements that will be more difficult to prove. For each of these "disputed elements," the attorney looks at the definitions or tests the courts use in determining whether the element is met, at examples of how those definitions or tests have been applied in analogous cases, and at each side's arguments. What factual arguments will the parties make? How will each side use the analogous cases? Given the purpose and policies underlying the statute or rule, what types of policy arguments might each side make? Finally, most attorneys make a prediction. Given the facts, rules, cases, and arguments, how will a court decide each element?

The discussion section reflects this process. It contains the same components — rules, analogous cases, arguments, and mini-conclusions — in the same order. At its simplest, and at its best, the discussion section analyzes the problem, walking the attorney step by step through the statute, cases, and arguments to the writer's prediction.

§ 7.8.1 Modify the Template So that It Works for Your Issue

Just as different people prefer different styles of houses, some attorneys prefer different styles of discussion sections: some prefer discussion sections written using what we call the script format, and others prefer discussion sections written using a more integrated format. Although neither format is inherently better than the other, the script format tends to be a bit easier to use. Thus, in this chapter we show you how to write a discussion section using that format. Then, once you have mastered the script format, turn to the next chapter for a description of how to write a discussion section using a more integrated format.

In studying Example 1 below, note how the template reflects the way attorneys think about problems involving an elements analysis. The first section is an introductory section in which the writer introduces and sets out the applicable statute or common law rule, the burden of proof, and any other general rules. At the end of this introductory section, most writers provide the attorney with a roadmap that tells the attorney which elements the party with the burden of proof can easily prove and which elements will be more difficult to prove. The writer then walks the attorney through the elements one by one. For the elements that the party with the burden of proof can easily prove, the writer simply sets out the specific rules for that element and applies them to the client's case. For the elements that will be more difficult to prove, the writer sets out the specific rules for those elements, provides the attorney with descriptions of analogous cases in which those rules have been applied, and then writes the "script" for the arguments related to that element. If that element were litigated, what would the party with the burden of proof argue? What would the other side argue? How would the court decide the question?

EXAMPLE 1 **Template for Discussion Section Written Using a Script Format**

Discussion

Introductory section *(Note: Do not include this subheading in the memo.)*

- If one or both sides will make a policy argument, describe the policies underlying the statute or rule.
- Introduce and set out the applicable statute(s) or common law rule.
- Explain which side has the burden of proof and what that burden is.
- Set out any other rules that apply to all of the elements.
- End by providing the attorney with a roadmap for the rest of the discussion.

A. First Element *(Note: Include a subheading that identifies the element.)*

- ■ If the first element is not likely to be in dispute, simply set out and apply applicable rule.
- ■ If, however, the first element will be in dispute, set out the following information:
    1. Specific rules for the first element
    2. Examples showing how the specific rules have been applied in analogous cases
    3. Arguments
    4. Mini-conclusion for the first element

B. Second Element *(Note: Include a subheading that identifies the element.)*

- ■ If the second element is not likely to be in dispute, simply set out and apply applicable rule.
- ■ If, however, the second element will be in dispute, set out the following information:
    1. Specific rules for second element
    2. Examples of how specific rules have been applied in analogous cases
    3. Arguments
    4. Mini-conclusion for the second element

C. Third Element *(Note: Include a subheading that identifies the element.)*

- ■ If the third element is not likely to be in dispute, simply set out and apply applicable rule.
- ■ If, however, the third element will be in dispute, set out the following information:
    1. Specific rules for the third element
    2. Examples of how specific rules have been applied in analogous cases
    3. Arguments
    4. Mini-conclusion for the third element

D. Fourth Element *(Note: Include a subheading that identifies the element.)*

- ■ If the fourth element is not likely to be in dispute, simply set out and apply applicable rule.
- ■ If, however, the fourth element will be in dispute, set out the following information:
    1. Specific rules for fourth element
    2. Examples of how specific rules have been applied in analogous cases
    3. Arguments
    4. Mini-conclusion for the fourth element

The template set out in Example 1 is, however, only a template. Just as a builder may need to modify a standard blueprint so that the house fits on the lot and satisfies the buyer's preferences, you may need to modify the template set out below in Example 2 so that it works for your issue. For example, if the applicable statute or rule has only two elements, you would need to modify the template so that it has only two subsections. Similarly, if the statute has five elements, you would need to modify the template so that it has five subsections.

In the Olsen case, the statute sets out three elements: (1) the complaint or petition must be left at the usual place of abode of the person being served, (2) the complaint or petition must be left with a person who is 15 years old or older who resides therein; and (3) the process server must inform the person served of the contents. Therefore, we modify the template so that it has three subsections. See Example 2.

> **PRACTICE POINTER**   In the Olsen case, we decided to combine the discussion of "residing therein" and "15 years or older." These two elements are closely related, and neither is in dispute.

EXAMPLE 2   **Revised Template**

Discussion

Introductory section:

Set out policies underlying § 48.031, Fla. Stat. (2013).

- Introduce and set out § 48.031, Fla. Stat. (2013).
- Explain which side has the burden of proof and what that burden is.
- Set out any other rules that apply to all of the elements.
- End with a roadmap that tells the attorney that the State can easily prove the second element but that it may not be able to prove the first and third elements.

A. Usual Place of Abode *(disputed element)*

1. Specific rules
2. Examples of how specific rules have been applied in analogous cases
3. Arguments
   - Ms. Olsen's arguments
   - The State's arguments
4. Mini-conclusion

B. Age and Residing Therein *(undisputed element)*

1. Set out applicable rules
2. Apply applicable rules

C. Informing of Contents *(disputed element)*

1. Specific rules
2. Examples of how specific rules have been applied in analogous cases
3. Arguments
   - Ms. Olsen's arguments
   - The State's arguments
4. Mini-conclusion

> **PRACTICE POINTER**   As a general rule, set out the party who has the burden of proof's arguments first. In the sample problem, Ms. Olsen has the burden of proof because the return of service is regular on its face.

§ 7.8.2   Draft the Introductory, or General Rule, Section

Drafting the introductory, or general rule, section is a three-step process. Decide what information to include, order that information, and draft the section.

a.   Decide What Information You Need to Include

The first step is to list the information that you want to include in your introductory section. In preparing this list, keep two things in mind. First, remember your audience. If the attorney for whom you are preparing the memo knows little or nothing about the area of law, provide the attorney with an overview of the area of law, distinguishing closely related doctrines and defining key terms. If, however, the attorney knows the area of law, do not include this type of information. Second, distinguish between general rules — that is, rules that apply to all of the elements — and specific rules — that is, rules that apply to only one element. Include only general rules in your introductory section. Save the specific rules for the discussion of the element to which they apply.

In the sample problem, you can presume that the attorney will have taken civil procedure as a law student and will, therefore, know the basics. Accordingly, in drafting the introductory section, you do not need to explain the difference between personal service and substituted service or define those terms. You do, though, need to set out the applicable portion of the statute and the rules relating to the burden of proof. In addition, you should set out two other "rules" that apply to all of the elements. First, because Ms. Olsen can make a policy argument, set out the policies underlying the statute. Second, tell your supervising attorney that the courts have said that the statute should be narrowly construed to assure due process. Finally, include a roadmap, which is what the name suggests: a map for the rest of the discussion.

b.   Order the Information

The next step is to order the items on the list. Most of the time, you will want to set out more general information before more specific information. Therefore, in drafting the introductory section, you will usually want to use an inverted pyramid: broad rules first, narrower rules next, and exceptions last.

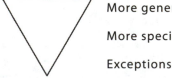

More general information

More specific information

Exceptions

Most attorneys would agree that the policies that underlie the statute are the most general piece of information, that the applicable portion of the statute is the next most general piece of information, and that the rules relating to the burden of proof are the most specific. Consequently, in our sample problem, you would want to set out the policies underlying the statute first, the applicable portions of the statute next, and the rules relating to the burden of proof last.

> PRACTICE
> POINTER
>
> If you are not sure which rules are the more general rules and which rules are the more specific rules, look at the cases. In most instances, the courts set out more general rules before more specific rules.

The approach is similar when there is more than one applicable statutory section: Instead of setting out the statutes in the order in which they appear in the code, set out the more general statutory sections first. For example, set out the section that explains the statute's purpose before the section that sets out the rule, and set out the section that contains the rule before the section that contains the definitions.

c. Prepare the First Draft

In preparing the first draft, do not do what the writer did in Example 3: String together a series of quotes, some of which set out the same rules using slightly different language.

EXAMPLE 3   **Poor Draft: Writer Has Simply Strung Together a Series of Quotes**

Discussion

"The purpose of service of process is to advise the defendant that an action has been commenced and to warn the defendant that he or she must appear in a timely manner to state such defenses as are available." *Torres v. Arnco Constr., Inc.*, 867 So. 2d 583 (Fla. 5th DCA 2004). It is well settled that the fundamental purpose of service is "to give proper notice to the defendant in the case that he is answerable to the claim of plaintiff and, therefore, to vest jurisdiction in the court entertaining the controversy." *Shurman v. Atl. Mortg. & Inv. Corp.*, 795 So. 2d 952, 953-54 (Fla. 2001) (citing *State ex rel. Merritt v. Heffernan*, 142 Fla. 496, 195 So. 145, 147 (1940)). Therefore, "a judgment entered without due service of process is void." *Torres*, 867 So. 2d at 586.

The statute specifically states:

Service of original process is made by delivering a copy of it to the person to be served with a copy of the complaint, petition, or other initial pleading or paper or by leaving the copies at his or her usual place of abode with any person residing therein who is 15 years of age or older and informing the person of their contents. Minors who are or have been married shall be served as provided in this section.

§ 48.031(1)(a), Fla. Stat. (2013).

"The statutes regulating service of process are to be strictly construed to assure that a defendant is notified of the proceedings." *Torres*, 867 So. 2d at 586. "Indeed, because statutes authorizing substituted service are exceptions to the general rule requiring a defendant to be served personally, due process requires strict compliance with their statutory requirements." *Id.*

Thus, because Ms. Olsen is challenging the validity of the service, she will have the burden of proof. Ms. Olsen will concede that the summons was left with a person who is 15 years old or older residing therein. In addition, she will probably concede that her sister was informed of the contents of the documents. She may, however, be able to prove that the summons was not left at her usual place of abode.

Instead of just cutting and pasting the rules from your research notes into your first draft, take the time to read, analyze, and synthesize the rules. Once you understand the rules, determine which rules apply to your case, and then set out each of the applicable rules once and only once.

> **PRACTICE POINTER**   Almost all attorneys will want you to quote the relevant portions of statutes. However, when it comes to other rules, for example, common law rules or rules that the courts have set out, different attorneys prefer different things. While some attorneys will want you to quote all of the rules, others find a series of quotes annoying and prefer that you set out close paraphrases of the rules. Therefore, before you do your first draft, check with your supervising attorney to see which style he or she prefers.

EXAMPLE 4   **Better Draft: Writer Has Set Out Each Rule Only Once**

Discussion

The fundamental purpose of service of process is to give defendants notice of claims that have been filed against them and to provide them with an opportunity to defend their rights. *Shurman v. Atl. Mortg. & Inv. Corp.*, 795 So. 2d 952, 953-54 (Fla. 2001). Because it is important that litigants receive notice of actions against them, courts strictly construe and enforce statutes governing service of process. *Id.* at 954.

In this case, the applicable section of the statute reads as follows:

> Service of original process is made by delivering a copy of it to the person to be served with a copy of the complaint, petition, or other initial pleading or paper or by leaving the copies at his or her usual place of abode with any person residing therein who is 15 years of age or older and informing the person of their contents. Minors who are or have been married shall be served as provided in this section.

§ 48.031(a)(1), Fla. Stat. (2013).

Although the party seeking to invoke the jurisdiction of the court has the burden of proving that service was proper, if the return is regular on its face, the courts presume that the service was valid. *Busman v. State, Dep't of Revenue*, 905 So. 2d 956, 958 (Fla. 3d DCA 2005); *Thompson v. State, Dep't of Revenue*, 867 So. 2d 603, 605 (Fla. 1st DCA 2004). In such instances, the party challenging the service has the burden of presenting clear and convincing evidence that the service was invalid. *Id.*

In this case, Ms. Olsen will have to concede that the summons was left with a person 15 years or older who was residing at the house where the summons and complaint were served. In addition, it is unlikely that Ms. Olsen will be able to prove that her sister was not informed of the contents of the documents. Ms. Olsen may, however, be able to present clear and convincing evidence that the summons was not left at her usual place of abode.

You do not, however, have to quote the entire statute. If only part of the statute is applicable, you can set out only that part.

| **EXAMPLE 5** | **Better Draft: Writer Has Quoted Only the Applicable Portion of the Statute** |

Discussion

The Florida courts have repeatedly stated that the fundamental purpose of service of process is to give defendants notice of claims that have been filed against them and to provide defendants with an opportunity to defend their rights. *E.g., Shurman v. Atl. Mortg. & Inv. Corp.*, 795 So. 2d 952, 953-54 (Fla. 2001). Because these rights are so important, the courts strictly construe and enforce statutes governing service of process. *Id.* at 954.

In the present case, the relevant portion of the statute reads as follows:

> (1)(a) Service of original process is made by delivering a copy of it to the person to be served with a copy of the complaint, petition, or other initial pleading or paper or by leaving the copies at his or her usual place of abode with any person residing therein who is 15 years of age or older and informing the person of their contents. . . .

§ 48.031(a)(1), Fla. Stat. (2013).

Although the party seeking to invoke the jurisdiction of the court has the burden of proving that service was proper, if the return is regular on its face, the courts presume that the service was valid. *Busman v. State, Dep't of Revenue*, 905 So. 2d 956, 958 (Fla. 3d DCA 2005); *Thompson v. State, Dep't of Revenue*, 867 So. 2d 603, 605 (Fla. 1st DCA 2004). In such instances, the party challenging the service has the burden of presenting clear and convincing evidence that the service was invalid. *Id.*

In this case, Ms. Olsen may be able to present clear and convincing evidence that the summons was not left at her usual place of abode. However, if the court decides that the summons was left at her usual place of abode, Ms. Olsen will have to concede that the summons was left with a person 15 years or older who was residing at the house where the summons and complaint were served. In addition, although Ms. Olsen can argue that her sister was not informed of the contents of the summons and complaint, it is unlikely that she can meet her burden of proof.

| **PRACTICE POINTER** | If your quotation has fifty words or more, you need to set it out as a block quote, indenting five spaces on the left and five spaces on the right and omitting the quotation marks. In contrast, if the quote has fewer than fifty words, you can include it in the text of your sentence. See Rule 38 in the *ALWD Guide to Legal Citation* and Rule 5.1 in *The Bluebook*. |

| **PRACTICE POINTER** | Read other lawyers' memos, briefs, wills, contracts, and other documents to learn how experienced attorneys organize their arguments and craft their writing. Do not just copy those documents, however: What worked in one situation may not work in another situation. Instead, adapt the examples so that they reflect the law that applies in your case. |

d.   Include a Citation to Authority for Each Rule

You must include a citation to authority for each rule that you set out in your memo. This authority may be a constitutional provision, a statute, a regulation, a court rule, or a case.

> **PRACTICE POINTER**   In drafting your memo, use the applicable citation rules. For example, if you are writing a memo to a Florida attorney about an issue governed by Florida law, use the Florida citation rules.

In choosing a citation for a rule, always choose mandatory, or binding, authority over persuasive authority. See section 2.3. For example, in choosing a case, always choose cases from your jurisdiction over cases from other jurisdictions. In addition, as a general rule, choose decisions from higher courts over decisions from lower courts and more recent decisions over older decisions. The exception might be when the decisions of the jurisdiction's highest court, for example, your state's highest court, are quite old and there are more recent decisions from your state's intermediate court of appeals. If the decisions from both your state's highest court and intermediate court are mandatory authority, you can choose to cite the more recent decision from the state intermediate court of appeals. Although there may be times when you want to list more than one case to show the attorney that the rule is well established, avoid long string cites, that is, listing more than two or three cases.

> **PRACTICE POINTER**   As a general rule, do not cite unpublished or unreported decisions as authority for a rule. Instead, cite a published decision, for example, the case or cases that the unpublished or unreported decision cited as authority for the rule.

§ 7.8.3   Draft the Discussion of the Undisputed Elements

More likely than not, one or more of the elements will not be in dispute. Although you cannot ignore these undisputed elements, you do not need to devote much space to them.

a.   Decide Where to Put Your Discussion of the Undisputed Elements

While some attorneys choose to raise and dismiss the undisputed elements at the end of their introductory section, others choose to discuss all of the elements in order. Compare the following examples. In Example 6, the writer has raised and dismissed the undisputed element in her roadmap at the end of her introductory section. In contrast, in Example 7, the writer has raised and dismissed the undisputed elements in their own subsections.

EXAMPLE 6	**Undisputed Elements Raised and Dismissed at the End of the Introductory Section**

[Note: The text of the first part of the introductory section is not shown.]

In this case, Ms. Olsen may be able to present clear and convincing evidence that the petition was not left at her usual place of abode. However, if the court decides that the petition was left at her usual place of abode, Ms. Olsen will have to concede that the summons was left with a person 15 years or older who was residing at the house where service was made. In addition, although Ms. Olsen can argue that her sister was not informed of the contents of the documents, it is unlikely that she can meet her burden of proof.

EXAMPLE 7	**Undisputed Elements Raised in Separate Subsections**

Introductory section

[Note: The first part of the introductory section is not shown.]

In this case, the second element is not in dispute: The summons was left with Ms. Webster at her home, and Ms. Webster is over the age of 15. In addition, more likely than not, a court would conclude that the process server told Ms. Webster about the contents of the document. Ms. Olsen may be able to prove, however, that service was not made at her usual place of abode.

A. Usual Place of Abode

[Disputed element; text not included in this example.]

B. Person 15 Years Old or Older Residing Therein

In addition to leaving the complaint or petition at the defendant's usual place of abode, the process server must leave the complaint or petition with a person 15 years old or older residing therein. If the court concludes that Ms. Olsen's sister's house was Ms. Olsen's usual place of abode, Ms. Olsen will have to concede that the petition was left with a person residing therein who is at least 15 years old: Ms. Webster is 32 years old, and the petition was left with her at her house.

C. Notified of Contents

[Disputed element; text not included in this example]

To see the full text of this example, see the memo set out in section 6.4.1.

---

b.   Prepare the First Draft of Your Discussion of the Undisputed Elements

In most instances, your discussion of an undisputed element will be very short: Identify the element, set out any applicable specific rules, and apply those rules to the facts of your case. While in some instances you will need to include brief case descriptions, in most instances such descriptions are not necessary. Compare the following examples.

PRACTICE POINTER	As a general rule, in a criminal case a defendant does not "concede" that an element is met. He or she makes the government prove each element of the crime. Accordingly, in a criminal case, do not

state that the defendant will concede that an element is met. Instead, frame the sentence in terms of what the government can prove.

EXAMPLE 8   **Poor Draft of Undisputed Element: Writer Has Set Out Conclusion Without Setting Out Facts that Support that Conclusion**

Ms. Olsen should concede that the second element, that the complaint or petition be left with a person 15 years or older residing therein, is met.

EXAMPLE 9   **Poor Draft of Undisputed Element: Writer Has Gone into Too Much Depth on Undisputed Element**

For substitute service of process to be valid at a defendant's "usual place of abode," the complaint or petition must be left with a person residing therein who is 15 years of age or older. § 48.031, Fla. Stat. (2013). Although the statute does not specify the period of time an individual must occupy a home to be regarded as "residing therein," the courts do not require extended habitation. *Compare Magazine v. Bedoya*, 475 So. 2d 1035 (Fla. 3d DCA 1985) (six-week stay long enough to establish residency), *with Gamboa v. Jones*, 455 So. 2d 613 (Fla. 3d DCA 1985) (ten-day visit not sufficient to establish residency). Because she is 32, Ms. Webster satisfies the age requirement. From the facts given, it is unclear how long Ms. Webster has lived at the home in question; however, the memo indicated that she was served at "her house." Consequently, unless other facts are presented, Ms. Webster appears to be the owner and a resident of the house, and she has lived there long enough to establish residency. Therefore, the residing therein requirement is met.

EXAMPLE 10   **Better Draft of Undisputed Element**

In addition to leaving the complaint or petition at the defendant's usual place of abode, the process server must leave the documents with a person 15 years old or older residing therein. If the court concludes that Ms. Olsen's sister's house was Ms. Olsen's usual place of abode, Ms. Olsen will have to concede that the summons was left with a person residing therein who is at least 15 years old: Ms. Webster is 32 years old, and the summons and complaint were left with her at her house.

EXAMPLE 11   **Better Draft of Undisputed Element**

A court will find that the second element is met. Because the summons and complaint were left with Ms. Olsen's 32-year-old sister, the age requirement is met. In addition, because Ms. Olsen's sister lives at the house where the summons and complaint were left, the residing therein requirement is met.

PRACTICE POINTER While some elements are clearly not in dispute and some are clearly in dispute, there will be elements that fall somewhere in between these two categories.

_____X_____

     Not in dispute   In dispute

When you have an element that falls into this "in between" category, you will usually do more than raise and dismiss the element but less than a full analysis. Alert the attorney to the fact that one side might have a weak argument, set out that argument, explain why the argument is weak, and then move on.

§ 7.8.4   Draft the Discussion of the Disputed Elements

You will usually want to create a separate subsection for each disputed element. Include a subheading that identifies the element and then set out, in paragraph form, the following information:

a. the specific rules for that element;
b. cases that illustrate how those specific rules have been applied;
c. each side's arguments; and
d. your prediction about how the court is likely to decide the element.

a.   Set Out the Specific Rules

Begin your discussion of a disputed element by setting out the rules that relate to that element. For example, if the courts apply a particular test in determining whether the element is met, set out that test. Similarly, if the courts have defined any terms, set out those definitions.

In drafting your specific rule paragraphs, use the same process that you used in drafting the introductory section. Begin by listing all of the information that you want to include in your specific rule paragraph, and then order that information, setting out more general information before more specific information. Finally, draft the specific rule paragraph or paragraphs.

In drafting these paragraphs, keep the following in mind. First, include only those rules that apply to the element that you are currently discussing. Do not repeat general rules that you set out in your introductory section, and do not set out rules that apply to other elements. Second, do not simply cut and paste the rules from your research notes into your draft. Instead, determine what the rules are, and then set out each rule once, and only once, using clear and concise language. Finally, remember to include a citation to authority for each rule that you set out. Compare Examples 12 and 13, both of which are examples of the specific rule paragraph for the usual place of abode element.

EXAMPLE 12   **Poor Draft: Writer Has Simply Cut and Pasted Rules from Research Notes into Draft**

The Florida courts have defined "usual place of abode" as "the fixed place of residence for the time being when the service is made." *Shurman v. Atl. Mortg. & Inv. Corp.*, 795 So. 2d 952, 953-54 (Fla. 2001). "If a person has more than one residence, a summons must be served at the residence at which the defendant is actually living at the time of service." *Id.* at 954. As the Florida Supreme Court noted in *Torres v. Arnco Const., Inc.*, 867 So. 2d 583, 586 (Fla. 5th DCA 2004), "the courts have frequently invalidated substituted service of process in cases where the defendant was not actually living at the place where service was made, even though process might have been delivered to a relative."

EXAMPLE 13   **Better Draft: Writer Has Identified the Rules and Then Set Out Each Rule Once, Using Language that Is Clear and Concise**

Although the statute does not define the phrase "usual place of abode," the courts have said that a defendant's usual place of abode is the place "where the defendant was actually living at the time of service." *E.g., Shurman v. Atl. Mortg. & Inv. Corp.*, 795 So. 2d 952, 953-54 (Fla. 2001); *Busman v. State, Dep't of Revenue*, 905 So. 2d 956, 957 (Fla. 3d DCA 2005).

b.   Describe the Analogous Cases

When an element is in dispute, most attorneys want to see not only the specific rules but also examples of how those specific rules have been applied in analogous cases. Therefore, if an element is in dispute and there are analogous cases, you will usually want to describe at least some of those cases.

In drafting the analogous case section, always keep in mind why you are including cases. Do not include analogous case descriptions just to show your supervising attorney that you found and read cases. The analogous case section is not there so that you can prove that you did a lot of work. Instead, include analogous case descriptions because the case descriptions will help the attorney understand the rules or because either your side or the other side is likely to use the cases to support its position.

Step 1: Identify the Analogous Cases

The first step is to go back through your research notes and identify the cases in which the court discussed the disputed element. In the Olsen case, there are about a dozen cases that discuss usual place of abode. (For a list of the Florida cases that discuss usual place of abode, see subheading 9 in the notes of decision following section 48.031 in Florida Statutes Annotated.)

PRACTICE POINTER   In looking for analogous cases, look first for cases from your jurisdiction. If you do not find any, you can then look for analogous cases from other jurisdictions. However, before deciding to use an out-of-state case, make sure that the other state's specific rules are the same as your state's specific rules.

Step 2: Sort the Analogous Cases

Once you have identified the analogous cases, sort those cases. Put the cases in which the court held that the element was met in one stack and the cases in which the court held that the element was not met in another stack.

| EXAMPLE 14 | **Chart Listing Cases** |

Cases in Which Element Was Not Met	Cases in Which Element Was Met
• *Shurman v. Atl. Mortg. & Inv. Corp.*, 795 So. 2d 952 (Fla. 2001) • *Heck v. Bank Liberty*, 86 So. 3d 1281) (Fla. 1st DCA 2012) • *Portfolio Recovery Assocs., LLC v. Gonzalez*, 951 So. 2d 1037 (Fla. 3d DCA 2007) • *Cordova v. Jolcover*, 942 So. 2d 1045 (Fla. 2d DCA 2006) • *Gilbert v. Storey*, 920 So. 2d 1173 (Fla. 3d DCA 2006) • *Busman v. State, Dep't of Revenue*, 905 So. 2d 956 (Fla. 3d DCA 2005) • *Thompson v. State, Dep't of Revenue*, 867 So. 2d 603 (Fla. 1st DCA 2004) • *Torres v. Arnco Const., Inc.*, 867 So. 2d 583 (Fla. 5th DCA 2004) [other entries not included]	• *State ex rel. Merritt v. Heffernan*, 195 So. 145 (Fla. 1940) • *Johnston v. Hudlett*, 32 So. 3d 700 (Fla. 4th DCA 2010)

Step 3: Analyze and Synthesize the Cases

It is at this step that the real work begins. Because you want to do more than provide the attorney with "book reports" on the cases that you have read, you need to analyze each of the cases and then synthesize the group of cases.

Analysis requires you to read the cases carefully and critically, identifying the issue that was before the court, the standard of review that the court applied, the facts that the court considered, the court's holding, and the court's reasoning.

PRACTICE POINTER The standard of review is the standard that an appellate court uses in reviewing a trial court's decision. If the standard of review is *de novo,* the appellate court does not defer to the trial court. Instead, the appellate court reviews the issue on the merits and can substitute its judgment for the judgment of the trial court. In contrast, if the standard of review is abuse of discretion, the appellate court defers to the trial court. When the standard of review is abuse of discretion, the appellate court will overturn the trial court only when the trial court abused its discretion.

> In general, the standard of review is *de novo* when the issue is an issue of law—for example, whether the trial court properly instructed the jury. In contrast, the standard of review is usually abuse of discretion if the issue is an issue of fact—for example, whether a particular expert is qualified.

If there is more than one case, you also need to do synthesis. When the cases are read as a group, what principle or principles can you draw from them? For example, in the Olsen case, what principle or principles can you draw from the group of cases in which the courts have held that the summons was not left at the defendant's usual place of abode?

One way of doing this analysis and synthesis is to prepare a chart in which, for each case, you identify the court, the date of the decision, the key facts, and the court's reasoning. Note that in Examples 15 and 16 there is not a column for the holding. This column is not necessary because the cases are grouped based on their holdings. Example 15 analyzes the cases in which the element was met, and Example 16 is an excerpt from the chart that analyzes cases in which the element was not met.

> **PRACTICE POINTER**
> There is more than one way to list the cases: You can list them in chronological order; in reverse chronological order; by court; or within a court, by district or division. In Example 15, we set out decisions from the Florida Supreme Court first. We then list the decisions from the Court of Appeals in reverse chronological order.

EXAMPLE 15   **Excerpt from Chart Analyzing Cases in Which the Court Held that Service Was Not Made at the Defendant's Usual Place of Abode**

Case	Court	Date	Facts	Reasoning
Shurman v. Atl. Mortg. & Inv. Corp.	Florida Supreme Court	2001	• Mortgage foreclosure action • Service left with D's wife. • D had been incarcerated for at least 9 months.	• D was actually living in the prison. • Substituted service, being in derogation of the common law, must be strictly construed. • In general, the courts presume that the defendant will receive notice of process if the summons is left with a competent member of his household who lives in his house. This presumption is not, however, valid when the head of the household is in prison.

Case	Court	Date	Facts	Reasoning
Portfolio Recovery Assocs., LLC v. Gonzalez	Fla. 3d DCA	2007	• Summons left with the woman who was mother of one D and mother-in-law of the other D. • Undisputed affidavit established that neither D had lived at residence for five years.	• DCA affirmed trial court because undisputed affidavit established that neither defendant had lived at residence for five years. Thus, residence was not their usual place of abode. • It does not describe the underlying cause of action.
Cordova v. Jolcover	Fla. 2d DCA	2006	• P sued D to enforce real estate contract. Summons was left with D's estranged wife, who told process server that the D was not in the country. D submitted his passport and police report that showed that he was living in Peru. Estranged wife also submitted affidavit saying that she and husband were estranged and that process server did not notify her of content.	• DCA reversed trial court because defendant presented clear and convincing evidence that service was not left at the defendant's usual place of abode. The return of service raised doubts and the defendant submitted proof that he was living in Peru.
Busman v. State, Dep't of Revenue	Fla. 3d DCA	2005	• Action to establish paternity. • Service was left with the defendant's half brother on July 16, 2003 • D testified that he had moved out of half brother's house on July 1, 2003, and presented lease and landlord's testimony.	• Although the sheriff's return of service was regular on its face, Busman presented clear, convincing, and uncontradicted evidence that the summons was not left at his "usual place of abode." • Statute must be strictly construed.
Thompson v. State, Dep't of Revenue	Fla. 1st DCA	2004	• Child support action. • Summons left with wife. • D filed affidavit stating that he had been separated from wife for three years, that he had not lived at the address where the summons was left for three years, and he did not authorize anyone to accept service on his behalf.	• DCA reversed and remanded for an evidentiary hearing. • Thompson's motion and affidavit are based on the fact that the service did not comply with §48.031 and was, therefore, legally deficient.

Case	Court	Date	Facts	Reasoning
Torres v. Arnco Const., Inc.	Fla. 5th DCA	2004	• Summons left with D's mother. • D had resided in NY for 57 years and at NY address for 12 years. • NY neighbors verified that D lived in house but that he traveled a lot. • Mother said that D would be home soon.	• Although standard of review is gross abuse of discretion, no live testimony. • P has the burden of proof. • P did not meet burden. • Mother's statement was ambiguous. • Dissent argues that D had burden of proof and that his statements were not sufficient. If D were visiting his family in Florida for substantial periods of time, the Florida house was his "usual abode" when he was served in Florida. It would also be consistent with the affidavit of the Florida process server who said that D's mother remarked that Torres "would be home soon, and she would see to it that he received the papers."
Alvarez v. State Farm	Fla. 3d DCA	1994	• Service was left with D's cousin at cousin's residence. • Affidavits, telephone bill, and marriage license established that D was not living with cousin at time of service and that D had not lived there for some time.	• Uncontradicted evidence established that D was not living at that address on the date of service or for some time before. Therefore, service of process was ineffective as a matter of law.

EXAMPLE 16   **Case in Which the Court Held that Service Was Made at the Defendant's Usual Place of Abode**

Case	Court	Date	Facts	Reasoning
State ex rel. Merritt v. Heffernan, 195 So. 145 (Fla. 1940)	Florida Supreme Court	1940	• Wife served one hour after D left to go back to Minnesota. • D had an office, voted, and paid taxes in Minnesota. • D had moved family to Florida two months earlier. • D had visited family twice "during season." • Summons was left with D's wife and, apparently, D received actual notice.	• Ct acknowledges that D's permanent residence was in Minnesota. • However, ct seems to think that it was more important that his family was in Florida, that D was on a train and not in Minnesota at the time of service, and that the evidence suggested that D intended to return to Minnesota.

In creating and examining your chart, you might discover that the cases in which the element was met (or not met) have one of the following in common:

- that all of the cases in which the element is met (or not met) have a particular fact or set of facts in common;
- that in all of the cases in which the element is met (or not met) the courts seem to focus on a particular policy underlying the rule;
- that different courts or different divisions of the same court seem to take a particular approach;
- that the rules seem to be evolving; or
- that the decisions seem to be result oriented.

When you determine what the cases have in common, or that they do not have anything in common, you have done synthesis.

Step 4: Write the Sentences Introducing Your Description of the Analogous Cases

Do not make your supervising attorney guess about how a case or group of cases contributes to the overall analysis. Instead, use topic sentences to introduce each case or group of cases. The language you use will depend on a number of factors, including the number of analogous cases and what you discovered in analyzing and synthesizing those cases.

In the Olsen case, the writer wants to illustrate how the courts have interpreted the phrase "usual place of abode" by providing her supervising attorney with examples of the types of fact situations in which the courts have concluded that service was made at the defendant's usual place of abode and with examples of the types of fact situations in which the courts have held that the service was not made at the defendant's usual place of abode. While the writer could introduce the first case with a sentence that says, "In State ex rel. Merritt v. Heffernan, 195 So. 145, 146 (Fla. 1940), service was made on the defendant's wife at the defendant's apartment in Florida," most attorneys expect more. They want to know why the case is important and why you included the case in your memo.

In charting the first group of cases, the writer discovered that there was only one analogous case, one from 1940, in which the court held that the service was made at the defendant's usual place of abode. In addition, in analyzing and synthesizing both the 1940 case and the more recent cases, the writer concluded that, although the 1940 case had never been overruled, in the more recent cases the courts have changed the way in which they view service on a relative. As a consequence, the writer begins her description of the 1940 case by placing the old case in its historical context, by telling the attorney that the case is one of the few published decisions, and by setting out the court's conclusion. See Example 17.

EXAMPLE 17   **Sentence Introducing Analogous Cases**

In an early case, and one of the few published decisions in which the court concluded that the defendant had been served at his usual place of abode, the court reasoned that, at the time of service, defendant's wife and children were living at the apartment where service was made. *State ex rel. Merritt v. Heffernan*, 195 So. 145, 146-47 (Fla. 1940). In that case, the defendant had relocated his family to Florida two months before service was made and had twice visited them while they were in Florida, the second time leaving the apartment to return to Minnesota just an hour before service was made. *Id.* Although the defendant argued that his usual place of abode was Minnesota, where he had an office, paid taxes, and voted, the court disagreed, stating that "[w]e do not hold the view that Florida was the permanent residence of the defendant, but we do feel that in the circumstance reflected in the record, it was his usual place of abode . . . ." *Id.* at 148.

However, when there is more than one analogous case, you want to do more than just tell your readers that there are two, three, or four cases. In these instances, draft a principle-based topic sentence.

A principle-based topic sentence is a sentence that tells your reader what "principle" you are using the cases to illustrate. Sometimes, the courts set out these principles. For instance, in our sample problem the courts have explicitly said that the phrase "usual place of abode" should be narrowly construed and, in fact, in their decisions they do construe the language narrowly. At other times, you will "discover" the principle while synthesizing the cases. In charting the cases, you may discover (1) that all or most of cases have a particular set of facts in common; (2) that in all or most of the cases the courts seem to focus on a particular policy underlying the rule; (3) that different courts or different divisions of the same court seem to take a particular approach; (4) that the rules seem to be evolving; or (5) that the decisions seem to be result oriented.

While in some situations the case law is so consistent that everyone who reads a group of cases draws the same principle or principles from those cases, in other situations there is more than one way to read the cases or, depending on the arguments that you think the parties are likely to make, you may want to emphasize different points. See Examples 18, 19, and 20. In each example, the principle-based topic sentence is in bold.

EXAMPLE 18   **Principle-Based Topic Sentence Used to Introduce a Group of Analogous Cases**

In contrast, in the more recent cases, the courts have emphasized that it is not enough that the complaint or petition is left with a relative. *See, e.g., Busman*, 905 So. 2d at 947; *Torres v. Arnco Const., Inc.*, 867 So. 2d 583 (Fla. 5th DCA 2004). For example, in *Busman*, the court concluded that service of process was not valid even though the summons and complaint had been left with the defendant's half brother. *Id.* at 958. Similarly, in *Torres*, the court concluded that service had not been made at the defendant's usual place of abode when, after trying unsuccessfully to serve the defendant at his New York apartment, the plaintiff served the defendant's mother at her home in Florida. *Id.* at 585, 587. Although the defendant's mother told the process server that her son "would be home soon," the court decided that this statement was, at best, ambiguous. *Id.* at 585; *accord Portfolio Recovery Assocs., LLC v. Gonzalez*, 951 So. 2d 1037, 1038 (Fla. 3d DCA 2007) (service was not made at the defendants' usual place of abode when the summons and complaint were left with a woman who was the mother of one defendant and the mother-in-law of the other defendant, but the defendants had not lived at the residence for five years).

EXAMPLE 19	**Principle-Based Topic Sentence Used to Introduce a Group of Analogous Cases**

In the most recent cases, the courts have held that the service was invalid or remanded the case for an evidentiary hearing when the defendant presented evidence that he was not actually living at the house where service was made. *See, e.g., Busman*, 905 So. 2d at 958; *Thompson*, 867 So. 2d at 605. For example, in *Busman*, the Third District Court of Appeals held that service was invalid when the defendant presented a lease agreement that corroborated his testimony that he had moved out of his half brother's house two and one-half months before his half brother was served. Likewise, in *Thompson*, the First District Court of Appeals reversed and remanded the case for an evidentiary hearing when the defendant submitted an affidavit in which he stated that he was separated from his wife, that he had not resided at that address for over three years, and that he did not authorize anyone to accept service of process on his behalf. *Id.* at 605.

EXAMPLE 20	**Principle-Based Topic Sentence Used to Introduce a Group of Analogous Cases**

In most of the cases in which the courts have held that the summons was not left at the defendant's usual place of abode, the defendant had not lived at the house where service was made for a substantial period of time. *See, e.g., Shurman v. Atl. Mortg. & Inv. Corp.*, 795 So. 2d 952 (Fla. 2001); *Portfolio Recovery Assocs. LLC v. Gonzalez*, 951 So. 2d 1037 (Fla. 3d DCA 2007). For instance, in *Shurman*, the defendant was incarcerated and had not lived at the family home for at least nine months, 795 So. 2d at 953, and in *Portfolio Recovery Assocs.*, the defendants had not lived at the house where service was made for five years, 951 So. 2d at 1038.

PRACTICE POINTER	When you have difficulty coming up with a good topic sentence (and there will be times when you do), try asking yourself the following questions:

1. Why am I including these cases in my memo?
2. What is the common thread that runs through this group of cases?
3. If the client's case is litigated, how will each side use these cases?

Step 5: Draft Your Descriptions of the Cases

Once you have drafted the topic sentence, the next step is to draft the case descriptions.

If there are only two or three analogous cases, you can describe all of them. If, however, there are a number of cases, describe only the "best" cases. In selecting these cases, use the following criteria:

■ Select cases from your jurisdiction over cases from other jurisdictions.
■ Select cases with published decisions over cases with unpublished, or unreported, decisions.
■ Select more recent cases over older cases.
■ Select cases from higher courts over cases from lower courts.

In addition, most of the time you will be using the cases to see where your case falls along the continuum of decided cases. Is your case more like the cases in which the court held that the element was met or more like the cases in which the court held that the element was not met? Accordingly, select cases that are more factually analogous over cases that are less factually analogous.

$$??\leftarrow \text{my case} \rightarrow ??$$

Cases in which element met   Cases in which element not met

How much you say about a case will depend on the point that you are using the case to illustrate. If you are using the case to illustrate a small point, then a sentence or even a clause, phrase, or word may be enough. In contrast, if you expect that one or both sides will rely heavily on the case, your description will be longer. The bottom line is that you need to include only that information that is relevant to the principle that you are using the case to illustrate and to set up the arguments based on that case.

Compare Examples 21, 22, and 23. In Example 21, the case descriptions are very short because the writer is using the cases to illustrate a small point. In contrast, in Example 22, the case description is longer because the writer wants to use the case to illustrate several points and because the writer expects that both sides will use the case. In Example 23, the writer sets out two medium-length case descriptions.

EXAMPLE 21   **Short Descriptions of Two Cases**

Although the statute does not specify how long the person who received the service must have been "residing therein," the courts do not require extended habitation. While in *Gamboa*, the court determined that a ten-day visit was not sufficient to establish residency, *id.* at 614, in *Magazine*, the court determined that a six-week stay was sufficient, *id.* at 1035.

EXAMPLE 22   **Longer Description in Which the Writer Sets Out Facts and the Court's Holding and Reasoning**

In an early case, and one of the few published decisions in which the court concluded that the defendant had been served at his usual place of abode, the summons was left with the defendant's wife at the family's apartment in Florida an hour after the defendant boarded a train to Minnesota. *State ex rel. Merritt v. Heffernan*, 195 So. 145, 146 (Fla. 1940). Although the defendant argued that his usual place of abode was Minnesota, where he had an office, paid taxes, and voted, the court disagreed, noting that the defendant had moved his family to the Florida apartment two months before his wife was served, that the defendant had visited his family at the apartment twice "during the season," and that the defendant's family had remained in Florida for some time after the defendant was served. *Id.* at 147. As the court stated, "We do not hold the view that Florida was the permanent residence of the defendant, but we do feel that in the circumstance reflected in the record, it was his usual place of abode . . . ." *Id.* at 148.

EXAMPLE 23	**Two Descriptions in Which the Writer Sets Out Facts and the Courts' Holdings and Reasoning**

In recent cases, the courts have either held that the service was invalid or remanded the case for an evidentiary hearing when the defendant produced evidence establishing that he was not actually living at the house where the summons was served. *See, e.g., Busman*, 905 So. 2d at 958; *Thompson*, 867 So. 2d at 605. For example, in *Busman*, the Third District Court of Appeals held that the service was not valid when the defendant presented a lease agreement that corroborated his testimony that he had moved out of his half brother's house two and one-half months before his half brother was served. *Id.* at 958. Likewise, in *Thompson*, the First District Court of Appeals reversed and remanded the case for an evidentiary hearing when the defendant submitted an affidavit in which he stated that he was separated from his wife, that he had not resided at that address for over three years, and that he did not authorize anyone to accept service of process on his behalf. *Id.* at 605.

Occasionally, you will not need to include a full description of an analogous case. For instance, you may not need to include a full description of a case if you are using the case to illustrate a single point or if you have already given full descriptions of one or two cases but want to tell the attorney about a third or fourth case, or when you simply want to illustrate one aspect of a rule. In these situations you can use parentheticals.

EXAMPLE 24	**Cases Described in Parentheticals**

Although the statute does not specify the period of time an individual must occupy a home to be regarded as "residing therein," the courts do not require extended habitation. *Compare Magazine v. Bedoya*, 475 So. 2d 1035 (Fla. 3d DCA 1985) (six-week stay sufficient to establish residency), *with Gamboa v. Jones*, 455 So. 2d 613 (Fla. 3d DCA 1985) (ten-day visit not sufficient to establish residency).

EXAMPLE 25	**Additional Cases Described in Parentheticals**

In contrast, in the more recent cases, the courts have emphasized that it is not enough that the complaint or petition is left with a relative. *See, e.g., Busman*, 905 So. 2d at 947; *Torres v. Arnco Const., Inc.*, 867 So. 2d 583 (Fla. 5th DCA 2004). For example, in *Busman*, the court concluded that service of process was not valid even though the summons and complaint had been left with the defendant's half brother. *Id.* at 958. Similarly, in *Torres*, the court concluded that service had not been made at the defendant's usual place of abode when, after trying unsuccessfully to serve the defendant at his New York apartment, the plaintiff served the defendant's mother at her home in Florida. *Id.* at 585, 587. Although the defendant's mother told the process server that her son "would be home soon," the court decided that this statement was, at best, ambiguous. *Id.* at 585; *accord Portfolio Recovery Assocs., LLC v. Gonzalez*, 951 So. 2d 1037, 1038 (Fla. 3d DCA 2007) (service was not made at the defendants' usual place of abode when the summons and complaint were left with a woman who was the mother of one defendant and the mother-in-law of the other defendant, but the defendants had not lived at the residence for five years).

| **PRACTICE POINTER** | In most instances, when you refer to a case by only one party's name, you should use the plaintiff's name. For example, when you refer to *Thompson v. State, Dep't of Revenue*, you would say "in *Thomp-* |

son," and when you refer to *Cordova v. Jolcover*, you would say, "in *Cordova*." There are, however, some exceptions to this general rule. When the plaintiff is the state, you will refer to the case using the defendant's name: "*State v. Smith*" becomes "*Smith*," and "*Commonwealth v. Jones*" becomes "*Jones*." In addition, if the courts typically refer to a case using the defendant's name, you should use that name. For more on short cites, see Rule 12.19 in the *ALWD Guide to Legal Citation* and Rule 10.9 in *The Bluebook*.

c.   Draft the Arguments

At this point your role changes dramatically. No longer are you just a "reporter" telling the attorney what you found in doing your research. To do a good job presenting each side's arguments, you must become an advocate, using your training, intellectual abilities, and creativity to construct the arguments each side is likely to make. You must think like the plaintiff's attorney and then like the defendant's attorney.

When you use the script format, you are, in effect, writing a "script" for the oral arguments on the issue. You begin by putting yourself in the shoes of the party with the burden of proof, setting out the arguments that side might make. You then step into the other side's shoes and set out that side's arguments. Finally, you assume the role of the judge, predicting how the court would decide the element and how it would justify its decision.

EXAMPLE 26   **"Script" for Arguments**

- ■ Party with the burden of proof's arguments
- ■ Responding party's arguments
- ■ Party with the burden of proof's rebuttal (optional)
- ■ Court's decision + rationale

Step 1: Identify Each Side's Arguments

The first step is to identify each side's arguments. If you wrote down possible arguments as you did your research, start with that list.

EXAMPLE 27   **List of Arguments from Research Notes**

Ms. Olsen's arguments

- ■ On the day that she was served, Ms. Olsen was living at the residential treatment house.
- ■ Service on a relative is not sufficient.

- Her more permanent address was the residential treatment house address. She had a room, etc., at the residential treatment house.
- *Heffernan* is an old case.
- In *Torres*, the court held that the defendant's mother's house was not the defendant's usual place of abode even though the mother indicated that the defendant would be home later.
- There is no indication that the State tried to serve Ms. Olsen at the residential treatment house.

The State's arguments

- Ms. Olsen stayed at her sister's house three nights a week.
- Ms. Olsen apparently received mail at her sister's house—the shoebox.
- Ms. Olsen listed her sister's address on her driver's license.
- In *Heffernan*, the court held that the apartment was the defendant's usual place of abode even though the defendant had left the apartment and was on a train back to his permanent residence.
- In *Torres*, the defendant had a permanent residence where he had lived for twelve years. He was just visiting his mother.

Do not, however, stop with the list that you came up with while research-ing the issue. Push yourself further, asking yourself whether the parties can make any of the other standard types of arguments. For example, can one or both of the parties make plain language arguments, arguments based on the analogous cases, or policy arguments?

1. Plain Language Arguments

A plain language argument is an argument in which you apply the plain language of a statute or rule to the facts of your case. For instance, in the service of process problem, you would make a plain language argument if you argued that, under the plain language of the statute, the service was not made at Ms. Olsen's "usual" place of abode because her sister's house was not the place where she "usually" stayed. During the month in which service was made, Ms. Olsen spent four nights a week at the residential treatment house and only three nights a week at her sister's house. Similarly, you would be making a plain language argument if you argued that, under the plain language of the rule that the courts have set out, Ms. Olsen was not "actually living" at her sister's house because the summons and complaint were served on a weekday and, during the week, Ms. Olsen "actually lived" at the residential treatment house. Note that a plain language argument has two components: a word or phrase from the statute or rule and facts that show that that element is or is not met.

> **PRACTICE POINTER**
> To make sure that you have considered all the plain language arguments, do two things. First, think about each word or phrase in the applicable part of the statute and/or rules, asking your-self what the plain meaning of that word or phrase requires. Second, go through each of your facts, asking yourself how each side might be able to use that fact.

2. Analogous Case Arguments

Under our system of law, judges usually decide like cases in a like manner. Therefore, if the analogous cases support the conclusion that you want the court to reach, you need to argue, first, that your case is like the analogous cases and, second, because your case is like the analogous cases, the court should reach the same result as the courts reached in those decisions. In contrast, if the analogous cases do not support the conclusion that you want the court to reach, you need to distinguish those cases. For example, in Ms. Olsen's case, she will want to argue that her case is like *Busman* and *Torres*, and she will want to distinguish *Heffernan*. Conversely, the State will want to distinguish *Busman* and *Torres* and argue that its case is more like *Heffernan*.

To make sure that you have considered all analogous case arguments, think about rules and the principles you drew from the cases and how the parties might be able to use those rules and principles to support their respective positions. In addition, go through the analogous cases one by one, thinking about how each side might be able to use that case.

PRACTICE POINTER	In constructing analogous case arguments, ask yourself the following questions:

- In what ways is the analogous case similar to my case?
- In what ways is it different?
- Is the case a relatively old case? If it is, how can each side use that fact?
- Is the case from an intermediate court of appeals or from the state's highest court? How can each side use that fact?
- Is the case well reasoned or poorly reasoned? How can each side use that fact?
- How have other cases used or distinguished the case?

3. Policy Arguments

In making a policy argument, look at the reasons why the legislature enacted a particular statute or a court adopted a particular rule and use those underlying reasons to support your client's position. For example, in the Olsen case you could use the policy behind the service of process statutes — to ensure that defendants have notice of actions filed against them — to argue that service was invalid because Ms. Olsen did not receive notice.

When your issue is one that is governed by a statute, you may be able to find the policies underlying the statute in a "finding" or "purpose" section of the act of which your statute is a part, or a legislative history may tell you what the legislature intended when it enacted the statute. In addition, in applying a statute, the courts frequently set out what they believe are the policies underlying the statutes. Therefore, to come up with policy arguments, look at the text of the statute, the statute's legislative history, and those parts of other courts' decisions that discuss the policies underlying the statute. Once you identify the various policies, determine how each side might be able to use those policies to support its position.

In situations in which the underlying reason for the statute is not explicitly laid out in the act, in its legislative history, or in court decisions, use common sense to determine why the statute was enacted. Ask yourself "what good was the legislature trying to promote" or "what harm was the legislature trying to prevent" when it enacted the statute.

| PRACTICE POINTER | At this initial stage, list all of the arguments (plain language, analogous case, and policy), no matter how weak they may seem. Later, you can go through these arguments, weeding out those that |

don't pass "the giggle test," that is, those that you could not make to a court without laughing.

You can use a chart like the one set out in Example 28 to keep track of the arguments that each side makes.

EXAMPLE 28   **List of Arguments**

Element	Olsen's Arguments	State's Arguments
Usual Place of Abode (in dispute)	Plain language arguments: Analogous case arguments: Policy arguments:	Plain language arguments: Analogous case arguments: Policy arguments:
Age and Residing Therein (not in dispute)		
Informing of Contents (in dispute)	Plain language arguments: Analogous case arguments: Policy arguments:	Plain language arguments: Analogous case arguments: Policy arguments

PRACTICE POINTER
If you find yourself staring at your computer screen unable to come up with more than one or two arguments, find an empty room and then stand up and make Ms. Olsen's arguments. After you have made all of her arguments, take a few steps to your right and make the State's arguments. In most instances, this process will trigger more ideas about what each side can argue. Thus, keep going to back and forth, making and then countering each side's arguments and "answering" questions that you think that a judge might ask you. While at first this exercise may feel a little silly, it will help you come up with additional arguments and it will help you develop the oral skills that you will need as a lawyer.

Step 2: Present the Arguments

After you have identified each side's arguments, you are ready to move to the second step: deciding how you want to present those arguments. Once again, you have some choices. For instance, you can do what we do in this chapter and set out the arguments using a script format, or you can do what we do in the next chapter and set out the rules using an integrated format.

Even under the script format, you have choices. One way to organize the arguments is by type of argument. If you choose this organizational scheme, set out the party with the burden of proof's plain language arguments in one paragraph, its analogous cases arguments in another paragraph or block of paragraphs, and its policy arguments in a third paragraph. Then set out the other side's arguments: Set out the other side's plain language arguments in one paragraph, its analogous case arguments in another paragraph or block of paragraphs, and its policy arguments in a third paragraph.

PRACTICE POINTER
If you organize your arguments around types of arguments, you will usually want to set out the plain language arguments first, analogous cases arguments second, and policy arguments third. This ordering reflects the weight that courts typically give to the different types of arguments. If a court can decide an issue by applying the plain language of the statute or common law to the facts of the case, it will usually do so. If, however, the court cannot decide the issue based on the plain language, it will look to the cases to see how the cases have applied the rules. If the cases do not resolve the issue, the court will then look to the policies underlying the statute.

In the alternative, organize the arguments around the principles that you identified when you analyzed and synthesized the cases. For example, if you determined that all of the cases have three facts in common, you could organize your arguments around those three facts. In setting out the party with the burden of proof's arguments, you would discuss the first fact in one paragraph or block of paragraphs, the second fact in a second paragraph or block of paragraphs, and the third fact in a third paragraph or block of paragraphs. Similarly, in setting out the other side's arguments, you would discuss the first fact in one paragraph or block of paragraphs, the second fact in a second paragraph or block of paragraphs, and the third fact in a third paragraph or block of paragraphs. Within the paragraphs discussing these facts, you would set out any plain language, analogous case, and/or policy arguments that relate to that fact.

A third, and more sophisticated, approach is to organize your arguments around "lines of argument." For example, if you have a burden of proof argument and an argument on the merits, you could organize the arguments around these two lines of argument. In setting out your arguments, set out the party with the burden of proof's arguments relating to the first line of argument in one paragraph or block of paragraphs and its arguments relating to the second line of argument in a second paragraph or block of paragraphs. Then set out the other side's arguments, putting the other side's points relating to the first line of argument in one paragraph and its points relating to the second line of argument in a second paragraph or block of paragraphs. In setting out these lines of argument, include the plain language, analogous case, or policy arguments that relate to that line of argument.

> **PRACTICE POINTER**
>
> If you use the second option—organizing your arguments around the principles you identified when you analyzed and synthesized the cases—you will usually want to discuss the principles in the same order that you set them out and illustrated them in your analogous case section. If you use the third approach—organizing your arguments around "lines of argument"—you should discuss threshold arguments first. In other words, if one argument builds upon another argument, set out the foundational argument first.

Example 29 illustrates the differences between these three organizational schemes.

EXAMPLE 29   Three Ways of Organizing the Arguments

Arguments Organized by Type of Argument	Arguments Organized by Principles	Arguments Organized by Lines of Argument
Party with burden of proof's arguments	**Party with burden of proof's arguments**	**Party with burden of proof's arguments**
• Plain language arguments	• Arguments relating to first principle (include any plain language, analogous case, and policy arguments)	• First line of argument (include any plain language, analogous case, and policy arguments)
• Analogous case arguments	• Arguments relating to second principle (include any plain language, analogous case, and policy arguments)	• Second line of argument (include any plain language, analogous case, and policy arguments)

Arguments Organized by Type of Argument	Arguments Organized by Principles	Arguments Organized by Lines of Argument
• Policy arguments	• Arguments relating to third principle (include any plain language, analogous case, and policy arguments)	
Responding party's arguments	**Responding party's arguments**	**Responding party's arguments**
• Plain language arguments	• Arguments relating to first principle (include any plain language, analogous case, and policy arguments)	• First line of argument (include any plain language, analogous case, and policy arguments)
• Analogous case arguments	• Arguments relating to second principle (include any plain language, analogous case, and policy arguments)	• Second line of argument (include any plain language, analogous case, and policy arguments)
• Policy arguments	• Arguments relating to third principle (include any plain language, analogous case, and policy arguments)	

Step 3: Draft the Arguments

In most instances, you should start your discussion of each side's arguments by setting out that side's general assertion. For example, in the Olsen case, start the usual place of abode arguments by setting out Ms. Olsen's general assertion: that her sister's house was not her usual place of abode. Similarly, start your discussion of the State's arguments by setting out the State's assertion: Ms. Olsen's sister's house was Ms. Olsen's usual place of abode or it was one of her usual places of abode. In addition, if you are going to make a number of different arguments, you may want to alert the attorney to that fact.

EXAMPLE 30   **Three Ways of Setting Out Ms. Olsen's General Assertion Relating to Usual Place of Abode**

1. Ms. Olsen will argue that her sister's house was not her usual place of abode.
2. Ms. Olsen will argue that she was not actually living at Ms. Webster's house and that, therefore, Ms. Webster's house was not her usual place of abode.
3. Ms. Olsen can make three arguments to support her assertion that her sister's house was not her usual place of abode. First, ...

| EXAMPLE 31 | **Three Ways of Setting Out the State's General Assertion Relating to Usual Place of Abode** |

1. In response, the State will argue that Ms. Webster's house was Ms. Olsen's usual place of abode.
2. The State will counter by arguing that Ms. Olsen was actually living at her sister's house.
3. The State can make three arguments to support its assertion that the service was made at Ms. Olsen's usual place of abode.

In addition to setting out each side's general assertion, you should also introduce and set out each side's subassertions. For example, if you have decided to organize the arguments around types of arguments, introduce each of these types of arguments, asserting that the plain language, the analogous cases, and the policies underlying the statute or rule support your general assertion. Likewise, if you are organizing your arguments around lines of arguments, include a sentence introducing each line of argument.

| EXAMPLE 32 | **Sentences Introducing Subassertions** |

■ First, Ms. Olsen can argue that under the plain language of the statute her sister's house was not her usual place of abode.

■ Second, Ms. Olsen can argue that her case is more like [case names] than it is like [case names].

■ Third, Ms. Olsen can argue that, as a matter of public policy, the court should hold that service was not left at Ms. Olsen's usual place of abode.

It is not, however, enough to just set out general assertions and subassertions. You also need to show the attorney how each side will support those assertions. One way to do this is to picture yourself standing in front of a judge. If you are making a plain language argument, what facts would you use, and how would you characterize those facts? If you are making an analogous case argument, what cases would you use, and how would you characterize and use those cases? If you are making a policy argument, what policies would you rely on, and how would you use those policies? Similarly, picture the other side presenting its arguments. How would its attorney use the facts, cases, and policies to support its position?

The following example, Example 33, is ineffective because the writer has not supported her assertions. For instance, in the first paragraph, the writer asserts that Ms. Olsen's sister's house was not Ms. Olsen's usual place of abode because the residential treatment house was her usual place of abode. The writer does not, however, back up this assertion with facts: She does not point out that Ms. Olsen had been a full-time resident of the residential treatment house for several months and that she was still spending four nights a week there. Similarly, although the writer asserts that Ms. Olsen's case is more like *Busman* and *Torres* than it is like *Heffernan*, she does not support this assertion by comparing and contrasting the facts in those cases to the facts in the Olsen case. Finally, although the writer sets out a rule relating to the burden of proof, she does not explain why or how that rule will produce a just result.

PRACTICE POINTER While almost every attorney wants citations to authority in the rule and analogous case sections of memos, not all attorneys want them in the argument sections. Thus, before you draft your memo, determine which approach the attorney that you are working for prefers. (In the following examples, citations are not included in the argument section.)

EXAMPLE 33   **Poor Example: The Writer Has Set Out Assertions but Has Not Supported Those Assertions**

General assertion
First subassertion

Second subassertion
Third subassertion

General assertion
First subassertion
Second subassertion

Third subassertion

In this case, Ms. Olsen can make three arguments to support her assertion that the summons and complaint were not left at her usual place of abode. First, she can argue that her sister's house was not her usual place of abode because the residential treatment house was her usual place of abode. Second, she can use the cases to support her position: her case is more like *Busman* and *Torres* than *Heffernan*. Finally, she can argue that as a matter of public policy the party seeking to invoke the jurisdiction of the court has the burden of proving that the service was valid.

In response, the State will argue that the summons and complaint were left at Ms. Olsen's usual place of abode. The facts establish that Ms. Olsen was, in fact, living at her sister's house at the time the summons and complaint were served. Accordingly, this case is like *Heffernan*. In addition, the State will distinguish *Busman* and *Torres* on the basis that, in those cases, the defendant was not spending any time at the house where the service was made. Finally, the State can argue that the service was valid because the defendant's sister's house was the place where she was most likely to receive notice.

Example 34, while not perfect, is much better. In addition to setting out his assertions, the writer has supported those assertions.

EXAMPLE 34   **Better Example: The Writer Has Set Out Assertions and Support for Those Assertions**

Ms. Olsen's general assertion
Ms. Olsen's first subassertion
Facts that support Ms. Olsen's first subassertion
Ms. Olsen's second subassertion
Explanation of how cases support Ms. Olsen's second subassertion

Ms. Olsen can make three arguments to support her assertion that her sister's house was not her usual place of abode. First, Ms. Olsen will argue that, under the plain language of the statute, her sister's house was not her usual place of abode. As the courts have stated, service must be made at the place where the defendant was actually living at the time service is made. In this case, the summons and petition were served on a weekday, and on weekdays Ms. Olsen was actually living at the residential treatment house.

Second, Ms. Olsen will argue that the facts in her case are more like the facts in *Busman* and *Torres* than the facts in *Heffernan*. Like Mr. Busman, who produced a lease that corroborated his testimony that he was not living with his half brother on the day that the summons and complaint were served, Ms. Olsen can produce evidence that establishes that on the day she was served she was living at the residential treatment house. Both Ms. Olsen's sister and the manager of the residential treatment house have said that they will testify that, during June and July, Ms. Olsen lived at the treatment house during the week and only visited her sister on weekends. In the alternative, Ms. Olsen can argue that the facts in her case are even stronger than the facts in *Torres*. While Mr. Torres's mother's statement that Mr. Torres "would be home soon" suggested that Mr. Torres would be returning to his mother's house that day, Ms. Olsen's sister told the process server that Ms. Olsen "isn't here today." In addition, Ms. Olsen can distinguish *Heffernan*: Although Mr. Heffernan had been at his family's apartment only an hour before the summons and complaint were served, Ms. Olsen had not been at her sister's house for several days.

Finally, Ms. Olsen can argue that, as a matter of public policy, the court should decide that the summons and petition were not left at her usual place of abode. The courts have stated that the statute should be narrowly construed, and this policy is particularly important in cases in which the State is seeking to terminate a mother's parental rights. In addition, this is not a case in which the State tried but could not locate Ms. Olsen: There is no evidence that the State tried to serve Ms. Olsen at the residential treatment house.

Ms. Olsen's third subassertion

Policies supporting Ms. Olsen's third subassertion

In response, the State will argue that Ms. Olsen was served at one of her usual places of abode.

State's main assertion

The courts have not required that the plaintiff be living at the house where the summons and complaint are served on the day on which the service is made. Therefore, while Ms. Olsen may not have been at her sister's house on the day that the summons and complaint were served, she had been there the previous weekend, and she was there the following weekend. In addition, Ms. Olsen had possessions at her sister's house.

State's first subassertion

Facts that support State's first subassertion

Therefore, the State will argue that the facts in this case are much stronger than the facts in *Heffernan*. While in *Heffernan*, Mr. Heffernan visited his family only "twice during the season," Ms. Olsen lived at her sister's house on weekends. In addition, while Mr. Heffernan had another permanent residence, Ms. Olsen was staying at a halfway house, which, by definition, is only a temporary residence. Finally, while in *Heffernan* there was no indication that Mr. Heffernan listed the Florida address on any documents, Ms. Olsen listed her sister's address on her driver's license, and there is evidence indicating that Ms. Olsen received other types of mail at her sister's house.

State's second subassertion

Cases that support State's second subassertion

The State will use these same facts to distinguish *Torres*. While in *Torres*, Mr. Torres presented evidence establishing that his permanent residence was in New York, in the present case, Ms. Olsen did not have a permanent residence. In the five months before service, she had been an inpatient in a treatment facility, she had lived at the treatment house, and she had lived with her sister. The State can also distinguish *Busman*. While in *Busman* the record indicated that the defendant had not lived at the house where service had been for several weeks, Ms. Olsen admits that she stayed at her sister's house on the weekend before her sister was served.

Cases that support State's second subassertion

Finally, the State will argue that, because the return was regular on its face, Ms. Olsen has the burden of proving, by clear and convincing evidence, that her sister's house was not her usual place of abode. In this instance, Ms. Olsen has not met that burden. When there is evidence that the defendant was in fact living at the house where service was made, the courts should not require plaintiffs to determine which house the defendant was living at on any particular day.

State's third subassertion

Policies supporting State's third subassertion

While in the prior example, the writer organized the arguments by type of argument, in the following example, the writer organized the arguments by lines of argument. Once again, the writer has not included pinpoint citations.

| EXAMPLE 35 | **Arguments Organized Around Lines of Argument** |

Ms. Olsen's strongest argument is that service was not made at the place where she was actually living. Although Ms. Olsen stayed at her sister's house on weekends, on the day that service was made, she was actually living at the residential treatment center. Consequently, this case is more like *Busman* and *Torres* than it is like *Heffernan*. Like Mr. Busman, who was not actually living with his half brother on the day that the summons and complaint were served, Ms. Olsen was not living with her sister on

July 24. Both Ms. Olsen's sister and the manager of the residential treatment house have said that they will testify that, during June and July, Ms. Olsen lived at the treatment house during the week and visited her sister only on weekends. This testimony makes this case stronger than *Torres*, in which the defendant's mother's statement that Mr. Torres "would be home soon" suggested that Mr. Torres would be returning to his mother's house that day. Ms. Olsen can also distinguish *Heffernan*: While Mr. Heffernan had been at his family's apartment only an hour before the summons and complaint were served, Ms. Olsen had not been at her sister's house for several days.

Ms. Olsen also has strong policy arguments. The courts have repeatedly said that the purpose of the statute is to ensure that defendants receive notice and that, to that end, the statute should be narrowly construed. In this case, the defendant will testify that she did not receive notice. Her sister states that instead of giving the summons to Ms. Olsen, she put the summons in a shoebox in the kitchen. Moreover, Ms. Olsen can argue that in cases involving the termination of parental rights, the courts should err on the side of ensuring that the parent receives notice. At a minimum, the State should have tried to serve Ms. Olsen at the residential treatment house.

The State can counter this policy argument with its own policy argument. When a defendant has two or more places of abode, the State should not have to determine which one the defendant is staying at on the day that service is actually made. Service can be made at any of the defendant's usual places of abode.

The State can also argue that Ms. Olsen has not met her burden of proving by clear and convincing evidence that she was not actually living at her sister's house on the day when service was made. Unlike Mr. Busman, who had proof that he had moved out of his half brother's house three weeks before service was attempted, Ms. Olsen had not moved out of her sister's house. In fact, she stayed at her sister's house both on the weekend before and the weekend after service was made. The State can also distinguish *Torres*. As the majority in that case noted, the mother's statement was ambiguous; in addition, there was nothing in Mr. Torres's affidavit that established where he was living on the date service was made. In contrast, in this case Ms. Olsen does not deny that she was living at her sister's house three nights a week during the month of July, the month during which service was made. Finally, the State can argue that this case is similar to *Heffernan* in that, as in that case, Ms. Olsen was moving back and forth between two residences. While in *Heffernan* there was no indication that Mr. Heffernan planned to return to the family home the next weekend, in this case Ms. Olsen did, in fact, go back to her sister's house.

d.   Predict How the Court Will Decide the Element

The final piece of information you need to include is your prediction about how a court is likely to decide the element. Is it more likely that the court will find that the element is met, or is it more likely that the court will decide that the element is not met?

In writing this section, you must once again change roles. Instead of playing the role of the reporter describing the rules and analogous cases or of the advocate making each side's arguments, you must play the role of judge. You must put yourself in the position of the particular court that will decide the issue — trial court, appellate court, state court, federal court — and decide how that court is likely to decide that element.

At least initially, you may be uncomfortable making such predictions. How can you predict what a court might do? The good news is that with time, and experience, you will get better and better at making predictions. In the meantime, read the statutes and cases carefully, and critically evaluate each side's arguments. Careful reading and careful consideration of arguments — plus common sense — will help you make reliable predictions. Remember, too, that you are predicting, not guaranteeing, an outcome.

In drafting your mini-conclusion, do two things: First, set out your prediction. Second, briefly explain why you believe the court will decide the element as you have predicted. As a general rule, do not include phrases like "I think" or "in my opinion."

In Example 36, the writer has set out his prediction but not his reasoning. As a consequence, the reader has to guess about why the writer reached the conclusion that he reached. Example 37 is better: In it, the writer has set out both his prediction and his reasoning.

EXAMPLE 36　　**Poor Draft: The Writer Has Set Out the Prediction but Not the Reasoning**

While both sides have strong arguments, the court will probably conclude that the summons was not left at Ms. Olsen's usual place of abode.

EXAMPLE 37　　**Better Draft: The Writer Has Set Out Both the Prediction and Reasoning**

While both sides have strong arguments, the court will probably conclude that the summons was not left at Ms. Olsen's usual place of abode. In the more recent cases, the courts have strictly construed the statute, holding that the service was not made at the defendant's usual place of abode when the defendant had a more permanent place of abode. Thus, because the residential treatment house was Ms. Olsen's more permanent residence, the court will probably conclude that it was Ms. Olsen's usual place of abode. In addition, the court may be influenced by two key facts: The record does not indicate that the State tried to serve Ms. Olsen at the residential treatment house, and Ms. Olsen states that she did not receive notice.

---

§ 7.8.5　Checklist for Critiquing a Discussion Section Written Using a Script Format

a.　Content

Introduction

- The writer has included a sentence or paragraph introducing the governing statute or common law rule.
- The writer has set out the general rule, quoting the applicable statutory sections and quoting or paraphrasing the common law rule.
- The writer has set out any other general rules.
- When appropriate, the writer has briefly described the policies underlying the statute or common law rule.
- The writer has included a roadmap.
- The writer has not included rules or information that the attorney does not need.
- The rules are stated accurately and objectively.
- For each rule stated, the writer has included a citation to authority.

Discussion of Undisputed Elements

- The writer has identified the element and, when there are specific rules, set out those specific rules.
- The writer has applied the rules to the facts of the client's case, explaining why the element is not in dispute.

Discussion of Disputed Elements

- For each disputed element, the writer has set out the specific rules, described cases that have interpreted and applied those rules, set out each side's arguments, and predicted how the court will decide the element.
- The writer has included all of the applicable specific rules and set out those rules accurately and objectively.
- The writer has introduced each group of analogous cases, telling the attorney what rule or principle the cases illustrate.
- The case descriptions illustrate the rule or principle and are accurate and objective.
- In setting out the arguments, the writer has set out both assertions and support for those assertions.
- The analysis is sophisticated: the writer has set out more than the obvious arguments.
- The writer has predicted how each element will be decided and given reasons to support those predictions.

b.   Large-Scale Organization

- The writer has presented the information in the order in which the attorney expects to see it. For example, the writer begins the discussion section with an introductory section in which he or she sets out the general rules. The writer then walks the attorney through each of the elements, raising and dismissing the undisputed elements and doing a more complete analysis of the disputed elements.

c.   Writing

- The attorney can understand the discussion with just one reading.
- The paragraph divisions are logical, and the paragraphs are neither too long nor too short.
- Transitions and dovetailing have been used to make the connection between ideas clear.
- In most sentences, the writer has used the actor as the subject of the sentence, and the subject and verb are close together.
- The writer has varied the length of the sentences and the sentence patterns so that each sentence flows smoothly from the prior sentence.
- The writing is concise and precise.
- The writing is grammatically correct and correctly punctuated.
- The discussion section has been proofread.

§ 7.9   Drafting the Formal Conclusion

You are not doing anything wrong. In drafting a formal memo, you do set out your conclusions in more than one place. If you included a brief answer, you set out your conclusion there. In addition, if your problem required an elements analysis, you set out mini-conclusions for each disputed element. And yes, you will now, once again, set out your conclusion, this time in a formal conclusion.

While some attorneys think that the typical memo has too many conclusions, other attorneys believe that each conclusion serves a useful purpose. The brief answer is exactly that: a brief answer. If the client is on the phone and the attorney has not had time to read the full memo, he or she can read the brief answer. The mini-conclusions serve a different purpose. They are part of the analysis and help the attorney understand which elements will be easy to prove and which may be more difficult to prove. The formal conclusion serves still a different purpose. It is the place where you pull all of the pieces together.

§ 7.9.1   Summarize Your Conclusions

In a one-issue memo, the formal conclusion is used to summarize the analysis of that one issue. For example, in the Olsen memo, you would use the formal conclusion to tell the attorney whether you think Ms. Olsen was properly served. In Example 1 below, the writer begins by answering the question set out in the issue statement. The writer does not, however, stop there. In addition to answering the question, she goes through the elements, element by element. In the second paragraph, the writer tells the attorney that Ms. Olsen will have to concede that the summons was left with a person of suitable age and discretion and that, more likely than not, the court will conclude that the process server told Ms. Olsen's sister about the contents. In the third paragraph, the writer discusses usual place of abode, briefly explaining why she thinks that Ms. Olsen can prove that the summons was not left at her usual place of abode.

Notice that in Example 1, the writer has not included citations to authority. Most legal readers do not expect citations in a formal conclusion.

EXAMPLE 1   **Formal Conclusion**

Conclusion

Because of the strong public policy in favor of ensuring that defendants receive notice of actions that have been filed against them, the court will probably decide that the substituted service of process was not valid and vacate the judgment terminating Ms. Olsen's parental rights.

Ms. Olsen will have to concede that her sister, Ms. Webster, is a person of suitable age and that Ms. Webster was residing at the house where the service was made. In addition, because the process server told Ms. Webster that Ms. Olsen needed to go to court, it seems unlikely that Ms. Olsen will be able to prove that Ms. Webster was not informed of the contents.

Ms. Olsen may, however, be able to prove that the summons and complaint were not served at her usual place of abode. In the more recent cases, the courts have concluded that service made on a relative was invalid when the defendants produced evidence establishing that they were not actually living with that relative on the day that service was made. While in most of these cases the defendants had not lived at the house where service was made for several months or several years, in the Olsen case the court may be swayed by three facts: This case involves the termination of Ms. Olsen's parental rights; there is no evidence that the State tried to personally serve Ms. Olsen or that it tried to serve Ms. Olsen at the residential treatment house; and Ms. Olsen states that she did not receive notice.

§ 7.9.2   Present Your Advice

While some attorneys just want conclusions, others may want you to go one step further and offer advice. What are the client's options? What action should the attorney take next? Is this the type of case that the firm should, or wants to, handle? When you are asked to include this type of information in the conclusion, add a paragraph like the one in Example 2.

EXAMPLE 2   **Paragraph Setting Out Advice**

Because Ms. Olsen has some strong arguments, I recommend that we move to quash the service of process and vacate the order terminating her parental rights.

---

§ 7.9.3   Checklist for Formal Conclusion

a.   Content

■ In a one-issue memorandum, the conclusion is used to predict how the issue will be decided and to summarize the reasons supporting that prediction.
■ When appropriate, the writer includes not only the conclusion but also strategic advice.

b.   Organization

■ The information is organized logically.

c.   Writing

■ The attorney can understand the conclusion with just one reading.
■ The paragraph divisions are logical, and the paragraphs are neither too long nor too short.
■ Transitions and dovetailing have been used to make the connection between ideas clear.
■ In most sentences, the writer has used the actor as the subject of the sentence, and the subject and verb are close together.
■ The writer has varied the length of the sentences and the sentence patterns so that each sentence flows smoothly from the prior sentence.
■ The writing is concise and precise.
■ The writing is grammatically correct and correctly punctuated.
■ The conclusion has been proofread.

Chapter 7 Quiz No. 3

Draft answers for each of the following questions. Make your points clearly and concisely, and write sentences that are easy to read and that are grammatical and correctly punctuated.

1. What is the difference between a disputed element and an undisputed element?
2. When should you include descriptions of analogous cases?
3. Why should you begin your descriptions of a group of analogous cases with a principle-based topic sentence?
4. In drafting the analogous case section, when might you use a parenthetical?
5. What distinguishes a good argument section from a weak one?

§ 7.10   Revising, Editing, and Proofreading the Memo

Yes, there are occasions when, because of time or money constraints, you will have to turn in a first draft of an in-house memo. You should not, however, get in the habit of submitting first drafts to your supervising attorney, and you should never submit a first draft to a court, to opposing counsel, or to your client. Unlike speech, which disappears as soon as the words are spoken, written words remain: While well-written documents can enhance your reputation, poorly written ones can damage it

As a consequence, whenever possible, do what we do in this section, and treat revising, editing, and proofreading as three separate processes.

§ 7.10.1 Revise Your Draft

Revising is the process of "re-visioning" what you have drafted. During this re-visioning process, step back from your draft, and look at it through the eyes of your reader. Have you given the attorney all of the information that he or she needs? Have you presented that information in the order that the attorney expects to see it?

During the revising stage, you need to be willing to make major changes. If, in revising the draft, you realize that you did not need to include one part of your discussion, delete that part, no matter how many hours you spent drafting it. Similarly, if in revising the draft, you realize that you did not research or discuss a major point, go back and do that research, analysis, and writing. Finally, if in revising your draft, you realize that your organizational scheme just does not work, start over, reorganizing one section or even the entire statement of facts or discussion section.

PRACTICE POINTER	Many writers do a better job revising when they print out a draft and lay out the pages side by side.

a. Check Content

In revising a draft, look first at its content. If there are problems with content, solving those problems must be your first priority.

In checking content, the first question to ask yourself is whether you have given the attorney the information that he or she requested. Did you research the assigned issue or issues? Did you locate all of the applicable statutes and cases? Did you identify and present the arguments that each side is likely to make? Did you evaluate those arguments and predict how the court is likely to rule?

b. Check to Make Sure that the Information Is Presented Accurately

In law, small errors can have serious consequences. The failure to cite check to make sure that a case is still good law, an omitted "not," or an "or" that should have been "and" can make the difference between winning and losing, between competent lawyering and malpractice.

Consequently, in writing the memo, exercise care. Because the attorney is relying on you, your research must be thorough. Make sure that you have located the applicable statutes and cases and that you have checked to make sure that those statutes and cases are still good law. In addition, make sure your analysis is sound. Did you read the statutes and cases carefully? Is the way in which you have put the pieces together sound? Finally, make sure you have presented the statutes and cases accurately and fairly. Did you correctly identify the issue in the analogous cases? Did you take a rule out of context? Did you misrepresent the facts or omit a key fact? Unless the attorney reads the statutes and cases you cite, he may not see an error until it is too late.

c. Check to Make Sure that the Discussion Section Is Well Organized

The next step is to check the discussion section's large-scale organization. Has the information been presented in the order that the attorney expects to see it?

One way to check large-scale organization is to prepare an after-the-fact outline. This is done either by labeling the subject matter of each paragraph and then listing those labels in outline form or by summarizing what each paragraph says.

d. Check to Make Sure that the Connections Are Explicit

Once you have revised for content and organization, look at your use of roadmaps, signposts, topic sentences, and transitions.

1. Roadmaps

A roadmap is just what the term implies: a "map" providing the reader with an overview of the document. For example, in our sample problem, the writer put a roadmap at the end of the introductory section that tells readers which elements will be easy to prove and which elements will be more difficult to prove.

EXAMPLE 1	**Roadmap Telling the Attorney Which Elements Will Be in Dispute and Which Elements Will Not Be in Dispute**

In this case, Ms. Olsen will have to concede that the summons was left with a person 15 years or older who was residing at the house where the summons and complaint were served. In addition, it is unlikely that Ms. Olsen will be able to prove that her sister was not informed of the contents of the documents. Ms. Olsen may, however, be able to present clear and convincing evidence that the summons was not left at her usual place of abode.

Note that in Example 1 above, the roadmap is substantive in nature. Instead of saying, "First I will discuss this and then I will discuss that," the writer has talked about what Ms. Olsen can and cannot prove.

2. Topic Sentences, Signposts, and Transitions

Topic sentences, signposts, and transitions serve the same function that directional signs serve on a freeway. They tell readers where they are, what to expect, and how the pieces are connected. While these directional signs may not be particularly important in some types of writing, they are essential in legal writing. Without them, the connections between paragraphs and between sentences may not be clear, making the analysis difficult to follow.

Similarly,　　　In contrast,　　　In addition,

Compare Example 2 below, in which the writer has not included topic sentences, signposts, or transitions, with Example 3. In Example 3, the topic sentences, signposts, and transitions are in boldface type.

EXAMPLE 2	**The Writer Has Not Included Topic Sentences, Signposts, or Transitions**

When a defendant has more than one residence, the service must be made at the place where the defendant was actually living at the time the summons and complaint were served. Ms. Olsen had more than one residence: During the week she lived at the treatment house, and on weekends she visited her sister. Because the summons and complaint were served on a Wednesday, a weekday, the service was not made at the place where Ms. Olsen was actually living.

Like Mr. Torres, who only visited his mother and who was not at his mother's house when service was made, Ms. Olsen only visited her sister and was not at her sister's house when the summons and complaint were served. While Mr. Torres's mother's statement that Mr. Torres "would be home soon" suggested that Mr. Torres would be returning to his mother's house that day, Ms. Olsen's sister told the process server that Ms. Olsen "isn't here today." While the plaintiff in *Torres* had tried on a number of occasions to serve Mr. Torres at his New York house, we do not know whether the defendant tried to serve Ms. Olsen personally or at the treatment house. While Mr. Heffernan had been at his family's apartment only an hour before the summons and complaint were served, Ms. Olsen had not been at her sister's house for several days and, while in *Heffernan* the summons and complaint were served on the defendant's wife, in the present case the summons and complaint were served on Ms. Olsen's sister. Since *Heffernan*, the courts have interpreted the service process statutes more narrowly.

The courts have repeatedly held that the service of process statutes should be strictly construed and that service on a relative is not, by itself, enough. *Shurman v. Atl. Mortg. & Inv. Corp.*, 795 So. 2d 952, 953-54 (Fla. 2001). Ms. Olsen did not receive notice.

EXAMPLE 3   The Writer Has Included Topic Sentences, Signposts, and Transitions

Ms. Olsen can make three arguments to support her assertion that her sister's house was not her usual place of abode. First, Ms. Olsen will argue that, under the plain language of the statute, her sister's house was not her usual place of abode. As the courts have stated, service must be made at the place where the defendant was actually living at the time the summons and complaint were served. **In this case,** the summons and complaint were served on a weekday, and on weekdays Ms. Olsen was actually living at the residential treatment house.

Second, Ms. Olsen will argue that the facts in her case are more like the facts in *Busman* and *Torres* than the facts in *Heffernan*. Like Mr. Busman, who produced a lease that corroborated his testimony that he was not living with his half brother on the day that the summons and complaint were served, Ms. Olsen can produce evidence that establishes that on the day she was served she was living at the residential treatment house. Both Ms. Olsen's sister and the manager of the residential treatment house have said they will testify that during June and July Ms. Olsen lived at the treatment house during the week and only stayed with her sister on weekends. **In the alternative,** Ms. Olsen can argue that the facts in her case are even stronger than the facts in *Torres*. While Mr. Torres's mother's statement that Mr. Torres "would be home soon" suggested that Mr. Torres would be returning to his mother's house that day, Ms. Olsen's sister told the process server that Ms. Olsen "isn't here today." **In addition,** Ms. Olsen can distinguish *Heffernan*: Although Mr. Heffernan had been at his family's apartment only an hour before the summons and complaint were served, Ms. Olsen had not been at her sister's house for several days.

Finally, Ms. Olsen can argue that, as a matter of public policy, the court should decide that the summons and petition were not left at her usual place of abode. The courts have stated that the statute should be narrowly construed, and this policy is particularly important in cases in which the State is seeking to terminate a mother's parental rights. **In addition,** this is not a case in which the State tried but could not locate Ms. Olsen: There is no evidence that the State tried to serve Ms. Olsen at the residential treatment house.

---

3. *Dovetailing*

Another technique that you can use to make the connections between ideas clear is dovetailing. You use dovetailing when you refer back to a point made in the prior sentence or paragraph.

A	B	Reference to B	C

In Examples 4 and 5, the writer has used dovetailing to make clear the connections between the first and second sentences. The language that is in bold is the dovetail.

| EXAMPLE 4 | **Dovetailing Used to Connect First and Second Sentences** |

During April, May, and June 2013, Ms. Olsen usually spent weeknights at the treatment house and Friday, Saturday, and Sunday nights at her **sister's house. Because she was spending time at her sister's house,** she moved some of her clothing and personal effects into her sister's house.

| EXAMPLE 5 | **Dovetailing Used to Connect First and Second Sentences** |

Although the party seeking to invoke the jurisdiction of the court has the burden of proving that service was proper, if the return is regular on its face, the courts presume that the service was valid. *Busman v. State, Dep't of Revenue*, 905 So. 2d 956, 958 (Fla. 3d DCA 2005); *Thompson v. State, Dep't of Revenue*, 867 So. 2d 603, 605 (Fla. 1st DCA 2004). **In such instances,** the party challenging the service has the burden of presenting clear and convincing evidence that the service was invalid. *Id.*

While in Examples 4 and 5 dovetailing was used to make clear the connections between sentences, in Example 6 it is used to make clear the connections between paragraphs. The first sentence in the second paragraph refers back to the information at the end of the first paragraph.

| EXAMPLE 6 | **Dovetailing Used to Connect Paragraphs** |

Thus, the plaintiff will argue that the facts in this case are much stronger than the facts in *Heffernan*. While in *Heffernan*, Mr. Heffernan visited his family only "twice during the season," Ms. Olsen lived at her sister's house three days a week. In addition, while Mr. Heffernan had another permanent residence, Ms. Olsen was staying at a treatment house, which by definition, is only a temporary residence. Finally, while in *Heffernan* there was no indication that Mr. Heffernan listed the Florida address on any documents, Ms. Olsen listed her sister's address on her driver's license.

The plaintiff will use these same facts to distinguish *Torres*. While in *Torres*, Mr. Torres presented evidence establishing that his permanent residence was in New York, in our case, Ms. Olsen did not have a permanent residence. In the five months prior to service, she had been an . . .

| PRACTICE POINTER | While roadmaps, topic sentences, signposts, transitions, and dovetailing are more important in legal writing than in many other types of writing, do not overuse them. For example, do not use dovetailing to connect all of your sentences or all of your paragraphs. |

The work is now almost done. When you step back from the memo and look at it through the attorney's eyes, you are pleased with its content and organization. You do, however, still need to edit and proofread your memo.

Although some writers mistakenly believe that revising, editing, and proofreading are the same, they are not. While during the revision process you "re-vision" your creation, during the editing process you make that vision clearer, more concise, more precise, and more accessible. Proofreading is different yet again. It is the search for errors. When you proofread, you are not asking yourself, "Is there a better way of saying this?" Instead, you are looking to see if what you intended to have on the page is in fact there.

Although the lines between revising and editing and between editing and proofreading blur at times, the distinctions among these three skills are important to keep in mind, if for no other reason than to remind you that there are three distinct ways of making changes to a draft and that the best written documents undergo all three types of changes.

§ 7.10.2   Edit Your Draft

Like revising, editing requires that you look at your work through fresh eyes. At this stage, however, the focus is not on the larger issues of content and organization but on sentence structure, precision and conciseness, grammar, and punctuation. The goal is to produce a professional product that is easy to read and understand. In this chapter, we focus on writing effective sentences and writing correctly; in Chapter 8, we focus on writing precisely and concisely.

a.   Writing Effective Sentences

Most writers can substantially improve their sentences by following four simple pieces of advice about writing:

1. Use the actor as the subject of most sentences.
2. Keep the subject and verb close together.
3. Put old information at the beginning of the sentence and new information at the end.
4. Vary sentence length and pattern.

1. Use the Actor as the Subject of Most Sentences

By using the actor as the subject of most of your sentences, you can eliminate many of the constructions that make legal writing hard to understand: overuse of the passive voice, most nominalizations, expletive constructions, and many misplaced modifiers.

(a) Passive Constructions

In a passive construction, the actor appears in the object rather than the subject slot of the sentence, or it is not named at all. For instance, in Example 7, although the jury is the actor, the word "jury" is used as the object of the preposition "by" rather than the subject of the sentence.

EXAMPLE 7	**Passive Voice**

A verdict was reached by the jury.

In the following example, the actor, "jury," is not named at all.

EXAMPLE 8	**Passive Voice**

A verdict was reached.

To use the active voice, simply identify the actor (in this case, the jury) and use it as the subject of the sentence.

EXAMPLE 9	**Active Voice**

The jury reached a verdict.

Now read each of the sentences in Example 10, marking the subject and verb and deciding whether the writer used the actor as the subject of the sentence. If the writer did not use the actor as the subject of the sentence, decide whether the sentence should be rewritten. As a general rule, the active voice is better unless the passive voice improves the flow of sentences or the writer wants to de-emphasize what the actor did.

> If the return is regular on its face, there is a presumption that the service was valid. *Thompson v. State, Dep't of Revenue*, 867 So. 2d 603, 605 (Fla. 1st DCA 2004); *Magazine v. Bedoya*, 475 So. 2d 1035, 1035 (Fla. 3d DCA 1985). In such instances, the defendant must prove that the service was invalid. *Thompson*, 867 So. 2d at 605; *Magazine*, 475 So. 2d at 1035.

Sentence 1

If the return is regular on its face, <u>there is</u> a presumption that the service was valid.

In writing Sentence 1, the writer used the passive voice. Instead of using the actor (the court) as the subject of the sentence, the writer has used an expletive construction: "there is." Because the writer did not have a good reason for using the passive voice, we have rewritten the sentence using the active voice.

EXAMPLE 10	**Rewrite Using the Active Voice**

However, if the return is regular on its face, the <u>courts</u> <u>presume</u> that the service was valid.

Sentence 2

In such instances, the <u>burden</u> of presenting clear and convincing evidence that the service was invalid is on the defendant.

Sentence 2 is also written in the passive voice. Instead of using the actor (the defendant) as the subject of the sentence, the writer has placed the actor in a prepositional phrase. Because the writer did not have a good reason for using the passive voice, we have shown three ways to rewrite the sentence.

EXAMPLE 11   **Edits Using the Active Voice**

In such instances, the <u>party</u> challenging the service <u>has</u> the burden of presenting clear and convincing evidence that the service was invalid.

In such instances, the <u>party</u> challenging the service <u>must</u> <u>prove</u> that the service was invalid by clear and convincing evidence.

In such instances, the <u>party</u> challenging the service <u>must</u> <u>prove</u>, by clear and convincing evidence, that the service was invalid.

| **PRACTICE POINTER** | Be sure to distinguish between the passive voice and past tense. A sentence written in the past tense may or may not use the passive voice. |

(b) Nominalizations

You create a nominalization when you turn a verb or an adjective into a noun.

Verb		**Nominalization**
apply	→	application
conclude	→	conclusion
decide	→	decision

Although there are times when you will want to use a nominalization, overusing nominalizations can make your writing harder to read and understand. In the following sentence, "presumption" is a nominalization.

EXAMPLE 12   **Nominalization**

If the return is regular on its face, there is a <u>presumption</u> that the service is valid.

To make this sentence better, identify the real actor (in this instance, the court) and then, in the verb, specifically state what action that actor has taken or will take. Note that "presumption" becomes "presume."

EXAMPLE 13   **Edit Without Nominalization**

If the return is regular on its face, the courts <u>presume</u> that the service is valid.

(c) Expletive Constructions

In an expletive construction, phrases such as "it is" or "there are" are used as the subject and verb of the sentence. Although it is sometimes necessary to use such a construction (note the use of an expletive construction in this sentence), such a construction gives the reader almost no information. Therefore, when possible, use a concrete subject and verb—that is, a subject and verb that describe something the reader can "see" in his or her mind.

EXAMPLE 14   **Expletive Constructions**

However, if the return is regular on its face, <u>there is a</u> presumption that the service was valid.

<u>It is</u> Ms. Olsen's argument that . . .

EXAMPLE 15   **Edits Without Expletive Constructions**

If the return is regular on its face, the <u>courts</u> <u>presume</u> that the service was valid.

<u>Ms. Olsen</u> <u>will argue</u> that . . .

PRACTICE POINTER   Note that expletive constructions and nominalizations often go hand in hand. Because you use a expletive construction, you are forced into using a nominalization:

If the return is regular on its face, <u>there</u> <u>is</u> a <u>presumption</u> that the service is valid.

(d) Dangling Modifiers

A dangling modifier is a modifier that does not reasonably modify anything in the sentence. For example, in the following sentence, the modifying phrase "Applying this test" does not reasonably modify anything in the sentence. It is not "it was held" that is doing the applying.

EXAMPLE 16   **Dangling Modifier**

Applying this test, it was held that the summons and complaint were not left at the defendant's usual place of abode.

The dangling modifier can be eliminated if the actor is used as the subject of the sentence.

EXAMPLE 17   **Edit Without Dangling Modifier**

Applying this test, the **court** held that the summons and complaint were not left at the defendant's usual place of abode.

Now the phrase "Applying this test" modifies something in the sentence: the court.

> **PRACTICE POINTER**   When you see a word ending in "ing" (a participle) in a phrase or clause near the beginning of a sentence, ask yourself who is doing the action. For example, in the preceding sentence, ask who is doing the "applying." Then look at the subject of the sentence. If the subject does not identify who is doing the action, then you have a dangling modifier.

2. Keep the Subject and Verb Close Together

Researchers have established that readers cannot understand a sentence until they have located both the subject and the verb. In addition, readers have difficulty remembering the subject if it is separated from the verb by more than seven or eight words: If there are more than seven or eight words, after finding the verb, many readers must go back and relocate the subject.

The lesson to be learned from this research is that, as a writer, you should try to keep your subject and verb close together. In Examples 18 and 19, the subject and verb are underlined.

EXAMPLE 18   **Subject and Verb Too Far Apart**

In such instances, the <u>burden</u> of presenting clear and convincing evidence that the service was invalid <u>is</u> on the party challenging the service.

EXAMPLE 19   **Edits with Subject and Verb Closer Together**

In such instances, the <u>party</u> challenging the service <u>has</u> the burden of presenting clear and convincing evidence that the service was invalid.

In such instances, the <u>defendant must prove</u> by clear and convincing evidence that the service was invalid.

---

3. Put Old Information at the Beginning of the Sentence and New Information at the End

Sentences, and the paragraphs they create, make more sense when the old information is placed at the beginning and the new information is placed at the end. When this pattern is used, the development progresses naturally from left to right without unnecessary backtracking.

EXAMPLE 20   **Old Information Is at the Beginning of the Sentence, and New Information Is at the End**

The only Florida case in which the summons was left with a relative with whom the defendant was visiting is *Torres*. *Id.* at 585. <u>In that case, the plaintiff tried for more than a month to serve Mr. Torres at the New York apartment where Mr. Torres had lived for 12 years.</u> *Id.* Although all

<u>attempts at service were unsuccessful</u>, the New York process server indicated in his affidavit that he had "verified" with a neighbor that "Mr. Torres lived at the New York address, but that he was often out of town, and was expected to return in two weeks." *Id.* Because it could not serve the defendant in New York, the plaintiff served Mr. Torres's mother at her residence in Florida. In his affidavit, the Florida process server stated that Mr. Torres mother told him that "he (presumably Mr. Torres) would be home soon." *Id.* Mr. Torres stated that he never received notice. In holding that the service was not valid, the court noted that while the standard of review was gross abuse of discretion, the trial court had not heard live testimony and the plaintiff had the burden of establishing that the service was valid. *Id.* at 587. It then went on to note that the evidence tended to support Mr. Torres's position that his usual place of abode was in New York and that Mr. Torres's mother's statement that Mr. Torres would be home soon was, at best, ambiguous. *Id.*

In the paragraph set out above, the first sentence, which is in bold, acts as a topic sentence, telling the attorney that there is only one Florida case that has facts similar to the facts in the client's case. That first sentence ends with a reference to the new information, which is the name of the case: "*Torres.*" In the second sentence, the name of the case is now the old information, and the second sentence begins with a reference back to that old information. The second sentence then ends with the new information: that the plaintiff had tried, on a number of occasions, to serve the defendant in New York. In the third sentence, the old information is that the plaintiff had tried to serve the defendant in New York. Thus, the author uses this old information to start the third sentence, putting the new information, that the neighbor had told the process server that the defendant was out of town, at the end of the third sentence.

PRACTICE POINTER	Note how putting "old" information at the beginning of the sentence allows you to use dovetailing.

4. Vary Sentence Length and Pattern

Even if writing is technically correct, it is not considered good if it is not pleasing to the ear. Read Example 21 aloud.

EXAMPLE 21	**All the Sentences Are About the Same Length and Use the Same Pattern**

A process server went to Ms. Webster's house on Wednesday, July 24, 2013. The process server asked for Elaine Olsen. Ms. Webster told the process server that "Elaine isn't here today." The process server then handed the summons and complaint to Ms. Webster. The process server told Ms. Webster that Ms. Olsen "needed to go to court."

In Example 21, the writing is not pleasing because the sentences are similar in length and all follow the same pattern. Although short, uncomplicated sentences are usually better than long, complicated ones, the use of too many short sentences results in writing that sounds choppy and sophomoric. As Example 22 illustrates, the passage is much better when the writer varies sentence length and pattern.

EXAMPLE 22	**The Writer Has Varied the Length of the Sentences and the Sentence Pattern**

On Wednesday, July 24, 2013, a process server went to Ms. Webster's house and asked for Elaine Olsen. When Ms. Webster told the process server that "Elaine isn't here today," the process server handed the summons to Ms. Webster and told her that Ms. Olsen "needed to go to court."

b.   Writing Correctly

For a moment, imagine that you have received the following letter from a local law firm.

EXAMPLE 23	**Sample Letter**

Dear Student:

Thank you for submitting an application for a position as a law clerk with are firm. Your grades in law school are very good, however, at this time we do not have any positions available. Its possible, however, that we may have a opening next summer and we therefore urge you to reapply with us then.

Sincerely,

Senior Partner

No matter how bad the market is, most students would not want to be associated with a firm that sends out a three-line letter containing three major errors and several minor ones. Unfortunately, the reverse is also true. No matter how short-handed they are, most law firms do not want to hire someone who has not mastered the basic rules of grammar and punctuation. Most firms cannot afford an employee who makes careless errors or one who lacks basic writing skills.

Consequently, at the editing stage you need to go back through your draft, correcting errors. Look first for the errors that potentially affect meaning (misplaced modifiers, incorrect use of "which" and "that") and for errors that educated readers are likely to notice (incomplete sentences, comma splices, incorrect use of the possessive, lack of parallelism). Then look for the errors that you know from past experience that you are likely to make.

§ 7.10.3   Proofreading

Most writers learn the importance of proofreading the hard way. A letter, brief, or contract goes out with the client's name misspelled, with an "or" where there should have been an "and," or without an essential "not." At a minimum, these errors cause embarrassment; at worst, they result in a lawsuit.

To avoid such errors, treat proofreading as a separate step in the revising process. After you have finished revising and editing, go back through your draft, looking not at content, organization, or sentence style, but for errors. Proofreading is most effective when it is done on hard copy several days (or, when that is not feasible, several hours) after you have finished editing. Force yourself to read slowly, focusing not on the sentences but on the individual words in the sentences. Is a word missing? Is a word repeated? Are letters transposed? You can force yourself to read slowly by using a clean piece of paper to cover up all but the line you are reading, by reading from right to left, or by reading from the bottom of the page to the top.

Also, force yourself to begin your proofreading by looking at the sections that caused you the most difficulty or that you wrote last. Because you were concentrating on content or were tired, these sections probably contain the most errors.

Finally, when you get into practice, don't rely on just your spelling and grammar checkers. Instead, make it a habit to have a second person proofread your work. Not only will someone else see errors that you missed, he or she is also less likely than you to "read in" missing words.

§ 7.10.4 Citations

As a legal writer, you have an extra burden. In addition to editing and proofreading the text, you must also edit and proofread your citations to legal authorities.

At the editing stage, focus on selection and placement of citations. Is the authority you cited the best authority? Did you avoid string cites (the citing of multiple cases for the same point)? Have you included a citation to authority for every rule stated? Did you include the appropriate signal? Have you over- or under-emphasized the citation? (You emphasize a citation by placing it in the text of a sentence; you de-emphasize it by placing it in a separate citation sentence.)

In contrast, at the proofreading stage, focus on the citation itself. Are the volume and page numbers correct? Are the pinpoint cites accurate? Have you included the year of the decision and any subsequent history? Is the spacing correct?

Chapter 7 Quiz No. 4

Draft answers for each of the following questions. Make your points clearly and concisely, and write sentences that are easy to read and that are grammatical and correctly punctuated.

1. What is the difference between revising, editing, and proofreading?
2. In the following sentences, has the writer used dovetailing? If your answer is yes, what is the dovetail?

   The State will use these same facts to distinguish *Torres*. While in *Torres*, Mr. Torres presented evidence establishing that his permanent residence was in New York, in the present case, Ms. Olsen did not have a permanent residence.

3. Rewrite the following sentence using the active voice.

   There are three arguments that the State can make to support its assertion.

4. Rewrite the following sentence eliminating the nominalization.

The court's conclusion was that the plaintiff had not met its burden of proof.

5. Rewrite the following sentence eliminating the dangling modifier.

Weighing these arguments, it is likely that the court will conclude that Ms. Olsen has met her burden of proving that service was not made at her usual place of abode.

Drafting Memo 2

For the purposes of this memo, presume that you are spending the summer working for a law firm in San Francisco. Although it is only your first week at the firm, your supervising attorney has given you the following assignment.

§ 8.1   The Assignment

To:	Legal Intern
From:	Supervising Attorney
Date:	October 13, 2013
Re:	Michael Garcia; Adverse Possession of Property in Washington State

- One of our longtime clients, Michael Garcia, has contacted our office regarding property that he owns in Washington State. Mr. Garcia is worried that an organization may have obtained title to this property through adverse possession.
- Mr. Garcia inherited the Washington property from his grandfather, Eduardo Montoya, in 1999.

- Mr. Montoya purchased the land in 1958. He and his family used the land every summer from 1958 until the early 1990s, when he became ill.
- When Mr. Montoya's family used the property, family members camped on the site and used a small dock for swimming, fishing, and boating.
- Mr. Garcia visited the property in the fall of 1999 but moved to California not long after that visit. He did not visit the property from 2000 until last August.
- The group that has been using Mr. Garcia's land since 1997 is called Doctors and Nurses Who Care (DNWC).
- DNWC has owned the five-acre parcel that is just to the north of Mr. Garcia's property since 1996. DNWC uses its property for summer camps for children who suffer from serious illnesses and disabilities. In a typical summer, DNWC runs two one-week camps for children with cancer, two one-week camps for children who are blind, two one-week camps for children with autism, and two one-week camps for children with diabetes.
- DNWC maintains and uses the campsites, the fire area, the outhouse, and the dock, all of which are on Mr. Garcia's property.
- During the summer of 2001, DNWC posted a no trespassing sign on the dock, and the sign is still there.
- Most of the time the children stay in cabins located on the DNWC property. However, DNWC uses Mr. Garcia's property for "campouts." One night each week, one group of about 10 children will camp out in tents on Mr. Garcia's property, the next night another group of 10 will camp out on his property, and so on. Thus, DNWC uses Mr. Garcia's land four or five nights a week for eight weeks each summer.
- During these campouts, the children pitch and stay in tents and cook over a fire.
- Mr. Garcia has paid all of the taxes and assessments.
- In about February 2001, Mr. Garcia received a letter from DNWC asking whether it could continue using his land for campouts. Mr. Garcia was busy and never responded to the letter.
- Last August, Mr. Garcia visited the property with the intent of spending a few days camping on the lake. When he got there, he discovered that there were children and their counselors on the property.
- Mr. Garcia went to the camp's headquarters and talked to the director, Dr. Liu, who was very nice. However, Dr. Liu told Mr. Garcia that it was his understanding that the land belonged to DNWC.
- Mr. Garcia did not spend the night at the property that night, but he did spend the next night there after the children left. No one from DNWC asked him to leave.
- Although over the years the land around the lake has become more and more developed, the area on which the camp is located

> is still relatively undeveloped. Most of the property owners use their land only during the summer.
>
> Because I am not familiar with Washington State law, can you please research this issue for me? Under Washington State law, can DNWC claim title to Mr. Garcia's land through adverse possession?

§ 8.2   Researching the Law

Unlike the first memo, which involved an issue governed by a state statute, this problem is governed by common law. To see how to research this problem using free sources, Lexis Advance®, WestlawNext™, Bloomberg Law, Lexis .com®, or Westlaw® Classic, go to *http://www.aspenlawschool.com/books/ oates_legalwritinghandbook/* and type in the access code that is on the card that came with this book. One you are on the website, click on the links to Sections 7.4.1-7.4.7.

§ 8.3   Understanding What You Have Found

A word to the wise: Do not put off analyzing and synthesizing the cases until you "finish" your research. Although in this book we talk about research, analysis, and writing in separate chapters, in practice they are part of a single, and often recursive, process.

§ 8.3.1   Organize Your Research Notes

Although there are many ways to organize your research notes, one way that works well is to record your findings using a research log like the one set out in Example 1. Although you can cut and paste the general and specific rules from the cases into your log, take the time to write your own "case briefs" for the cases you think you may want to use as analogous cases. In addition, as you think of them, write down arguments that each side might make.

EXAMPLE 1   **Research Log for Memo 2**

Issue: Whether DNWC has obtained a right to Mr. Garcia's land through adverse possession?
Type of Law: State common law and statutes
Jurisdiction: Washington

Introductory Section

General Rules

■ *ITT Rayonier, Inc. v. Bell*, **112 Wn.2d 754, 774 P.2d 6 (1989) (cite checked; still good law)**

Quote from pages 757-58:
"In order to establish a claim of adverse possession, there must be possession that is: (1) open and notorious, (2) actual and uninterrupted, (3) exclusive, and (4) hostile. *Chaplin v. Sanders*, 100 Wash.2d 853, 857, 676 P.2d 431 (1984). Possession of the property with each of the necessary concurrent elements must exist for the statutorily prescribed period of 10 years. RCW 4.16.020."

■ *Chaplin v. Sanders*, **100 Wn.2d 853, 676 P.2d 431 (1984) (cite checked; still good law)**

Quote from page 857:
"In order to establish a claim of adverse possession, the possession must be: 1) exclusive, 2) actual and uninterrupted, 3) open and notorious and 4) hostile and under a claim of right made in good faith."

■ *Riley v. Andres*, **107 Wn. App. 391, 27 P.3d 618 (2001) (cite checked; still good law)**

Quote from page 395:
"To claim title to property by adverse possession, a party must possess the property for 10 years in a manner that is actual, uninterrupted, open and notorious, exclusive, and hostile."

■ **RCW 4.16.020. Actions to be commenced within 10 years—Exception (cite checked; this is the applicable version of the statute)**

"The period prescribed for the commencement of actions shall be as follows:
Within 10 years:
(1) For actions for the recovery of real property, or for the recovery of the possession thereof; and no action shall be maintained for such recovery unless it appears that the plaintiff, his or her ancestor, predecessor or grantor was seized or possessed of the premises in question within ten years before the commencement of the action."

Burden of Proof

■ *ITT Rayonier, Inc. v. Bell*, **112 Wn.2d 754, 774 P.2d 6 (1989) (cite checked; still good law)**

Quote from pages 757-58:
"As the presumption of possession is in the holder of legal title, *Peeples v. Port of Bellingham*, 93 Wash.2d 766, 773, 613 P.2d 1128 (1980), *overruled on other grounds, Chaplin v. Sanders, supra,* the party claiming to have adversely possessed the property has the burden of establishing the existence of each element. **758 Skansi v. Novak*, 84 Wash. 39, 44, 146 P. 160 (1915), *overruled on other grounds, Chaplin v. Sanders, supra.*"

Other General Rules

■ *Chaplin v. Sanders*, **100 Wn.2d 853, 676 P.2d 431 (1984) (cite checked; still good law)**

Quote from page 863:
"[A]dverse possession is a mixed question of law and fact. Whether the essential facts exist is for the trier of fact; but whether the facts, as found, constitute adverse possession is for the court to determine as a matter of law." *Peeples v. Port of Bellingham, supra* at 771, 613 P.2d 1128.

Policies Underlying Doctrine

■ *Chaplin v. Sanders*, 100 Wn.2d 853, 676 P.2d 431 (1984) (cite checked; still good law)

Quote from pages 859-60:

"The doctrine of adverse possession was formulated at law for the purpose of, among others, assuring maximum utilization of land, encouraging the rejection of stale claims and, most importantly, quieting titles. 7 R. Powell, *Real Property* ¶ 1012[3] (1982); C. Callahan, *Adverse Possession* 91-94 (1961). Because the doctrine was formulated at law and not at equity, it was originally intended to protect both those who knowingly appropriated the land of others and those who honestly entered and held possession in full belief that the land was their own. R. Powell, at ¶ 1013[2]; C. Callahan, at 49-50; 3 Am.Jur.2d *Advancements* § 104 (1962). Thus, when the original purpose of the adverse possession doctrine is considered, it becomes apparent that the claimant's motive in possessing the land is irrelevant and no inquiry should be made into his guilt or innocence. *Accord Springer v. Durette*, 217 Or. 196, 342 P.2d 132 (1959); *Agers v. Reynolds*, 306 S.W.2d 506 (Mo.1957); *Fulton v. Rapp*, 59 Ohio Law Abs. 105, 98 N.E.2d 430 (1950); *see also* Stoebuck, *The Law of Adverse Possession in Washington*, 35 Wash. L. Rev. 53, 76-80 (1960)."

1. Open and Notorious

A.　Specific Rules

Riley v. Andres, 107 Wn. App. 391, 27 P.3d 618 (2001) (cite checked; still good law)

Quote from page 396:

"A claimant can satisfy the open and notorious element by showing either (1) that the title owner had actual notice of the adverse use throughout the statutory period or (2) that the claimant used the land such that any reasonable person would have thought he owned it."

Anderson v. Hudak, 80 Wn. App. 398, 907 P.2d 305 (1995) (cite checked; still good law)

Quote from pages 404-05:

"The open and notorious requirement is met if (1) the true owner has actual notice of the adverse use throughout the statutory period, or (2) the claimant uses the land so any reasonable person would assume that the claimant is the owner."

B.　Analogous Cases

Element Met:

Riley v. Andres, 107 Wn. App. 391, 397, 27 P.3d 618 (2001) (cite checked; still good law)

Facts:

The claimants planted trees and shrubs and maintained land up to the point where the title owners' landscaping began. In particular, the claimants watered and pruned the plants, spread beauty bark, and pulled weeds.

Holding:

Although the court set out the two-part test listed above, it applied a slightly different test. It began by stating that a party who claims adverse possession must show that its use is that of a true owner. It then states that the landscaping was the typical use of land of that character.

Element Not Met:

Anderson v. Hudak, 80 Wn. App. 398, 907 P.2d 305 (1995) (cite checked; still good law)

Facts:

The claimant (Anderson) planted a row of trees on a fifteen-foot strip of land that she thought belonged to her. There was, however, no evidence establishing that she did anything else on the land.

Holding:

The court stated that there was no evidence establishing that any of the true owners had actual notice of her possession of the trees. In addition, the court stated that the evidence was insufficient to establish that Anderson had used the land so that any reasonable person would assume that the claimant was the owner. Thus, the appellate court held that there was insufficient evidence to support the trial court's finding that Anderson's possession was open and notorious. *Id.* at 405.

C.   DNWC's Arguments

Letter provided Mr. Garcia with actual knowledge that DNWC was using his land.

The way in which DNWC used the land would have led any reasonable person to assume that it owned the land. In fact, the DNWC director seemed to think that DNWC owns the land.

Our case is more like *Riley* than *Anderson*. DNWC did more with the land than the Rileys did, and the court held that the Rileys' use of the land was sufficient to establish that their use was open and notorious.

D.   Garcia's Arguments

It does not appear as if Garcia has an argument on actual notice. A court would probably find that the letter gave Mr. Garcia actual notice. However, even if the letter is not enough to establish actual notice, DNWC's acts are probably enough to establish that a reasonable person would have thought that DNWC owned the land.

2. Actual and Uninterrupted

A.   Specific Rules

[The rest of the log is not shown.]

---

§ 8.3.2   Make Sure You Understand the Big Picture

Before you start to write, take a step back and make sure that you see the big picture. For instance, in Garcia's case, do you understand the policies underlying the doctrine of adverse possession? Historically, why did the courts create the doctrine? Why have most state legislatures left the common law rules intact, only enacting statutes that set out the time period for which the common law elements must be met?

§ 8.3.3   Make Sure You Understand the Common Law Rule and Any Applicable Statutes

In addition to making sure that you understand the big picture, make sure that you understand the common law rule. If the common law rule is complicated, diagram it using the same techniques that you would use to diagram a complicated statute. If the common law rule is not complicated, simply read the rule carefully, making sure that you know how many elements there are and whether those elements are connected by an "and" or an "or." Finally, make sure that you understand the relationship between the common law rule and any statutes that might apply. For example, in the Garcia case, make sure that you understand the relationship between the common law rule, which lists the elements, and the statutes, which list the time periods for which the elements must be met.

§ 8.3.4   Make Sure You Understand the Burden of Proof

In many cases, the determinative factor is the burden of proof. Therefore, make sure that you know which side has the burden of proof and what that burden is.

While in most civil cases the plaintiff has the burden of proof, that is not true in adverse possession cases. In adverse possession cases, the party claiming the property through adverse possession has the burden of proof regardless of whether it filed the action claiming title to the land through adverse possession or whether it was the true owner who filed an action to quiet title. There is only one exception: If the claimant proves that it used the land as if the land were its own, then the true owner has the burden of proving that that use was permissive.

§ 8.3.5   Make Sure You Understand the Specific Rules and the Cases that Have Applied Those Rules

Finally, make sure you understand the law. Sometimes, this part of the process is easy: The courts have set out, clearly and concisely, the rules that they apply in determining whether a particular element is met, and the courts apply those rules consistently. Unfortunately, however, this is not always the case. Sometimes the rules are complicated, sometimes the courts set out what seem to be conflicting rules, and sometimes the courts set out one rule but seem to apply a different one. In addition, in some situations, it can be difficult to distinguish between the test for one element and the test for another element. An example of this type of situation is adverse possession: In many states, the tests for actual possession, open and notorious, and hostile are very similar.

To make sure that you understand the specific rules and the cases that have interpreted and applied them, look first at that section of your research log in which you have set out the specific rules for a particular element. In discussing that element, do all of the courts set out the same rule? If they do, you have the rule. If, though, different courts seem to be setting out different rules, your job is more difficult. Begin by rereading the specific rules. Are the courts setting out the same rule using different language, or are they setting out different rules? If the courts are setting out the same rules using different language, you have the rule.

If, though, the courts are setting out different rules, you need to try to reconcile the courts' statements. Are the courts doing what the Washington Supreme Court did in *Chaplin v. Sanders* and overruling or abandoning one rule and adopting a new one? If they are, you need to determine which rule applies in your client's case. In the alternative, do different divisions of the same court apply different rules, or do the courts apply different rules in different types of situations? For instance, does Division I of the Washington Court of Appeals apply one rule and Division II a different rule, or do all of the divisions apply one rule when the land is in a rural area and another rule when the land is in an urban area?

Once you have figured out the specific rules, look at how the courts have applied the rules in the analogous cases. Do the courts apply the rules they set out? If they do not, what is the difference between the rules they set out and the rules they apply? Also look at the issue that was before the court. Was the issue whether the trial court erred in granting summary judgment? If it was, the appellate court will review the issue de novo and apply the same test that the trial court applied in deciding whether to grant or deny the motion. Keep in mind, though, that a decision that the trial court erred does not mean that the other side wins; instead, in most instances, it means that the appellate court will remand the case for a trial on the merits. In contrast, if the issue is whether there was sufficient evidence to support the jury's verdict, then the appellate court's review is much more limited. If there is sufficient evidence to support the jury's verdict, the appellate court cannot substitute its judgment for the judgment of the jury.

After you have analyzed all of the elements, compare them, making sure that you understand the difference between the specific rules for each of the elements. An easy way to do this part of the analysis is to make a chart in which you compare the specific rule for each element. See Example 2.

| **EXAMPLE 2** | **Chart Comparing Specific Rules** |

Open and Notorious	**Actual and Uninterrupted**	**Exclusive**	**Hostile**
The open and notorious requirement is met if (1) the true owner has actual notice of the adverse use throughout the statutory period, <u>or</u> (2) the claimant uses the land so any reasonable person would assume that the claimant is the owner. *Riley v. Andres*, 107 Wn. App. 391, 396, 27 P.3d 618 (2001).	The Washington courts have not set out a test for actual possession. 17 *Wash. Prac., Real Estate: Property Law* § 8.10 (2d ed.) In discussing "uninterrupted," the courts have held that the claimants' use was "continuous" even though they used the property only during the summer. The requisite possession requires such possession and dominion as ordinarily marks the conduct of owners in general in holding, managing, and caring for property of a like nature and condition. *Howard v. Kunto,* 3 Wn. App. 393, 477 P.2d 210 (1970).	"While possession of property by a party seeking to establish ownership of it by adverse possession need not be absolutely exclusive," "the possession must be of a type that would be expected of an owner. . . ." *ITT Rayonier*, 112 Wn.2d 754, 758, 774 P.2d 6 (1989).	"The 'hostility/claim of right' element of adverse possession requires only that the claimant treat the land as his own as against the world throughout the statutory period. The nature of his possession will be determined solely on the basis of the manner in which he treats the property. His subjective belief regarding his true interest in the land and his intent to dispossess or not dispossess another is irrelevant to this determination. Under this analysis, permission to occupy the land, given by the true title owner to the claimant or his predecessors in interest, will still operate to negate the element of hostility. The traditional presumptions still apply to the extent that they are not inconsistent with this ruling." *ITT Rayonier*, 112 Wn.2d at 761.

> **PRACTICE POINTER** If you have trouble distinguishing the test used for one element from the test used for another element, look for a case, a law review article, or a practice book that explains how the elements are the same and how they are different.

§ 8.4   Drafting the Heading

As you discovered in drafting your first memo, drafting the heading is easy: Just complete the "To," "From," "Date," and "Re" blocks. If the memo will only be filed in the client's file, the "Re" entry can be quite general. If, however, the memo will be filed not only in the client's file but also in a "memo bank," include words that will allow other people in your office who are researching similar issues to find your memo.

EXAMPLE 1   **Example 1   Sample Heading**

To: Supervising Attorney

From: Your name

Date: November 2, 2013

Re: Michael Garcia
        Adverse Possession; Washington Law

---

§ 8.5   Drafting the Statement of Facts

In drafting the statement of facts for this chapter's sample memo, use the same process that we used in drafting the statement of facts for Memo 1, which is set out in Chapter 7: (1) identify the legally significant, emotionally significant, background, and unknown facts; (2) select an organizational scheme; and (3) present the facts accurately and objectively.

§ 8.5.1   Decide What Facts to Include

To identify the legally significant facts, create a chart similar to the one set out below. In the first column, list the elements, and in the second column list the facts that the court would consider in determining whether those elements are met. For more on identifying the legally significant facts, see section 7.5.1a.

EXAMPLE 1	**Chart Listing Elements and the Facts that the Court Would Consider in Deciding Whether the Element Is Met**

Elements	Facts that the Court Would Consider in Deciding Whether the Element Is Met
Open and Notorious	
Actual and Uninterrupted	
Exclusive	
Hostile	

To identify the emotionally significant facts, think about which facts might influence a judge's or a jury's decision. In Garcia's case, is the fact that the claimant is a group of doctors and nurses that is running a camp for ill and disabled children likely to influence the jury's or the judge's decision? If it is, then you should include that fact in the statement of facts. Similarly, is the fact that the land has been in Mr. Garcia's family for more than fifty years something that will influence the judge's or the jury's decision? If it is, you should include that fact in your statement of facts. For more on identifying the emotionally significant facts, see section 7.5.1b.

Finally, identify the facts that you need to tell the story and the unknown facts. If you cannot analyze the issue without the unknown facts, ask your supervising attorney for permission to obtain those facts. If, however, you can analyze the issue without the unknown facts, do so. For more on identifying background and unknown facts, see section 7.5.1c and d.

§ 8.5.2   Select an Organizational Scheme

Once you have decided which facts need to be included, select an organizational scheme. As you learned in Chapter 7, the two most common organizational schemes are chronological and topical.

If you use a chronological organizational scheme, set out the facts in date order: Start the story with Mr. Garcia's grandfather giving the land to Mr. Garcia, and end with Mr. Garcia's visit to the property. In contrast, if you use a topical organizational scheme, set out the facts relating to the Garcia property in one paragraph or block of paragraphs, the facts relating to DNWC's property and DNWC's use of the Garcia property in a second paragraph or block of paragraphs, and the facts relating to the dispute in a third paragraph or block of paragraphs. In all instances, start the statement of facts with a paragraph in which you identify the parties and the issue.

EXAMPLE 2	Statement of Facts Written Using a Chronological Organizational Scheme

Michael Garcia has contacted our office regarding property that he owns in Washington State. Mr. Garcia is concerned that the organization that owns the property next to his, Doctors and Nurses Who Care (DNWC), may be able to claim title to his property through adverse possession.

Mr. Garcia's property is on Lake Chelan in eastern Washington. Mr. Garcia's grandfather, Eduardo Montoya, purchased the two-acre waterfront parcel in 1958, and the family used the land every summer from 1958 until Eduardo Montoya became ill in the early 1990s. When they used the land, the family would camp on the site and use a small dock for swimming, fishing, and boating.

In 1996, DNWC purchased the five-acre parcel that adjoins Mr. Montoya's property. Since 1997, DNWC has used its land as a summer camp for children with serious illnesses or disabilities. In a typical summer, DNWC runs two one-week camps for children with cancer, two one-week camps for children who are blind, two one-week camps for children with autism, and two one-week camps for children with diabetes.

Most of the time the children stay in cabins located on DNWC property. However, DNWC uses the Garcia property for "campouts." One night each week, one group of about 10 children will camp out in tents on Mr. Garcia's property; the next night another group of 10 will camp out on his property, and so on. Thus, DNWC has been using the Garcia property four or five nights a week for eight weeks each summer since 1997. During these campouts, the children pitch and stay in tents, cook over a fire, and use the dock. To facilitate these campouts, DNWC has maintained the campsite, the fire area, the outhouse, and the dock.

In 1999, Mr. Garcia's grandfather died and left the property to him. Although Mr. Garcia spent one weekend at the property in the fall of 1999, he moved to California in 2000 and did not visit the property again until last August. He has, however, continued to pay all of the taxes and assessments.

In February 2001, DNWC sent Mr. Garcia a letter asking him whether it could continue using his land for campouts. Mr. Garcia was busy and did not respond to the letter. Sometime during the summer of 2001, DNWC posted a no trespassing sign on the dock, and the sign is still there.

Last August Mr. Garcia visited the property with the intention of spending a few days camping on the lake. When he got there, he discovered children and their counselors on the property.

After discovering the children on his land, Mr. Garcia went to DNWC's camp headquarters and talked to the director, Dr. Liu, who told Mr. Garcia that it was his understanding that the land belonged to DNWC. Although Mr. Garcia did not spend that night on the property, he did spend the next night there after the children left. DNWC did not ask him to leave.

Although over the years the land around the lake has become more and more developed, the area in which the camp is located is still relatively undeveloped. Most of the property owners use their land only during the summer.

EXAMPLE 3	Statement of Facts Written Using a Topical Organizational Scheme

Michael Garcia has contacted our office regarding property that he owns in Washington State. Mr. Garcia is concerned that the organization that owns the property next to his, Doctors and Nurses Who Care (DNWC), may be able to claim title to his property through adverse possession.

Mr. Garcia's property is located on Lake Chelan in eastern Washington. Mr. Garcia's grandfather, Eduardo Montoya, purchased the two-acre waterfront parcel in 1958. From 1958 until Eduardo Montoya became ill in the early 1990s, the family used the land every summer. The family would camp on the site and use a small dock for swimming, fishing, and boating. In 1999, Mr. Garcia's grandfather died and left the property to Mr. Garcia. Although Mr. Garcia spent one weekend on the property in 1999, he moved to California in 2000 and did not visit the property from 1999 until last August. He has, however, continued to pay all of the taxes and assessments.

DNWC purchased the five-acre parcel that is to the north of Mr. Garcia's property in 1996. Since 1997, DNWC has used its land for a summer camp for children who suffer from serious illnesses and disabilities. In a typical summer, DNWC runs two one-week camps for children with cancer, two one-week camps for children who are blind, two one-week camps for children with autism, and two one-week camps for children with diabetes. While normally the children stay in cabins located on DNWC property, DNWC uses Mr. Garcia's property for "campouts." For example, on one night of the week, one group of about 10 children will camp out in tents on Mr. Garcia's property, the next night another group of 10 will camp out on his property, and so on. During these campouts, the children pitch and stay in tents and cook over a fire. To facilitate these campouts, DNWC has maintained the campsites, the fire area, the outhouse, and the dock. In the summer of 2001, DNWC posted a no trespassing sign on the dock, and the sign is still there.

In February 2001, DNWC sent a letter to Mr. Garcia asking him if it could continue using his land for campouts. Mr. Garcia was busy and never responded to the letter.

Late last August, Mr. Garcia visited the property with the intention of spending a few days camping on the lake. When he got there, he discovered children and their counselors on the property. Upon making this discovery, Mr. Garcia went to DNWC's camp headquarters and talked to the director, Dr. Liu, who was very nice. However, Dr. Liu told Mr. Garcia that the land belonged to DNWC. Although Mr. Garcia did not spend that night on his property, he did spend the next night there after the children had gone. DNWC did not ask him to leave.

While the land around the lake has become more and more developed, the area in which the camp is located is still relatively undeveloped. Most of the property owners only use their land during the summer.

§ 8.5.3   Present the Facts Accurately and Objectively

Finally, in writing the statement of facts, make sure that you present the facts accurately and objectively. Do not set out facts that are not in your case file; do not set out legal conclusions; and do not present the facts in a light that favors your client or the other side.

§ 8.5.4   Checklist for Critiquing the Statement of Facts

a.   Content

- The writer has included all of the legally significant facts.
- When appropriate, the writer has included emotionally significant facts.
- The writer has included enough background facts that a person not familiar with the case can understand what happened.
- The writer has identified the unknown facts.
- The writer has presented the facts accurately.
- The writer has presented the facts objectively.
- The writer has not included legal conclusions in the statement of facts.

b. Organization

- The writer has included an introductory sentence or paragraph that identifies the parties and the nature of the dispute.
- The writer has used one of the conventional organizational schemes: chronological, topical, or a combination of chronological and topical.

c. Writing

- The attorney can understand the facts of the case after reading the statement of facts once.
- The paragraph divisions are logical, and the paragraphs are neither too long nor too short.
- Transitions and dovetailing have been used to make the connection between ideas clear.
- In most sentences, the writer has used the actor as the subject of the sentence, and the subject and verb are close together.
- The writer has varied the length of the sentences and the sentence patterns so that each sentence flows smoothly from the prior sentence.
- The writing is concise and precise.
- The writing is grammatically correct and correctly punctuated.
- The statement of facts has been proofread.

§ 8.6   Drafting the Issue Statement

§ 8.6.1   Select a Format: The "Whether" Format

Although the "under-does-when" format is the easiest format to use, some attorneys prefer the more traditional "whether" format. When you use the "whether" format, begin your issue statement with the word "whether" and then set out the legal question and the key facts. Although you do not need to include a reference to the rule of law, you may incorporate one into your statement of the legal question.

Compare the following examples. In Example 1 the writer uses the "under-does-when" format, and in Examples 2 and 3 the writers use the "whether" format. While in Examples 1 and 2 the writers use the parties' names, in Example 3 the writer uses more generic labels.

EXAMPLE 1   **Issue Statement Written Using the "Under-Does-When" Format, the Parties' Names, and Enumeration**

Issue

Under Washington common law, has Doctors and Nurses Who Care (DNWC) obtained a right to Mr. Garcia's land through adverse possession when (1) DNWC has used the land for campouts several nights a week for eight weeks each summer since 1997; (2) to facilitate these campouts, DNWC has maintained the campsites, fire area, outhouse, and dock; (3) in 2001, DNWC sent a letter to Mr. Garcia asking him if it could continue using the land for campouts, but Mr. Garcia did not respond to the letter; and (4) Mr. Garcia has paid the taxes but did not visit the land from 1999 until August 2013?

EXAMPLE 2	**Issue Statement Written Using the "Whether" Format, the Parties' Names, and Enumeration**

Issue

Whether Doctors and Nurses Who Care (DNWC) has obtained a right to Mr. Garcia's land through adverse possession when (1) DNWC has used the land for campouts several nights a week for eight weeks each summer since 1997; (2) to facilitate these campouts, DNWC has maintained the campsites, fire area, outhouse, and dock; (3) in 2001, DNWC sent a letter to Mr. Garcia asking him if it could continue using the land for campouts, but Mr. Garcia did not respond to the letter; and (4) Mr. Garcia has paid the taxes but did not visit the land from 1999 until August 2013.

EXAMPLE 3	**Issue Statement Written Using the "Whether" Format But Not the Names of the Parties or Enumeration**

Issue

Whether a claimant may obtain a right to land through adverse possession when the claimant used the disputed land for campouts several nights a week for eight weeks each summer since 1997; when the claimant has maintained the campsites, fire area, outhouse, and dock; when the claimant sent a letter to the title owner asking him if it could continue using the land for campouts but the title owner did not respond to the letter; and when the title owner has paid the taxes but did not visit the land for more than 10 years.

---

§ 8.6.2   Make Sure Your Issue Statement Is Easy to Read

As we stated in section 7.6.2, it is not enough to include the right information in your issue statement. You must also present that information in a way that is easy to read.

One key to making an issue statement easy to read is to use the subject, verb, and object slots in the issue statement for the legal question.

Look again at Examples 1, 2, and 3 set out above.

EXAMPLE 4	**Subject-Verb-Object for Examples 1 and 2**

DNWC	has obtained	a right
subject	*verb*	*object*

EXAMPLE 5	**Subject-Verb-Object for Example 3**

claimant	has obtained	a right
subject	*verb*	*object*

In addition, in listing the key facts, remember to use parallel constructions for all of the items in the list. If you are not sure whether the items in the list are parallel, try setting them out in a vertical list. See Example 6.

EXAMPLE 6　　　**Key Facts Set Out in a Vertical List**

Whether Doctors and Nurses Who Care (DNWC) has obtained a right to Mr. Garcia's land through adverse possession when

(1) DNWC has used the land for campouts several nights a week for eight weeks each summer since 1994;

(2) to facilitate these campouts, DNWC has maintained the campsites, fire area, outhouse, and dock;

(3) in 2001, DNWC sent a letter to Mr. Garcia asking him if it could continue using the land for campouts, but Mr. Garcia did not respond to the letter; and

(4) Mr. Garcia has paid the taxes but did not visit the land from 1999 until August 2013.

Once you have created the list, compare the items. Do all of the items have the same grammatical structure? For instance, in the example, can each item stand by itself as a complete sentence?

Finally, check your punctuation. First, as a general rule, do not include a colon unless the material before the colon is grammatically complete, that is, it has a subject, verb, and object. Second, if the items in your list are long or have internal commas, use semicolons to separate the items, including the next to the last and the last items in your list.

EXAMPLE 7　　　**Issue Statement that Is Punctuated Correctly**

Whether Doctors and Nurses Who Care (DNWC) has obtained a right to Mr. Garcia's land through adverse possession when (1) DNWC has used the land for campouts several nights a week for eight weeks each summer since 1997; (2) to facilitate these campouts, DNWC has maintained the campsites, fire area, outhouse, and dock; (3) in 2001, DNWC sent a letter to Mr. Garcia asking him if it could continue using the land for campouts, but Mr. Garcia did not respond to the letter; and (4) Mr. Garcia has paid the taxes but did not visit the land from 1999 until August 2013.

PRACTICE POINTER　At first, some writers are bothered by the fact that issue statements written using the "whether" format are incomplete sentences. If you are one of those writers, remember that the "whether" is shorthand for "The question is whether . . ." Because a "whether" issue statement is a statement and not a question, put a period and not a question mark at the end.

§ 8.6.3   Checklist for Critiquing the Issue Statement

a.   Content

- The reference to the rule of law is neither too broad nor too narrow.
- The legal question is properly focused.
- The most significant of the legally significant facts have been included.
- Legal conclusions have not been set out as facts.

b.   Format

- The writer has used one of the conventional formats, for example, the "under-does-when" format or the "whether" format.

c.   Writing

- The issue statement is easy to read and understand.
- In setting out the legal question, the writer has used a concrete subject and an action verb.
- In listing the facts, the writer has used parallel constructions for all of the items in the list.
- If the list of facts is long, the writer has used enumeration or has repeated key structural cues, for examples, words like "when" and "that."

§ 8.7   Drafting the Brief Answer

§ 8.7.1   Use One of the Conventional Formats

As we explained in Chapter 7, the brief answer answers the question asked in the issue statement. By convention, most brief answers begin with a one- or two-word answer, which is followed by a one-, two-, or three-sentence explanation.

In writing the brief answer, think about what you would tell the attorney if he or she stopped you in the hallway and asked you for a quick answer.

Attorney: Has DNWC obtained a right to Mr. Garcia's property through adverse possession?

You: It looks as if it may have. DNWC can easily prove that its possession was open and notorious, actual and uninterrupted, and exclusive. In addition, it looks like DNWC can prove that its possession was hostile. It has been using the property as if it were its own and, because Mr. Garcia did not respond to the letter asking for permission, DNWC has a good argument that its use was not permissive.

EXAMPLE 1   **Example 1   Brief Answer**

Brief Answer

Probably. DNWC can easily prove that its possession was open and notorious, actual and uninterrupted, and exclusive. In addition, DNWC can probably prove that its possession was hostile: It used the land as a true owner would have used it and, although initially it may have been using the property with either the permission of Mr. Garcia's grandfather or Mr. Garcia, it appears that it has been using the property without permission since 1999. Because all of the elements are met for the statutory period, which is 10 years, DNWC has a right to the land through adverse possession.

PRACTICE POINTER	Before you include a brief answer, check with your supervising attorney to see whether he or she wants one in the memo.

§ 8.7.2   Checklist for Critiquing the Brief Answer

a.   Content

- The writer has predicted but not guaranteed how the issue will be decided.
- The writer has briefly explained his or her prediction, for example, the writer has explained which elements will be easy to prove and which will be more difficult and why.

b.   Format

- A separate brief answer has been included for each issue statement.
- The answer begins with a one- or two-word short answer. This one- or two-word short answer is then followed by a short explanation.

c.   Writing

- The brief answer is easy to read and understand.
- Most of the sentences have concrete subjects and action verbs.
- There are no grammatical or punctuation errors.

§ 8.8   Drafting the Discussion Section Using an Integrated Format

Sometimes novice legal writers ask which is better to use: the script format used in the memo in Chapter 7 or the more integrated format used in the memo in this chapter. Like so much else in law, the answer is "it depends." While some attorneys prefer the script format because it is easy to see what each side will argue, other attorneys prefer a more integrated format because memos written using an integrated format are shorter. Consequently, as a law clerk or new attorney, you need to know how to organize a memo using both formats.

The script and integrated formats have much in common. For example, when the problem involves an elements analysis, the large-scale organization is the same. Regardless of whether you use a script or integrated format, you will begin the discussion section with an introductory section in which you set out the general rule. In addition, regardless of which format you use, you will then walk the attorney through the elements one by one, spending less time on those that are not in dispute and more time on those that are.

Finally, your discussion of the disputed elements will include the same types of information: rules, descriptions of analogous cases, arguments or analysis, and conclusions.

In fact, the script and integrated format differ from each other in only two ways. The first difference is a difference in the way that you organize your analysis of the disputed elements. When you use the script format, you present the information using inductive reasoning. You set out the specific rules, illustrate how those rules have been applied in analogous cases, set out each side's arguments, and end by setting out your conclusion. In contrast, when you use an integrated format, you use deductive reasoning and set out your conclusion before your reasoning. See Example 1.

EXAMPLE 1	Inductive vs. Deductive Reasoning

Script Format **Inductive Reasoning** **(specific to general)**	**Integrated Format** **Deductive Reasoning** **(general to specific)**
Specific Rules	Specific Rules
Descriptions of Analogous Cases	Descriptions of Analogous Cases
Party with Burden of Proof's Arguments	Mini-Conclusion/Prediction
■ First Argument ■ Second Argument ■ Third Argument	Reasoning
	■ First Reason (Summarize and evaluate each side's arguments)
Responding Party's Arguments	■ Second Reason (Summarize and evaluate each side's arguments)
■ First Argument ■ Second Argument ■ Third Argument	■ Third Reason (Summarize and evaluate each side's arguments)
Rebuttal (if any)	
Mini-Conclusion/Prediction	

The second difference is a difference in perspective. When you use a script format, your role is similar to that of a writer setting out the script for an oral argument. In contrast, when you write a memo using a more integrated format, you assume a perspective that is similar to that of a judge drafting an opinion. After setting out the specific rules and analogous cases, you set out your conclusion and then your reasoning. In doing so, you do what most judges do. You summarize each side's arguments and then explain why one side's arguments are more persuasive than the other side's.

Example 2 illustrates the ways in which the script and integrated formats are the same and different.

EXAMPLE 2   **Same Discussion Using the Script and an Integrated Format**

Script Format	Integrated Format
Introductory Section	**Introductory Section**
■ If one or both sides will make a policy argument, describe the policies underlying the statute or rule. ■ Introduce and set out the applicable statute(s) or common law rule. ■ Explain which side has the burden of proof and what that burden is. ■ Set out any other rules that apply to all of the elements. ■ End the introduction by providing the attorney with a roadmap for the rest of the discussion.	■ If one or both sides will make a policy argument, describe the policies underlying the statute or rule. ■ Introduce and set out the applicable statute(s) or common law rule. ■ Explain which side has the burden of proof and what that burden is. ■ Set out any other rules that apply to all of the elements. ■ End the introduction by providing the attorney with a roadmap for the rest of the discussion.
A. First Element (not in dispute)	**A. First Element (not in dispute)**
■ Set out and apply applicable rule.	■ Set out and apply the applicable rule.
B. Second Element (in dispute)	**B. Second Element (in dispute)**

■ Specific rules for second element
■ Examples of how specific rules have been applied in analogous cases
■ Arguments
   ■ Party with burden of proof's arguments
   ■ Responding party's arguments
■ Mini-conclusion for second element
	■ Specific rules for second element
	■ Examples of how specific rules have been applied in analogous cases
	■ Mini-conclusion/prediction
	■ Reasoning
	
	Note: Instead of setting out the cases in a separate section, you can integrate them into the reasoning.

C. Third Element (in dispute)	**C. Third Element (in dispute)**

■ Specific rules for third element
■ Examples of how specific rules have been applied in analogous cases
■ Arguments
   ■ Party with burden of proof's arguments
   ■ Responding party's arguments
■ Mini-conclusion for third element
	■ Specific rules for third element
	■ Examples of how specific rules have been applied in analogous cases
	■ Mini-conclusion/prediction
	■ Reasoning
	
	Note: Instead of setting out the cases in a separate section, you can integrate them into the reasoning.

PRACTICE POINTER   The discussion of a disputed element written using the integrated format should contain the same information as a discussion of that element written using the script format. If you are leaving out information, you are doing something wrong.

§ 8.8.1   Draft the Specific Rule Section

The specific rule section is the same regardless of whether you use the script or the integrated format. Set out more general rules before more specific rules and exceptions, do more than just string together a series of quotes, and include a citation to authority for each rule that you set out. For more on drafting the specific rule section, see section 7.8.4a.

EXAMPLE 3   **Specific Rule Section for a Discussion Section Written Using the Script Format and for a Discussion Section Written Using an Integrated Format**

Specific Rules—Script Format	Specific Rules—Integrated Format
D. Hostile	**D. Hostile**
Since 1984, the claimant's subjective intent has been irrelevant. *Chaplin v. Sanders*, 100 Wn.2d 853, 860-61, 676 P.2d 431 (1984) (overruling cases in which the courts considered the claimant's subjective intent). Thus, under current Washington law, the claimant must prove only that it used the land as if it were its own for the statutory period. *Id.; Miller v. Anderson*, 91 Wn. App. 822, 828, 964 P.2d 365 (1998). If the claimant proves that it used the land as if it were its own, the use was hostile unless the true owner can prove that it gave the claimant permission to use the land. *Id.*	Since 1984, the claimant's subjective intent has been irrelevant. *Chaplin v. Sanders*, 100 Wn.2d 853, 860-61, 676 P.2d 431 (1984) (overruling cases in which the courts considered the claimant's subjective intent). Thus, under current Washington law, the claimant must prove only that it used the land as if it were its own for the statutory period. *Id.; Miller v. Anderson*, 91 Wn. App. 822, 828, 964 P.2d 365 (1998). If the claimant proves that it used the land as if it were its own, the use was hostile unless the true owner can prove that it gave the claimant permission to use the land. *Id.*
Permission can be express or implied. *Miller v. Anderson*, 91 Wn. App. at 829, *citing Granston v. Callahan*, 52 Wn. App. 288, 759 P.2d 462 (1988) (case involved a prescriptive easement and not adverse possession). The courts infer that the use was permissive when, under the circumstances, it is reasonable to assume that the use was permitted. *Id.* If there was permission, the party claiming adverse possession bears the burden of proving that permission terminated either because (1) the servient estate changed hands through death or alienation or (2) the claimant has asserted a hostile right. *Id.*	Permission can be express or implied. *Miller v. Anderson*, 91 Wn. App. at 829, *citing Granston v. Callahan*, 52 Wn. App. 288, 759 P.2d 462 (1988) (case involved a prescriptive easement and not adverse possession). The courts infer that the use was permissive when, under the circumstances, it is reasonable to assume that the use was permitted. *Id.* If there was permission, the party claiming adverse possession bears the burden of proving that permission terminated either because (1) the servient estate changed hands through death or alienation or (2) the claimant has asserted a hostile right. *Id.*

PRACTICE POINTER   In setting out citations to authority, you can use parentheticals to provide the attorney with additional information about the cases. For instance, in the preceding example, the writer used a parenthetical to tell the attorney that, in *Chaplin*, the Washington Supreme Court overruled those cases in which the courts had considered the claimant's subjective intent in determining whether the claimant's use was hostile. Similarly, the writer used a parenthetical to tell the attorney that, while the *Miller* court cited *Granston* as authority, *Granston* involved a prescriptive easement and not adverse possession.

§ 8.8.2   Draft the Analogous Case Section

The specific rules section is not the only section that is the same under the script and integrated formats. If you set out the descriptions of analogous cases in a separate analogous case section, that section will be the same regardless of whether you use a script or an integrated format.

In drafting the analogous case section, remember why you are including descriptions of analogous cases. You are not including them to prove that you read cases. Instead, you are including them to provide the attorney with examples of how the specific rules have been applied in cases that are factually similar to your case. As a consequence, to write the analogous case section for a discussion section written using an integrated format, you need to go through the same process that you went through in drafting the analogous case section for a discussion section using a script format: (a) identify the analogous cases; (b) sort the analogous cases, putting the cases in which the element was met in one stack and the cases in which the element was not met in another stack; (c) go through the cases in both stacks, analyzing each case and then synthesizing each group of cases; (d) draft a sentence introducing each group of cases; and (e) draft your case descriptions. For more on each of these steps, see section 7.8.4b.

EXAMPLE 4   **Analogous Case Section for a Discussion Section Written Using the Script Format and for a Discussion Section Written Using an Integrated Format**

Analogous Case Section Script Format	Analogous Case Section Integrated Format
In deciding whether the claimant was using the land as if it were its own, the courts consider whether the claimant made improvements to the land, whether the claimant maintained the property, and whether the claimant used the land on a regular basis. *See, e.g., Chaplin*, 100 Wn.2d at 855-56; *Timberlane*, 79 Wn. App. at 310-11. For example, in *Chaplin*, the court held that the claimants were using the land as if it were their own when the claimants built a road across the disputed land, cleared and maintained the disputed land, installed utility lines, and used the area for recreational activities. *Id.* at 855-56. Similarly, in *Timberlane*, the court held that claimants had used land belonging to the homeowners' association as if it were their own when they built and maintained a fence and a concrete patio and the claimants' children played on the land. *Id.* at 310-11.	In deciding whether the claimant was using the land as if it were its own, the courts consider whether the claimant made improvements to the land, whether the claimant maintained the property, and whether the claimant used the land on a regular basis. *See, e.g., Chaplin*, 100 Wn.2d at 855-56; *Timberlane*, 79 Wn. App. at 310-11. For example, in *Chaplin*, the court held that the claimants were using the land as if it were their own when the claimants built a road across the disputed land, cleared and maintained the disputed land, installed utility lines, and used the area for recreational activities. *Id.* at 855-56. Similarly, in *Timberlane*, the court held that claimants had used land belonging to the homeowners' association as if it were their own when they built and maintained a fence and a concrete patio and the claimants' children played on the land. *Id.* at 310-11.

<table>
<tr><td>**PRACTICE POINTER**</td><td>Remember to use a principle-based topic sentence to introduce each group of cases. For example, include a topic sentence that tells the attorney what principle you are using a group of cases to</td></tr>
</table>

illustrate. In addition, use a transition to tell the attorney whether a second case illustrates the same or different point from the first case.

While most of the time you will want to set out the cases in a separate analogous case section, if the case descriptions are very short, you may want to integrate the case descriptions into your reasoning. See Example 5.

EXAMPLE 5   **Case Description Integrated into Reasoning**

In addition, the court will probably conclude that DNWC's use of the property was uninterrupted. Although DNWC only used the property during the summer, in other cases the courts have held that such use was sufficient. For example, in *Howard v. Kunto*, 3 Wn. App. 393, 397, 477 P.2d 210 (1970), the court held that the claimants' use was continuous even though the claimants only used the beach house during the summer. As the court noted in that case, "the requisite possession requires such possession and dominion 'as ordinarily marks the conduct of owners in general in holding, managing, and caring for property of like nature and condition.'" Therefore, because the land is recreational land, DNWC's use of the land only in summer is consistent with how the owners of similar land hold, manage, and care for their property.

---

§ 8.8.3   Draft the Mini-Conclusion

The first subsection that is different is the mini-conclusion. While in the script format the mini-conclusion goes after the argument, in an integrated format your mini-conclusion goes before your reasoning. Example 6 illustrates the differences.

EXAMPLE 6   **Mini-Conclusion for a Discussion Section Written Using the Script Format and for a Discussion Section Written Using an Integrated Format**

Mini-Conclusion Script Format	Mini-Conclusion Integrated Format
D. Hostile Specific Rules [not shown]	**D. Hostile** Specific Rules [not shown]

Mini-Conclusion Script Format	Mini-Conclusion Integrated Format
Analogous Cases [not shown]	Analogous Cases [not shown]
Arguments [not shown] DNWC's arguments [not shown]	Mini-Conclusion In this case, the court will probably conclude that DNWC has met its burden of proving that its use of the Garcia land was hostile. First, the court will probably conclude that DNWC has met its burden of proving that it used the land as if it were its own. [Rest of reason 1 goes here.]
Mr. Garcia's arguments [not shown]	Second, the court will probably conclude that DNWC's use of the Garcia land was not permissive. [Rest of reason 2 goes here.]
Mini-Conclusion In this case, DNWC appears to have the stronger arguments. First, although DNWC has the burden of proof, it will probably be able to prove that it used Mr. Garcia's land as if it were its own when it maintained and used the campsites, the fire area, the outhouse, and the dock during the peak season. Second, DNWC will probably be able to prove that its use was not permissive. Although it is possible that initially DNWC was using the land with Mr. Garcia's grandfather's permission, that permission terminated when Mr. Garcia's grandfather died and left the property to Mr. Garcia. In addition, even though DNWC asked for permission to continue using the property, Mr. Garcia never responded to that request, and DNWC did an act that indicated its hostile intent when it posted the no trespassing sign and continued to use the property as its own. Third, it seems unlikely that a court would conclude that Mr. Garcia allowed DNWC to use his land as a neighborly accommodation. Although it may not be uncommon for farmers to allow a neighbor to use a driveway, it is uncommon for an owner of recreational land to allow a neighbor to use his land through the peak season. Thus, because DNWC used the property as its own and did an act that would have terminated the permission, the court will probably hold that it has proven that its use was hostile.	Finally, the court will probably conclude that Mr. Garcia did not allow DNWC to use his land as a neighborly accommodation. [Rest of reason 3 goes here.]

> ### PRACTICE POINTER
>
> When you use an integrated format, you can use your mini-conclusion both to set out your conclusion and as a roadmap for the paragraphs setting out your reasoning.

EXAMPLE 7   **Mini-Conclusion Also Acts as a Roadmap for the Reasoning**

In this case, the court will probably conclude that DNWC's use of Mr. Garcia's land was hostile for two reasons: (1) DNWC was using the land as if it were its own, and (2) DNWC's use of Mr. Garcia's land was not permissive.

First, the court will probably conclude that DNWC has met its burden of proving that it used the land as if it were its own. [Rest of the analysis goes here.]

Second, the court will probably conclude that DNWC's use of Mr. Garcia's land was not permissive. [Rest of the analysis goes here.]

---

§ 8.8.4   Draft the Arguments

When you set out the arguments using the script format, you organize the arguments by party. You set out the party with the burden of proof's arguments and then the responding party's arguments. In contrast, when you use an integrated format, you organize the arguments, or analysis, around "reasons." You set out the mini-conclusion and then the first reason, the second reason, and so on.

EXAMPLE 8   **Outline Showing Organizational Scheme for Arguments Presented Using the Script Format and Using an Integrated Format**

Script Format (Arguments organized by party)	Integrated Format (Arguments organized by reasons)
Party with Burden of Proof's Arguments ■ Party with burden of proof's general assertion ■ Party with burden of proof's first subassertion and support for that subassertion ■ Party with burden of proof's second subassertion and support for that subassertion Responding Party's Arguments ■ Responding party's first subassertion and support for that subassertion ■ Responding party's second subassertion and support for that subassertion	Mini-Conclusion Reason 1 ■ Integrated discussion of moving and responding parties' arguments Reason 2 ■ Integrated discussion of moving and responding parties' arguments Reason 3 ■ Integrated discussion of moving and responding parties' arguments

| **EXAMPLE 9** | **"Argument Section" for a Discussion Section Written Using the Script Format and for a Discussion Section Written Using an Integrated Format** |

Arguments **Script Format**	**Conclusions and Reasoning** **Integrated Format**
DNWC can argue that its use of Mr. Garcia's land was hostile because (1) it has treated Mr. Garcia's land as its own and (2) since 1999, it has not had either express or implied permission to use the land. DNWC will begin by arguing that it used the land as if the land were its own. Like the claimants in *Chaplin* and *Timberlane*, DNWC maintained the disputed land: Not only did it maintain the campsites and fire area, but it also maintained the outhouse and the dock. In addition, like the claimants in *Chaplin* and *Timberlane*, DNWC used the property on a regular basis by holding campouts on the land several nights a week for eight weeks every summer. DNWC will also argue that its use was not permissive. Unlike *Granston*, in which the parties were related, in this case there are no facts indicating that any of DNWC's members are related to Mr. Garcia. In addition, unlike the title owners in *Miller* who allowed their neighbors to use their driveway, owners of recreational property do not typically allow their neighbors to use their land throughout the summer months. In contrast, Mr. Garcia can argue that DNWC was not using the property as if it were its own or, even if it was, it was using the land with his implied permission. Mr. Garcia will argue that the facts do not support a conclusion that DNWC was using the land as if it were its own. Although DNWC maintained the campsites, fire area, outhouse, and dock, it did not build any new structures. In addition, although it used the land, it did so for only a few days a week during the summer. Therefore, the facts in this case can be distinguished from the facts in *Chaplin* and *Timberlane*. While in both of those cases, the claimants made substantial improvements to the land, for example, building a road or building a fence and a patio, in this case DNWC did not build anything new. In the alternative, Mr. Garcia can argue that even if DNWC was using the land as if it were its own, it was doing so with his permission. In its 2001 letter to Mr. Garcia, DNWC acknowledged that it was using the land with Mr. Garcia's permission, and it requested permission to continue using the land. Because Mr. Garcia did not revoke his permission, it is reasonable to assume that DNWC used the land with Mr. Garcia's implied permission. Consequently, this case is	The court will probably conclude that DNWC's use of Mr. Garcia's land was hostile. First, the court will probably conclude that DNWC used Mr. Garcia's land as if it were the true owner. Although DNWC did not build any new structures on Mr. Garcia's land, it maintained the campsites, the fire area, the outhouse, and the dock. In addition, although DNWC did not use the property year round, it did use the property during the summer, which is how a typical owner would have used the land. Thus, this case is similar to *Chaplin* and *Timberlane*, in which the claimants maintained and used the disputed land as a true owner would have used it. While in *Chaplin* and *Timberlane* the claimants built new structures (in *Chaplin*, the claimants built a road and, in *Timberlane*, they built a fence and a patio), the courts have held that the claimant does not have to do everything that a title owner might do. Second, the court will probably conclude that DNWC's use of Mr. Garcia's land was not permissive. Unlike *Granston*, in which the parties were related and had a close relationship, there is no evidence that the members of DNWC are related to Mr. Garcia. In addition, unlike *Miller*, in which the title owners allowed the claimants, their neighbors, to use their driveway, the typical owners of recreational land do not allow a neighboring property owner to use their land several days a week during the peak season. While Mr. Garcia can argue that the letter that DNWC sent to him establishes that DNWC's use of the land was permissive, the court will probably reject this argument. First, the court will conclude that if Mr. Garcia's grandfather gave DNWC permission to use his land, that permission terminated when his grandfather died. In addition, the court will probably conclude that even if DNWC used Mr. Garcia's land with Mr. Garcia's implied permission from the time of his grandfather's death until it sent the letter in February of 2001, that permission terminated in the summer of 2001 when the DNWC posted the no trespassing sign and continued to use the property as its own.

Arguments Script Format	Conclusions and Reasoning Integrated Format
more like *Miller* than it is *Lingvall*. Like the title owners in *Miller*, who allowed the claimants to use their driveway as a neighborly accommodation, Mr. Garcia allowed DNWC to use his land as a neighborly accommodation. In addition, unlike *Lingvall* in which there was an antagonistic relationship between the parties, in this case there was not. In response, DNWC can argue that even if its initial use was permissive, that permission would have terminated when Mr. Garcia's grandfather died. See *Granston*, 52 Wn. App. at 294-95. Likewise, even if DNWC had Mr. Garcia's implied permission to use the land, that permissive use ended in 2001 when, after not receiving a response from Mr. Garcia, the DNWC posted a no trespassing sign on the dock and continued to use the property as if it were its own.	

§ 8.8.5   Avoid the Common Problems

The two most common problems that writers encounter when using an integrated format are (a) that they do not give appropriate weight to each side's arguments and (b) that, in trying to give appropriate weight to each side's arguments, they write sentences that are hard to read.

a.   Give Appropriate Weight to Each Side's Arguments

While the script format forces writers to give appropriate weight to each side's arguments, the integrated format does not. As a consequence, as the writer, you need to make a special effort to tell the attorney what each side is likely to argue and why one set of arguments is more persuasive than another set. Compare Examples 10 and 11.

EXAMPLE 10	Poor Example: The Writer Sets Out Only the Arguments that Support Her Conclusion

First, the court will probably conclude that DNWC used Mr. Garcia's land as if it were the true owner. DNWC maintained the campsites, the fire area, the outhouse, and the dock. In addition, DNWC used the land for eight weeks each summer, which would be typical for that type of property. Consequently, this case is similar to *Chaplin* and *Timberlane*, in which the claimants maintained and used the disputed land as if it were their own.

EXAMPLE 11	Better Example: The Writer Sets Out Both Sides' Arguments

First, the court will probably conclude that DNWC used Mr. Garcia's land as if it were the true owner. Although DNWC did not build any new structures on Mr. Garcia's land, it maintained the campsites, the fire area, the outhouse, and the dock. In addition, although DNWC did not use the property year round, it did use the property during the summer, which is how a typical owner would have used the land. Therefore, this case is similar to *Chaplin* and *Timberlane*, in which the claimants maintained and used the disputed land as a true owner would have used the land. While in *Chaplin* and *Timberlane* the claimants built new structures (in *Chaplin*, the claimants built a road and in *Timberlane*, they built a fence and a patio), the courts have held that the claimant does not have to do everything that a title owner might do.

PRACTICE POINTER	In switching from the script format to an integrated format, you should not lose any content.

b.   Write Sentences that Are Easy to Read

Writing sentences that give appropriate weight to each side's arguments can be difficult. If you are having trouble with a sentence, try one of the following strategies.

Strategy 1:   Put the Weaker Argument in a Dependent Clause and the Stronger Argument in the Main Clause

One of the easiest ways to give appropriate weight to each side's argument is to put the weaker argument in a dependent clause and the stronger argument in the main clause.

Although [weaker argument], [stronger argument].

In Example 12, the dependent clauses are underlined, and the main clauses are in bold.

EXAMPLE 12	**Weaker Argument in the Dependent Clause and Stronger Argument in the Main Clause**

<u>Although DNWC did not build any new structures on Mr. Garcia's land,</u> **it maintained not only the campsites and the fire area but also the outhouse and the dock.** In addition, <u>although DNWC did not use the property year round,</u> **it did use the property during the summer, which is how a typical owner would have used the land.**

The problem, of course, is that if you use this construction too often your writing becomes monotonous. Sometimes you can solve the problem by changing the word that you use to introduce the dependent clause. Instead of using "although," you can use "even though," or "while." At other times, though, you will need to break the pattern by using another strategy.

<table>
<tr><td>**PRACTICE POINTER**</td><td>Many attorneys think that the word "though" is too informal for use in a formal memo or a brief. Instead, use the more formal "although" or "even though."</td></tr>
</table>

Strategy 2:   Use a "This and Not That" Sentence Structure

Another strategy that can work well is a "this and not that" sentence. When you use this strategy, remember to include a sentence that explains why your case is more like Case A than it is Case B.

EXAMPLE 13   **"This But Not That" Sentence Structure**

Thus, this case is more like Case A than it is Case B. Unlike Case B, in which . . . , in this case, . . . Instead, as in Case A, . . .

Strategy 3:   Set Out One Side's Argument in One Sentence or Set of Sentences and the Other Side's Argument in a Second Sentence or Set of Sentences

When you use an integrated format, you do not need to set out both side's arguments in a single sentence. When the arguments are complicated, set out one side's arguments in one sentence or set of sentences and the other side's arguments in a separate sentence or set of sentences. Note that it is often a good idea to start the other side's argument with a transitional word or phrase.

EXAMPLE 14   **Each Side's Arguments Set Out in Separate Sentences**

(Mr. Garcia's argument is underlined, and DNWC's argument is in bold.)

Mr. Garcia has paid all of the taxes and assessments on the disputed piece of property. **Nevertheless, the courts have consistently found that payment of taxes and assessments is not enough to defeat an adverse possession claim.**

EXAMPLE 15   **Each Side's Arguments Set Out in Separate Sentences**

(Mr. Garcia's arguments are underlined, and DNWC's arguments are in boldface type.)

Some actions taken by DNWC and Mr. Garcia suggest that both sides knew the property was his. In about February 2001, DNWC wrote Mr. Garcia, asking whether it could continue using his land for campouts. In addition, in August of 2013, Mr. Garcia visited the property with the intent of spending a few days camping on the lake. Arguably, both of these actions suggest that Mr. Garcia was asserting his rights as an owner. **Other actions, however, suggest that DNWC was successfully asserting its adverse claim. First, when Mr. Garcia did not respond to the DNWC letter, DNWC put up a no trespassing sign. There is no evidence that Mr. Garcia had ever put up a no trespassing sign, nor is there evidence that he removed DNWC's no trespassing sign. Second, when Mr. Garcia found children and counselors on the property, he did not tell them to leave. Instead he was the one who left, returning only the following evening after they had gone.**

Strategy 4:   Use the "Plaintiff Will Argue, Defendant Will Argue" Language

It is also not wrong to include an occasional "the plaintiff will argue" or "the defendant will respond." Just make sure to organize the arguments around the lines of argument and not each side's arguments.

EXAMPLE 16   **Using the Phrase "the Plaintiff Will Argue" and "the Defendant Will Respond" to Set Out the Arguments**

We can argue that the letter that DNWC sent to Mr. Garcia establishes that DNWC's use of the land was permissive. However, the court will probably reject this argument on the ground that even though Mr. Garcia did not respond, DNWC continued using his land for more than 10 years.

PRACTICE POINTER   In reading cases, pay attention to the ways in which the courts present each side's arguments. In particular, note which types of sentences are easy to read and understand and which are more difficult. You can then use some of the easy-to-read sentence patterns in your own writing.

§ 8.8.6   Checklist for Discussion Section Written Using an Integrated Format

a.   Content

Introduction

- The writer has included a sentence or paragraph introducing the governing statute or common law rule.
- The writer has set out the general rule, quoting the applicable statutory sections and quoting or paraphrasing the common law rule.
- The writer has set out any other general rules.
- When appropriate, the writer has briefly described the policies underlying the statute or common law rule.
- The writer has included a roadmap.
- The writer has not included rules or information that the attorney does not need.

- The rules are stated accurately and objectively.
- For each rule stated, the writer has included a citation to authority.

Discussion of Undisputed Elements

- The writer has identified the element and, when there are specific rules, set out those specific rules.
- The writer has applied the rules to the facts of the client's case, explaining why the element is not in dispute.

Discussion of Disputed Elements

- For each disputed element, the writer has set out the specific rules, described cases that have interpreted and applied those rules, stated her conclusion or prediction, and summarized her reasoning.
- The writer has included all of the applicable specific rules and set out those rules accurately and objectively.
- The writer has introduced each group of analogous cases, telling the attorney what rule or principle the cases illustrate.
- The case descriptions illustrate the rule or principle and are accurate and objective.
- In setting out the reasoning, the writer has given appropriate weight to each side's arguments.
- The analysis is sophisticated.

b.   Large-Scale Organization

- The writer has presented the information in the order in which the attorney expects to see it. For example, the writer begins the discussion section with an introductory section in which she sets out the general rules. The writer then walks the attorney through each of the elements, raising and dismissing the undisputed elements and doing a more complete analysis of the disputed elements.

c.   Writing

- The attorney can understand the discussion with just one reading.
- The paragraph divisions are logical, and the paragraphs are neither too long nor too short.
- Transitions and dovetailing have been used to make the connection between ideas clear.
- In most sentences, the writer has used the actor as the subject of the sentence, and the subject and verb are close together.
- The writer has varied the length of the sentences and the sentence patterns so that each sentence flows smoothly from the prior sentence.
- The writing is concise and precise.
- The writing is grammatically correct and correctly punctuated.
- The discussion section has been proofread.

§ 8.9   Draft the Conclusion

The last section of the memo is the formal conclusion. In a one-issue memo, use your formal conclusion to summarize your analysis of that issue. Set out your conclusion and then summarize your analysis. In Example 1, the writer sets out his conclusion in the first sentence and then, in the following paragraphs, summarizes his analysis of the elements.

EXAMPLE 1   **Conclusion**

Conclusion

More likely than not, DNWC will be able to establish title to Mr. Garcia's land through adverse possession.

To prove that its possession was open and notorious, DNWC only needs to show that Mr. Garcia had actual notice of its use of his land throughout the statutory period or that it used his land in such a way that any reasonable person would have thought that it owned this land. In this case, DNWC can use the letter that it sent to Mr. Garcia to prove that he had actual notice, and it can show that its use of the land for campouts was such that any reasonable person would have thought that DNWC owned the land.

To prove that its possession was actual and uninterrupted, DNWC need only show that it actually used the land and that its use was consistent with how the true owner might have used the land. The case law suggests that DNWC's maintenance of the campsites, fire area, outhouse, and dock were sufficient to establish actual possession. In addition, although DNWC only used the land during the summer months, the court is likely to find that such use was uninterrupted because most owners of recreational land only use their land during certain seasons.

To prove that its use of the land was exclusive, DNWC will have to show that it did not share the land with anyone else. Although we could try to argue that DNWC's use was not exclusive because it allowed campers to use the land, this argument is weak because the campers used the land under DNWC's supervision.

Finally, to prove that its use was hostile, DNWC will have to prove that it used the land as if it were its own and that it did not do so with Mr. Garcia's permission. DNWC's maintenance and use of the property is probably sufficient to establish that it used Mr. Garcia's land as if it were its own. In addition, DNWC will be able to prove that its use was not permissive. Even if DNWC's initial use of the property was with Mr. Garcia's grandfather's permission, that permission terminated when Mr. Garcia's grandfather died. In addition, although in its 2001 letter DNWC asked Mr. Garcia for permission to continue using the property, DNWC has a strong argument that it did a hostile act that terminated permission when, even after Mr. Garcia did not respond, it continued maintaining and using the property and it posted the no trespassing sign.

Because all of these elements have been met for the statutory period, which is 10 years, DNWC has established a right to title to the land through adverse possession.

In contrast, if your memo discusses more than one issue, use your conclusion to summarize your analysis of each issue and to explain the interrelationships among those issues.

Chapter 8 Quiz No. 1

Draft answers for each of the following questions. Make your points clearly and concisely, and write sentences that are easy to read and that are grammatical and correctly punctuated.

1. In reading a discussion of a disputed element, what types of information does an attorney expect to see? What information does the attorney expect to see first? Second? Third? Fourth?
2. What is the difference between inductive and deductive reasoning?
3. Why should you discuss the elements one at a time rather than as a group?
4. What is the relationship between the IRAC formula that is used to brief a case or draft an exam answer and the IRAC formula that is used to discuss a disputed element?
5. How is the discussion of a disputed element written using an integrated format the same as and different from the discussion of a disputed element written using the script format?

§ 8.10   Revising and Editing Your Draft

As you learned in writing your first memo, your first draft should not be your last draft. Because so much is as stake for the client, for the firm, and for you, make the time to revise, edit, and proofread your memo.

§ 8.10.1   Revise for Content and Organization

In revising the draft, focus first on content and organization. Begin by checking the memo's content. Have you given the attorney the information that he or she needs to evaluate the case? If you did not, add that information. Did you include information that the attorney does not need? If you did, delete that information. Did you present the information accurately and objectively? If you have misstated a rule or misrepresented a case, correct those errors.

Next, check the large-scale organization. Did you present the information in the order that the attorney expects to see it? For example, did you start with an introductory section and then walk the attorney through the elements one by one? In walking the attorney through the disputed elements, did you use one of the standard organizational schemes — for example, did you use the script format or an integrated format? In setting out the specific rules, did you set out more general rules before more specific rules and exceptions? If you did not do all of these things, stop and make the necessary revisions.

Finally, check your small-scale organization. Have you used roadmaps, signposts, topic sentences, and transitions? One way to check the small-scale organization is to look at the first sentence of each paragraph. Does that sentence accurately identify the topic of that paragraph? Is there a transition that tells the attorney how that paragraph is related to the prior paragraphs?

Also check to make sure that the discussion of the various elements is "coherent." For example, make sure that you have repeated key terms and phrases. What terms and phrases are in the specific rules? Do those same terms and phrases appear in the descriptions of the analogous cases? In the arguments? In the mini-conclusion? In Example 1, note how the writer has repeated the key terms and phrases, which are "actual notice" and "used the land such that any reasonable person would have thought that the claimant owned it." The references to "actual notice" are in bold, and the references to "used the land such that any reasonable person would have thought that the claimant owned it" are underlined.

EXAMPLE 1	**Good Example: The Writer Has Repeated Key Terms**

A claimant can satisfy the open and notorious element by showing either (1) that the title owner had **actual notice** of the adverse use throughout the statutory period or (2) that the claimant used the land such that any reasonable person would have thought that the claimant owned it. *Riley v. Andres,* 107 Wn. App. 391, 396, 27 P.3d 618 (2001).

In this case, DNWC can prove both that Mr. Garcia had **actual notice** of its adverse use and that any reasonable person would have thought that DNWC owned the land. To prove that Mr. Garcia had **actual notice** of DNWC's use of the land, DNWC can point to the letter that it sent to Mr. Garcia in 1998 asking for continuing permission to use his land for campouts. To prove that a reasonable person would have thought that DNWC owned the land, DNWC will point out that it not only used the land for campouts but also maintained the campsites, fire area, outhouse, and dock. In addition, it posted a no trespassing sign.

§ 8.10.2   Edit Your Draft

In section 7.10.2, we set out four pieces of advice that will help you to write effective sentences: (1) use the actor as the subject of most of your sentences; (2) keep your subjects and verbs close together, (3) put old information at the beginning of the paragraph and new information at the end, and (4) vary sentence length and patterns. You should apply that same advice to this second memo. In particular, pay particular attention to the sentences that tend to be more difficult to write: the sentence setting out the issue, the sentences setting out complex rules, and, when you use an integrated format, the sentences in which you set out the parties' arguments and your evaluation of those arguments.

In this chapter, we add two more recommendations: (a) make sure that your writing is concise and (b) make sure that your writing is precise.

a.   Write Concisely

Although writing sentences with strong subject-verb units eliminates much unnecessary language, you also need to edit out such throat-clearing expressions as "it is expected that . . ." and "it is generally recognized that . . ." and redundancies like "combined together" and "depreciate in value." In Example 2, without the citation, the first draft has 73 words, and the revised draft has 54 words.

Example 2 Delete Unnecessary Words and Phrases

First Draft (73 Words)

It is generally recognized that a claimant can satisfy the open and notorious element by showing one of two things. The claimant can show either (1) that the title owner had real and actual notice of the adverse use of the claimant's land throughout the statutory period or (2) that the claimant used the land in such a way that any reasonable person would have thought or believed that the claimant owned it. *Riley v. Andres*, 107 Wn. App. 391, 396, 27 P.3d 618 (2001).

Revised Draft (54 Words)

A claimant can prove that its possession was open and notorious by showing either (1) that the title owner had actual notice of the adverse use throughout the statutory period or (2) that the claimant used the land in such a way that any reasonable person would have thought that the claimant owned it. *Riley v. Andres*, 107 Wn. App. 391, 396, 27 P.3d 618 (2001).

In Example 2, the writer reduced the number of words by 25 percent by doing some simple editing. Writers using the same technique throughout a draft can get a ten-page draft down to seven and one-half pages.

b.   Write Precisely

If conciseness is the first hallmark of excellent legal writing, precision is the second. Make sure that you use correct terms, that you use those terms consistently, that subjects and verbs are paired correctly, and that in making your arguments you compare or contrast like things.

1. Select the Correct Term

In the law, many words have specific meanings. For example, the words "held," "found," and "ruled" have very different meanings. In most instances, use "held" when you are setting out the appellate court's answer to the issue raised on appeal. In contrast, use "found" to refer to the trial court's or jury's findings of fact, and "ruled" when talking about the court's ruling on a motion or objection.

Compare the following examples. In Example 3, the writer used "held" incorrectly. Because the writer is not setting out the court's holding, "held' is incorrect. In contrast, in Example 4, the writer has used "held' correctly. Similarly, in Examples 5 and 6, the writer uses "found" and "ruled" correctly.

"Held" Used Incorrectly

For example, in *Chaplin*, the court **held** that the claimants had built a road across the disputed land, cleared and maintained the disputed land, installed utility lines, and used the disputed land for recreational activities.

EXAMPLE 4	**"Held" Used Correctly**

For example, in *Chaplin*, the court **held** that the claimants had proven that their use of the property was hostile when they built a road across the disputed land, cleared and maintained the disputed land, installed utility lines, and used the disputed land for recreational activities. *Id.* at 864.

EXAMPLE 5	**"Found" Used Correctly**

For example, in *Chaplin*, the trial court **found** that the claimants had built a road across the disputed land, cleared and maintained the disputed land, installed utility lines, and used the disputed land for recreational activities.

EXAMPLE 6	**"Ruled" Used Correctly**

The court **ruled** that the evidence was inadmissible.

2. Use Terms Consistently

In addition to making sure that you use the correct term, also make sure that you use terms consistently. If something is an "element," continue referring to it as an element. Do not switch and suddenly start calling it a "factor" or a "requirement."

EXAMPLE 7	**Poor Example: Inconsistent Use of Terms**

To prove adverse possession, the claimant must prove four **elements:** that its possession was (1) exclusive, (2) actual and uninterrupted, (3) open and notorious, and (4) hostile for the statutory period. *ITT Rayonier, Inc. v. Bell*, 112 Wn.2d 754, 757, 774 P.2d 6 (1989); *Chaplin v. Sanders*, 100 Wn.2d 853, 857, 676 P.2d 431 (1984). In this case, the statutory period is 10 years. RCW 4.16.020(1). Whether a particular **factor** is met is a mixed question of law and fact. *Chaplin*, 100 Wn.2d at 863. Whether the essential facts exist is for the trier of fact to decide; but whether the facts, as found, satisfy the **requirement** is for the court to determine as a matter of law. *Id.*

EXAMPLE 8	**Good Example: Consistent Use of Terms**

To prove adverse possession, the claimant must prove four **elements:** that its possession was (1) exclusive, (2) actual and uninterrupted, (3) open and notorious, and (4) hostile for the statutory period. *ITT Rayonier, Inc. v. Bell*, 112 Wn.2d 754, 757, 774 P.2d 6 (1989); *Chaplin v. Sanders*, 100 Wn.2d 853, 857, 676 P.2d 431 (1984). In this case, the statutory period is 10 years. RCW 4.16.020(1). Whether a particular **element** is met is a mixed question of law and fact. *Chaplin*, 100 Wn.2d at 863. Whether the essential facts exist is for the trier of fact to decide, but whether the facts, as found, satisfy the **element** is for the court to determine as a matter of law. *Id.*

3. Make Sure the Subjects and Verbs Go Together

In addition to making sure that you have selected the right word and used it consistently, also make sure that the subjects of your sentences go with the verbs and objects. For instance, while courts "state," "find," "rule," and "hold," they do not "argue." It is the parties who present arguments. Thus, in Example 9, the subject and verb do not go together.

| EXAMPLE 9 | Poor Example: Subject and Verb Mismatch |

While a **court** can **argue** that DNWC was not using the land as if it were its own, this argument is not a strong one.

| EXAMPLE 10 | Good Example: Subject and Verb Go Together |

While **Mr. Garcia** can **argue** that DNWC was not using the land as if it were its own, this argument is not a strong one.

| PRACTICE POINTER | You can, however, say that the dissent argued. |

4. Compare or Contrast Like Things

In setting out the arguments, you will often want to show how your case is similar to or different from other cases. For instance, you will want to compare or contrast the facts in your case to the facts in another case. In making these comparisons, make sure that you are comparing apples with apples and oranges with oranges. For example, do not compare a case name to a party or a party to a fact.

In Example 11, the writer has not compared similar things. She compared a case (*Crites*) to a person (Mr. Garcia).

| EXAMPLE 11 | Poor Example: The Writer Has Not Compared Similar Things |

Unlike *Crites*, in which the title owner allowed the claimants to use his land as a neighborly accommodation, **Mr. Garcia** did not allow DNWC to use his land as a neighborly accommodation.

| EXAMPLE 12 | Good Example: The Writer Has Compared Similar Things |

Unlike *Crites*, in which the title owner allowed the claimants to use his land as a neighborly accommodation, **in this case,** Mr. Garcia did not allow DNWC to use his land as a neighborly accommodation.

> **PRACTICE POINTER**
>
> Remember that when a name is italicized, the reference is to the court's decision. When the name is not italicized, the reference is to a person. Thus, in the following sentence, "*Crites*" is a reference to the court's decision in *Crites v. Koch*, and the reference to "Crites" is a reference to the plaintiff, Mr. Crites.
>
> In *Crites*, the court held that Koch allowed Crites to use his land as a neighborly accommodation.

§ 8.10.3　Proofread the Final Draft

The final step in the process is to proofread your draft, checking for spelling errors, grammatical and punctuation errors, typographical errors, and citation errors. The easiest way to proofread is to print out a copy of your memo and read through it word by word, spending the most time on the sections that you worked on last or when you were the most tired.

For a copy of the completed memo, see section 6.4.2.

Chapter 8 Quiz No. 2

Draft answers for each of the following questions. Make your points clearly and concisely, and write sentences that are easy to read and that are grammatical and correctly punctuated.

1. What technique can you use to make your discussion of an element more coherent?
2. How might you revise the following paragraph to make the same points more concisely?

> Second, more likely than not it will probably be the court's conclusion that DNWC's use of the land belonging to Garcia was not permissive. In reaching this conclusion, it is likely that the court will probably point out that, unlike the court in *Granston*, in which the parties were related and had a close relationship, in the case before the court there is no evidence that the members of DNWC are related to Mr. Garcia in any way. In addition, unlike the court's decision in *Miller*, in which the owners of the land allowed the claimants, who were their neighbors, to use their driveway, it is more typical that owners of recreational land are not so generous as to allow a neighboring property owner to use their land several days a week during the peak seasons of the year, which in this case the summer months. [146 words]

3. What is the difference between an element and a factor?
4. In the following example, has the writer compared like things? If not, how could you rewrite the sentences?

> Unlike *Chaplin* and *Timberlane* in which the claimants built new structures, DNWC did not do anything other than maintain existing improvements.

5. Does the following paragraph contain any errors? If yes, how would correct those errors?

In deciding whether the claimant was using the land as if it were its own, the primary consideration appears to be whether the plaintiff made any improvements to the land, the type of maintenance, and how much the claimant used the land. [citations omitted.] For example, in *Chaplin*, the court ruled that the claimants' were using the land as if it were there own when the claimants built a road across the disputed land, cleared and maintained the disputed land, installed utility lines and used the area for recreation.

Drafting Memos Requiring Other Types of Analysis

In Chapters 7 and 8, we showed you one of the most common types of legal analysis, an elements analysis. There are, however, other types of analysis, and this chapter provides you with templates for three of those types: section 9.1 provides you with a template for issues that require the analysis of a set of factors; section 9.2, with a template for issues that require the balancing of competing interests, and section 9.3, with templates for issues of first impression.

§ 9.1   Factor Analysis

While in an elements analysis the party with the burden of proof must prove all of the elements, in a factor analysis no one factor is determinative. The court can find for a party even when one or more of the factors favor the other side. For example, in most states, the legislature has set out a list of factors that the courts must consider in deciding child custody cases. Although the statutes may state that a particular factor, or set of factors, should be given the most weight, the courts can find for a parent even when the majority of the factors favor the other parent.

§ 9.1.1   Templates for Issues Involving a Factor Analysis

The templates for issues involving a factor analysis are very similar to the templates for issues involving an elements analysis. In both instances, you begin the discussion section with an introductory section, and in both instances you then walk your reader through the analysis step by step: In an elements analysis you walk the reader through the elements, and in a factor analysis you walk the reader through the factors. The primary difference is that, in a factor analysis, you need to add a section in which you weigh the factors. Taken as a group, do the factors weigh in favor of the plaintiff, or do they weigh in favor of the defendant?

In the following examples, Example 1 sets out the templates for an elements and factor analysis using the script format, and Example 2 sets out the templates for an elements and factor analysis using a more integrated format. For the purposes of both examples, presume that, for the issue involving an elements analysis, there are three elements, one of which is not likely to be in dispute and two that will be in dispute. Likewise, for the issue involving a factors analysis, presume that there are three factors: Even though the first factor is not "in dispute," the second and third factors are.

> **PRACTICE POINTER**
>
> When you use a script format, you use inductive reasoning and organize the analysis around the parties' arguments: You set out all of one side's arguments and then all of the other side's arguments. See section 8.7. On the other hand, when you use a more integrated format, you use deductive reasoning: You set out your conclusion and then your reasoning. For more on the script and integrated formats, see section 8.7.

EXAMPLE 1   **Templates for an Elements and Factor Analysis Using a Script Format**

Elements Analysis	Factor Analysis
Discussion	**Discussion**
Introductory Section	**Introductory Section**
■ If one or both sides will make a policy argument, describe the policies underlying the statute, common law rule, or court rule. ■ Introduce and set out the applicable statute, common law rule, or court rule. ■ If one of the parties has the burden of proof, explain which side has the burden of proof and what that burden is. ■ Set out any other rules that apply to all of the elements. ■ End the introductory section by providing the attorney with a roadmap for the rest of the discussion.	■ If one or both sides will make a policy argument, describe the policies underlying the statute, common law rule, or court rule. ■ Introduce and set out the applicable statute, common law rule, or court rule. ■ If one of the parties has the burden of proof, explain which side has the burden of proof and what that burden is. ■ Set out any other rules that apply to all of the factors. ■ End the introductory section by providing the attorney with a roadmap for the rest of the discussion.

Elements Analysis	Factor Analysis
A. First Element (not in dispute)	**A. First Factor (not in dispute)**
■ Set out and apply the applicable rule and/or definitions.	■ Set out and apply the applicable rule and/or definitions.
B. Second Element (in dispute)	**B. Second Factor (in dispute)**
■ Set out the specific rules or definitions for the second element. ■ If there are analogous cases that discuss the second element and descriptions of those analogous cases would help your supervising attorney understand how the courts have interpreted this element, include descriptions of analogous cases. ■ Set out arguments: 　■ Party with burden of proof's arguments 　■ Responding party's arguments. ■ Evaluate each side's arguments and set out mini-conclusion for the second element.	■ Set out the specific rules or definitions for the second factor. ■ If there are analogous cases that discuss the second factor and descriptions of those analogous cases would help your supervising attorney understand how the courts have interpreted this factor, include descriptions of analogous cases. ■ Set out arguments: 　■ Party with burden of proof's arguments 　■ Responding party's arguments. ■ Evaluate each side's arguments and set out mini-conclusion for the factor.
C. Third Element (in dispute)	**C. Third Factor (in dispute)**
■ Set out the specific rules or definitions for the third element. ■ If there are analogous cases that discuss the second element and descriptions of those analogous cases would help your supervising attorney understand how the courts have interpreted this element, include descriptions of analogous cases. ■ Set out each side's arguments: 　■ Party with burden of proof's arguments 　■ Responding party's arguments. ■ Evaluate each side's arguments and set out mini-conclusion for the third element.	■ Set out the specific rules or definitions for the third factor. ■ If there are analogous cases that discuss the second factor and descriptions of those analogous cases would help your supervising attorney understand how the courts have interpreted this factor, include descriptions of analogous cases. ■ Set out each side's arguments: 　■ Party with burden of proof's arguments 　■ Responding party's arguments. ■ Evaluate each side's arguments and set out mini-conclusion for the third factor.
Conclusion	**Evaluation of Factors**
■ Set out your conclusion and advice.	■ Using either a script or an integrated format, weigh the factors and set out your mini-conclusion. Note: if doing so would help your reader, describe how the courts have weighed the factors in analogous cases, and then show how the parties would use those cases to support their arguments (script format) or how the court might use those cases in making its decision (integrated format).
	Conclusion
	■ Set out your conclusion and advice.

EXAMPLE 2	Templates for an Elements and Factor Analysis Using a More Integrated Format

Elements Analysis	Factor Analysis
Discussion	**Discussion**
Introductory Section	**Introductory Section**
■ If one or both sides will make a policy argument, describe the policies underlying the statute, common law rule, or court rule. ■ Introduce and set out the applicable statute, common law rule, or court rule. ■ If one of the parties has the burden of proof, explain which side has the burden of proof and what that burden is. ■ Set out any other rules that apply to all of the elements. ■ End the introductory section by providing the attorney with a roadmap for the rest of the discussion.	■ If one or both sides will make a policy argument, describe the policies underlying the statute, common law rule, or court rule. ■ Introduce and set out the applicable statute, common law rule, or court rule. ■ If one of the parties has the burden of proof, explain which side has the burden of proof and what that burden is. ■ Set out any other rules that apply to all of the factors. ■ End the introductory section by providing the attorney with a roadmap for the rest of the discussion.
A. First Element (not in dispute)	**A. First Factor (not in dispute)**
■ Set out and apply the applicable rule and/or definitions.	■ Set out and apply the applicable rule and/or definitions.
B. Second Element (in dispute)	**B. Second Factor (in dispute)**
■ Set out the specific rules or definitions for the second element. ■ If there are analogous cases that discuss the second element and descriptions of those analogous cases would help your supervising attorney understand how the courts have interpreted this element, include descriptions of analogous cases. ■ Set out your conclusion. ■ Set out your reasoning, summarizing and evaluating each side's arguments.	■ Set out the specific rules or definitions for the second factor. ■ If there are analogous cases that discuss the second factor and descriptions of those analogous cases would help your supervising attorney understand how the courts have interpreted this factor, include descriptions of analogous cases. ■ Set out your conclusion. ■ Set out your reasoning, summarizing and evaluating each side's arguments.
C. Third Element (in dispute)	**C. Third Factor (in dispute)**
■ Set out the specific rules or definitions for the third element. ■ If there are analogous cases that discuss the third element and descriptions of those analogous cases would help your supervising attorney understand how the courts have interpreted this element, include descriptions of analogous cases. ■ Set out your conclusion. ■ Set out your reasoning, summarizing and evaluating each side's arguments.	■ Set out the specific rules or definitions for the third factor. ■ If there are analogous cases that discuss the third factor and descriptions of those analogous cases would help your supervising attorney understand how the courts have interpreted this factor, include descriptions of analogous cases. ■ Set out your conclusion. ■ Set out your reasoning, summarizing and evaluating each side's arguments.

Elements Analysis	Factor Analysis
Conclusion	**Evaluation of Factors**
■ Set out your conclusion and advice.	Using an integrated format, weigh the factors and set out your mini-conclusion. Note: if doing so would help your reader, describe how the courts have weighed the factors in analogous cases, and then show how the court might use those cases in making its decision.
	Conclusion
	Set out your conclusion and advice.

You must, of course, modify the templates so that they work for your issue and your readers. For instance, if there are four and not three factors, discuss each of those four factors. However, if there are more than three or four factors, think about whether you need a separate subsection for each factor. Can you raise and dismiss some of the factors at the end of your introductory section? If some of the factors are closely related, can you combine your discussions of the related factors?

In addition, modify your template so that it is consistent with your supervising attorney's preferences. While some attorneys love subheadings and will want you to use lots of them, others don't. Likewise, while in a factor analysis some attorneys will want you to include both a section in which you weigh the factors and a formal conclusion, others will say that the formal conclusion is repetitive and that you can either (1) delete the formal conclusion or (2) keep the formal conclusion but move the weighing of the factors out of the discussion section and into that formal conclusion. When in doubt, use common sense or ask your supervising attorney what he or she prefers.

§ 9.1.2　Draft the Introductory or General Rule Section

In both a memo involving an elements analysis and a memo involving a factor analysis, the introductory section serves the same function. It places the issue in context, it sets out the general rules, and it provides the reader with a roadmap for the rest of the discussion.

In deciding what to include in your introductory section, think about how much your supervising attorney knows about the area of law. If the area is one that she knows well, the section can be short. In most instances, include only the following information:

- a sentence introducing the applicable law;
- the applicable law, for example, the applicable portions of the statute, common law rule, or court rule;
- any other rules that apply to all of the factors; and
- a roadmap that tells your supervising attorney which factors appear to be in dispute and which factors are not in dispute.

If, however, the area of law is not one that your supervising attorney knows, you will usually want to include at least some background information. Depending on the issue and the types of arguments that you expect that the parties may make, explain how the law developed, the policies underlying the law, and the rules relating to the burden of proof.

> **PRACTICE POINTER**   While most attorneys will want you to quote the applicable portions of statutes and regulations, you can paraphrase common law and other rules.

As a general rule, set out more general rules before more specific rules. Thus, set out the policies underlying the rules before the rules themselves and the rules before the exceptions to the rules. Also remember to include a citation to authority for each rule that you set out. Finally, in most instances, keep the focus on the rule by putting the citation not at the beginning of the sentence, but in a separate citation sentence after the rule.

§9.1.3   Draft the Discussion of the Undisputed Factors

Most likely, not all of the factors will be in dispute. Sometimes the factor will favor one side but not the other side; at other times, the factor helps — or hurts — both sides equally.

For these undisputed factors, you have a choice. You can either raise and dismiss these factors at the end of the introductory section, or you can discuss them in separate, but very short, subsections. For example, if you are working on a child custody case and both parents want custody of their 3-year-old child, you could raise and dismiss the factor that relates to the parents' and child's preferences either at the end of the general rule section or in a separate subsection.

> **PRACTICE POINTER**   Even if the factor is not in dispute, you need to discuss it, both initially and in the section where you weigh the various factors.

§ 9.1.4   Draft the Discussion of the Disputed Factors

Just as disputed elements require more analysis, so do disputed factors. In some instances, the dispute will be a purely factual dispute. For example, in a custody case, the mother might argue that she has the more flexible work schedule while the father argues that his schedule is the more flexible schedule. In this situation, you do not need to include descriptions of the analogous cases. Simply set out the facts and each side's arguments based on those facts using either a script or integrated format.

There will, of course, be times when you will need to do more than just set out the factual arguments. If the rules are ambiguous and there are analogous cases, set out the rules, provide the attorney with the examples of how those rules have been applied in analogous cases, and then set out each side's arguments and your mini-conclusion using either a script or an integrated format. For more on drafting the descriptions of analogous cases, and in particular, drafting the description of analogous cases using a principle-based analysis, see sections 7.8.4b and 8.8.2.

§ 9.1.5   Draft the Paragraph or Block of Paragraphs in Which You Weigh the Factors

Unlike an elements analysis in which your discussion section is done once you have discussed each of the elements, in a factor analysis you need to go one step further. You need to weigh the factors.

There are several ways to organize this part of the discussion section. If you use a script format, set out the rules first, the descriptions of any analogous cases second, the plaintiff's arguments third, the defendant's arguments fourth, and your mini-conclusion at the end. If you use a more integrated format, begin by setting out the rules, then set out the description of any analogous cases, and end by setting out your conclusion and reasoning.

EXAMPLE 3	Organizational Schemes for Section Weighing the Factors

Script Format	Integrated Format
■ Set out the rules or tests that the courts use in weighing the factors. ■ If there are analogous cases that illustrate how the courts have weighed the factors in situations that are analogous to your situation, include descriptions of those analogous cases. ■ Set out each side's arguments: 　■ Party with burden of proof's arguments 　■ Responding party's arguments. ■ Evaluate each side's arguments and set out your conclusion.	■ Set out the rules or tests that the courts use in weighing the factors. ■ If there are analogous cases that illustrate how the courts have weighed the factors in situations that are analogous to your situation, include descriptions of those analogous cases. ■ Set out your conclusion. ■ Set out your reasoning, summarizing and evaluating each side's arguments.

Whichever organizational scheme you choose, take the time to think critically and carefully about each side's arguments and about how a court might view those arguments. If there is a statute, begin by reviewing the statute. Has the legislature stated that one factor or one set of factors should be given the most weight? Similarly, if the issue is governed by a common law or court rule, review the cases. Do the courts give one factor or set of factors more weight? In creating and applying the rules, what policies have the courts emphasized or tried to promote?

Do not, however, stop there. Push yourself to construct each side's story. For example, in a custody case, how will the mother use the factors to tell her story and persuade the court that it would be in the best interests of the children to grant her custody? How will the father use the factors to construct his story? Then ask yourself which story a court is likely to find most compelling.

| **EXAMPLE 4** | **Block of Paragraphs in Which the Writer Weighs the Factors** |

In this case, even though three of the four factors favor Ms. Morris, the court will probably find in favor of Ms. Springer. The three factors that favor Ms. Morris are position of authority, susceptibility, and the public nature of the comment. As Ms. Morris's basketball coach, Ms. Springer was in a position of authority over Ms. Morris, and given that Ms. Morris cried during her meeting with Ms. Springer, Ms. Springer knew that Ms. Morris was susceptible to statements about her weight. In addition, Ms. Springer made the comments about Ms. Morris's weight publicly on the basketball court in front of players, parents, and scouts.

The factor that favors Ms. Springer is that the case involves a single statement. Given that there are no cases in which the courts have held that a single statement by a defendant constituted extreme and outrageous conduct, the court is likely to find that Ms. Springer's comment, although inappropriate behavior for a coach, does not rise to the level of extreme and outrageous conduct. Other factors that are likely to contribute to the decision that the conduct was not extreme and outrageous are that the statement was made at the end of an emotionally charged basketball game between two elite teams, no racial slurs were involved, and Ms. Morris was almost 18 and not a young child.

§ 9.2   Balancing of Competing Interests

Another common type of analysis is an analysis that requires the balancing of competing interests. For example, in a criminal case, the trial court will balance the probative value of admitting particular evidence against the prejudicial value of allowing the jury to view that evidence, and in a nuisance case, the court will balance one individual's right to use his or her land against the rights of adjoining landowners.

§ 9.2.1   Templates for Issues Requiring the Balancing of Competing Interests

As with an elements analysis and factor analysis, there is more than one way to organize the discussion of an issue that requires the balancing of competing interests. However, regardless of which organizational scheme you choose to use, you need to do two things: identify the competing interests, and do the balancing.

Example 1 sets out two templates: The template in the left-hand column shows how to organize the discussion section using a script format while the template in the right-hand column shows how to organize the discussion section using a more integrated format. As you look at these templates, note that there is no one "right place" for the descriptions of analogous cases. While sometimes it will make more sense to put the descriptions of the analogous cases in a separate section, at other times it will make more sense to integrate them into the parties' arguments or into your reasoning.

In making the decision about where to put the cases, think about how you are going to use the cases. If you are going to use a case or set of cases extensively, showing how both sides would use the cases or how the court would treat the cases, it will probably make more sense, and be more efficient, to put the descriptions of those cases in a separate analogous case section. If, however, you are using the case to illustrate only a small point, it will probably make more sense to integrate your description of the case into your discussion of that point. For more on drafting the descriptions of analogous cases, and in particular, drafting the description of analogous cases using a principle-based analysis, see sections 7.8.4b and 8.8.2.

EXAMPLE 1	**Templates for an Issue Requiring the Balancing of Competing Interests**

Script Format	Integrated Format
Discussion	**Discussion**
Introductory Section	**Introductory Section**
■ If one or both sides will make a policy argument, describe the policies underlying the general rule (constitutional provision, statute, common law rule, or court rule). ■ Introduce and set out the general rule, identifying the competing interests and explaining the burden of proof. ■ Set out any other general rules or exceptions.	■ If one or both sides will make a policy argument, describe the policies underlying the general rule (constitutional provision, statute, common law rule, or court rule). ■ Introduce and set out the general rule, identifying the competing interests and explaining the burden of proof. ■ Set out any other general rules or exceptions.
[If appropriate, descriptions of analogous cases]	**[If appropriate, descriptions of analogous cases]**
Plaintiff's or Moving Party's Arguments	**Conclusion**
■ Set out the plaintiff's or moving party's assertion. ■ Summarize the plaintiff's arguments, including any plain language, analogous case, and policy arguments.	■ Set out your conclusion. (In this case, which interest outweighs the other interest?)
Defendant's or Responding Party's Arguments	**Reasoning**
■ Set out the defendant's or responding party's assertion. ■ Summarize the defendant's or responding party's arguments, including any plain language, analogous case, and policy arguments. ■ Set out your mini-conclusion (in this case, which interest outweighs the other interest?) and explain your reasoning.	■ Set out your first reason, incorporating and evaluating each side's arguments. (Often this will be a discussion of the first interest.) ■ Set out your second reason, incorporating and evaluating each side's arguments. (Often, this will be a discussion of the second interest.) ■ Set out your third reason, incorporating and evaluating each side's arguments. (Often, this will be where you balance the competing interests.)
Conclusion	**Conclusion**
[Put your formal conclusion here. In this conclusion, explain why one party's interests outweigh the other party's interests.]	**[Put your formal conclusion here.]**

§ 9.2.2   Draft the Introductory or General Rule Section

In a memo involving the balancing of competing interests, the introductory section serves the same function that the introductory section serves in memos involving other types of analysis. It introduces and sets out the applicable law, and it provides the reader with a roadmap for the rest of the discussion.

However, for issues involving the balancing of competing interests, the introductory section serves an additional function. While there are always exceptions, in most instances, you will want to use the introductory section to explain the competing interests and describe the policies that underlie them. How much you say will, of course, depend on the issue and what your supervising attorney knows about that issue. At one end of the continuum are those instances in which your supervising attorney knows the area of law and the application of the law to your client's facts is relatively easy. In these situations, your description of the competing interests and the underlying policies can be very short. At the other end of the continuum are cases in which your supervising attorney is not familiar with the area of law, the rules are evolving, the application of the law to the facts of your case is nuanced, and/or a lot is at stake. While you never want to turn a memo into a law review article, in these situations, your descriptions of the interests and the underlying policies needs to be more thorough.

PRACTICE POINTER	Remember to include a citation to authority for each rule that you set out. In addition, when possible, cite to mandatory authority.

§ 9.2.3   Draft the Discussion of the Competing Interests

In most instances, your discussion of the competing interests will have three components: an analysis of each interest; an analysis of how a court, or other decision maker, is likely to balance those competing interests; and a conclusion. How you organize those components depends on whether you use a script format or a more integrated format.

If you use the script format, begin by setting out one side's arguments in a paragraph or, more likely, a block of paragraphs. In setting out your client's arguments, begin by setting out your assertion, which will usually consist of a statement that your client's interests outweigh the other side's interests. Then set out your support for your assertion, showing your supervising attorney how you can use the facts, analogous cases, and underlying policies to support that assertion. While sometimes you will want to organize these arguments by type of argument — for example, putting your plain language arguments first, your analogous case arguments second, and your policy arguments last — it is usually better to organize the arguments around lines of argument, showing your supervising attorney how you can weave together the facts, analogous cases, and policies to make a particular point. After you have set out your client's arguments, then set out the other side's arguments using the same format: Set out the other side's assertion and the arguments that it can make to support that assertion. Finish by setting out your prediction and your reasoning. How do you think the court will balance the competing interests? What reasons do you think that the court will give for finding that one party's interests are stronger than the other party's interests?

> **PRACTICE POINTER**   Sometimes there are more than two competing interests. For instance, in a land use case, the court, or another decision maker, may not only have to balance the interests of two parties but also the interests of the public at large. In such situations, discuss and balance all of the competing interests.

If you use a more integrated format, begin by setting out your conclusion. How do you think that the court will balance the competing interests? Then, in a paragraph or block of paragraphs, walk your supervising attorney through your reasoning. If you have several reasons, you will usually want to start your discussion of each reason by setting out a subassertion that builds on a rule, the cases interpreting that rule, or one of the underlying policies. You will then want to set out your reasoning in much the same way that a court might discuss its reasoning in a judicial decision. Just make sure that you do not omit or give short shrift to the losing side's arguments. To do her job well, your supervising attorney needs thorough analysis of each side's potential arguments.

> **PRACTICE POINTER**   In moving from a script to an integrated format, you should not lose any arguments. For more on avoiding the common problems, see section 8.8.5.

Depending on the format that you use, your supervising attorney's preferences, and whether your memo discusses just one issue or several issues, you may or may not need a formal conclusion. If you are analyzing a single issue using a script format, you may be able to use your mini-conclusion, that is, the paragraph or block of paragraphs in which you predict how the court will balance the interests and how it will explain its decision, as your formal conclusion. On the other hand, if your memo has more than one issue statement and, thus, more than one part to the discussion section, include a formal conclusion.

§ 9.3   Issue of First Impression

Some of the most interesting, and most challenging, issues that you will work on are issues of first impression, that is, issues that have not been decided by the courts in your jurisdictions.

Issues of first impression have two things in common: They require you to predict what rule the court is likely to apply, and they require you to apply that rule, and in some instances, alternative rules, to the facts of your case. Unfortunately, though, that is about all that issues of first impression have in common. You will, therefore, need to use the following templates as starting, and not ending, points for determining what types of information you need to include in your discussion section and the best way of organizing that information.

§ 9.3.1   Circuit Split

One of the most common scenarios is one in which there is a "circuit split." In the federal system, a circuit split occurs when one or more of the federal circuits adopt one rule or approach while one or more of the other circuits adopt a different rule or approach. In the state systems, a "split" occurs when one or more of the divisions of a state's intermediate court of appeals adopt one rule or approach and one or more of the other divisions adopt a different rule or approach. Until the United States Supreme Court or the state's highest court resolves the split, other circuits or divisions are free to adopt whichever rule or approach that they choose.

In discussing an issue in which there is a circuit split, you need to do the following:

- You need to tell your supervising attorney that your jurisdiction has not decided the issue and that there is a circuit split, with other circuits taking two or more different approaches.
- You need to describe the different approaches, telling your supervising attorney which circuits have taken which approach and the reasons that the courts have given for selecting one approach over other approaches. If different courts have adopted the same approach for different reasons, make that point clear.
- You need to evaluate the different approaches, predict which approach your jurisdiction is likely to take, and explain your reasoning.
- You need to apply the rules to the facts of your case. If you are confident that your jurisdiction will adopt a particular rule, just apply that rule to the facts of your case. If, however, it is not clear which rule your jurisdiction will adopt, you should do an alternative analysis, applying the various rules to the facts of your case.

Example 1 shows two templates for organizing this information.

EXAMPLE 1　　**Templates for Organizing a Discussion of First Impression Involving a Circuit Split Using the Script and a More Integrated Format**

Script Format	Integrated Format
Introductory Section ■ Introduce the issue and explain (1) that in your jurisdiction the issue is an issue of first impression and (2) that in other jurisdictions the courts have adopted different rules or taken different approaches.	**Introductory Section** ■ Introduce the issue and explain (1) that in your jurisdiction the issue is an issue of first impression and (2) that in other jurisdictions the courts have adopted different rules or taken different approaches.
Majority Rule ■ If the majority of jurisdictions have adopted a particular rule or approach, begin by introducing that rule or approach, telling your supervising attorney which jurisdictions have adopted that rule or approach, and summarizing the courts' reasons for adopting that rule or approach.	**Majority Rule** ■ If the majority of jurisdictions have adopted a particular rule or approach, begin by introducing that rule or approach, telling your supervising attorney which jurisdictions have adopted that rule or approach, and summarizing the courts' reasons for adopting that rule or approach.
Minority Rule ■ Set out the minority rule, telling your readers which jurisdiction or jurisdictions have adopted that rule or approach and explaining the court's or courts' reasons for adopting that rule or approach.	**Minority Rule** ■ Set out the minority rule, telling your readers which jurisdiction or jurisdictions have adopted that rule or approach and explaining the court's or courts' reasons for adopting that rule or approach.
Arguments ■ Set out the plaintiff's or moving party's assertion about which rule or approach the court should adopt and the arguments that the plaintiff or moving party is likely to make. ■ Set out the defendant's or responding party's assertion about which rule or approach the court should adopt and the arguments that the defendant or responding party is likely to make.	**Conclusion and Reasoning** ■ Tell your supervising attorney which rule or approach you think the court is likely to adopt. ■ Set out your reasoning, incorporating into your reasoning a discussion and evaluation of each side's arguments.
Conclusion and Reasoning ■ Tell your supervising attorney which rule you think the court is likely to adopt and why you think that the court will adopt that rule.	**Application of Rule or Approach to Facts** ■ Apply the rule or approach that you predict the court will adopt to the facts of your case. If the application of the rule will be in dispute, set out the plaintiff's or moving party's assertion and arguments, the defendant's or responding party's assertion and arguments, and your mini-conclusion using either a script or integrated format. Note: If that rule or approach requires an elements analysis, a factor analysis, or the balancing of competing interests, do that analysis using the templates set out in Chapters 7 and 8 and sections 9.1 and 9.2.
Application of Rule or Approach to Facts ■ Apply the rule or approach that you predict the court will adopt to the facts of your case. If the application of the rule or approach will be in dispute, set out the	

Script Format	Integrated Format
plaintiff or moving party's assertion and arguments, the defendant's or responding party's assertion and arguments, and your mini-conclusion. Note: If that rule or approach requires an elements analysis, a factor analysis, or the balancing of competing interests, do that analysis using the templates set out in Chapters 7 and 8 and sections 9.1 and 9.2. ■ If you think that there is a possibility that the court will adopt a different rule or approach, do an alternative analysis. If the application of the other rule or approach will be in dispute, set out the plaintiff's or moving party's assertion and arguments, the defendant's or responding party's arguments, and your mini-conclusion. Note: If that rule or approach requires an elements analysis, a factor analysis, or the balancing of competing interests, do that analysis using the templates set out in Chapters 7 and 8 and sections 9.1 and 9.2.	■ If you think that there is a possibility that the court will adopt a different rule or approach, apply that different rule or approach to the facts of your case. If the application of the rule will be in dispute, set out the plaintiff or moving party's assertion and arguments, the defendant's or responding party's assertion and arguments, and your mini-conclusion using a script or an integrated format. Note: If that rule or approach requires an elements analysis, a factor analysis, or the balancing of competing interests, do that analysis using the templates set out in Chapters 7 and 8 and sections 9.1 and 9.2.

§ 9.3.2   The Statute Is Ambiguous, and There Are No Regulations or Cases that Have Interpreted that Statute

Another common scenario is one in which the statute is ambiguous and there are no regulations or cases that have resolved that ambiguity.

In this situation, you will usually want to start your discussion section by introducing and quoting the relevant statutory language, identifying the ambiguity, and telling your supervising attorney that there are no regulations or cases that have resolved the ambiguity. What else you include, and how you order that other information, will depend on what you found in doing your research and what arguments you think the parties are likely to make.

§ 9.3.3   Arguments Based on Agency Decisions

If, in doing your research, you located administrative memos or decisions that interpret the statute, you will need to do a *Chevron* analysis[1] to determine

---

1. In *Chevron U.S.A., Inc. v. Natural Resources Defense Council, Inc.*, 67 U.S. 837 (1984), the United States Supreme Court set out a two-part test to determine whether courts should defer to an administrative agency's interpretation of a statute. Under the first part of this test, the courts look to see whether the statute is ambiguous or whether there is a "gap" in the statute that Congress intended the agency to fill. If the statute is ambiguous, the courts then look to see whether the agency's interpretation of the statute is reasonable. If the agency's decision is reasonable, the courts will defer to the agency; if the agency's decision is not reasonable, the courts will substitute their judgment for the agency's. In more recent cases, some courts have added a "Step Zero," in which they look to see if an agency's interpretation has the force of law, for example, whether the agency followed the notice and comment provisions of § 553 of the Administrative Procedure Act. See Cass R. Sunstein, *Chevron Step Zero*, 92 Va. L. Rev. 187 (2006). While the courts do not have to defer to

whether the courts will defer to the agency's interpretation. Because the courts sometimes do the Step Zero analysis first and sometimes they do it last, Example 2 shows two ways of organizing a *Chevron* analysis.

EXAMPLE 2	**Templates for Doing a *Chevron* Analysis**

Option 1	Option 2
A. *Chevron* Analysis	A. *Chevron* Analysis
■ Explain *Chevron*, including a brief description of the two-part test. ■ Do a *Chevron* Step Zero analysis, using a script or integrated format to discuss whether the agency's decision has the force of law. ■ Do a *Chevron* Step One analysis, discussing whether the statutory language is, in fact, ambiguous. (If this step of the analysis is not in dispute, you can simply raise and dismiss this issue.) ■ Do a *Chevron* Step Two analysis, using a script or integrated format to discuss whether the agency's interpretation of the statute is reasonable.	■ Explain *Chevron*, including a brief description of the two-part test. ■ Do a *Chevron* Step One analysis, discussing whether the statutory language is, in fact, ambiguous. (If this step of the analysis is not in dispute, you can simply raise and dismiss this issue.) ■ Do a *Chevron* Step Two analysis, using a script or integrated format to discuss whether the agency's interpretation of the statute is reasonable. ■ If, given your facts, there is an issue about whether the agency's decision has the force of law, do a *Chevron* Step Zero analysis.

§ 9.3.4 Policy Arguments

If there are no agency decisions interpreting a statute, or if you believe that the courts will find that an agency's decision is unreasonable or does not have the force of law, think policy. In doing your research, did you locate a "findings" or "purpose" section in which Congress or the state legislature explained why it enacted the statute and/or what its purpose or goal was in enacting that statute? (These sections are often set out in a separate section or sections at the beginning of the act or of the chapter in which your statute has been placed.) If there isn't a findings or purpose section, is there anything in the legislative history that the parties might use to support their assertions about how the statute should be interpreted? Last, but certainly not least, take a step back. Given the facts of your case, and the larger social, political, and economic context in which that case is being decided, what will each side argue is the "right" or "just" way to interpret the statute?

If there is a finding and/or purposes section, make those arguments first. Then move to any arguments based on the legislative history and, if you think the parties will use them, any broader policy arguments. See Example 3.

---

agency interpretations that do not have the force of law, the courts often give these interpretations substantial weight.

<table>
<tr><td>**PRACTICE POINTER**</td><td>If you did a legislative history but did not find any relevant information, include that fact in your discussion section.</td></tr>
</table>

EXAMPLE 3   **Templates for Organizing Policy and Legislative History Arguments Using the Script and a More Integrated Format**

Script Format	Integrated Format
B. Policy Arguments	**B. Policy Arguments**
If you are going to include more than one type of policy argument, include a roadmap that alerts your supervising attorney to that fact.	If you are going to include more than one type of policy argument, include a roadmap that alerts your supervising attorney to that fact.
1. Arguments based on a findings and/or purpose section ■ Introduce and quote the relevant portions of any findings or purpose sections. ■ Set out the plaintiff's or moving party's assertion and support for those assertions. ■ Set out the defendant's or responding party's assertion and support for those assertions. ■ Set out your mini-conclusion.	1. Arguments based on a findings and/or purpose section ■ Introduce and quote the relevant portions of any findings or purpose sections. ■ Set out your prediction. ■ Set out your first reason, summarizing and evaluating the arguments that each side is likely to make. ■ If you have additional reasons, set out those additional reasons, summarizing and evaluating the arguments that each side is likely to make.
2. Arguments based on legislative history ■ Describe and, if appropriate, quote, relevant portions of legislative history. ■ Set out the plaintiff's or moving party's assertions and support for those assertions. ■ Set out the defendant's or responding party's assertion and support for those assertions. ■ Set out your mini-conclusion.	2. Arguments based on legislative history ■ Describe and, if appropriate, quote, relevant portions of legislative history. ■ Set out your conclusion ■ Set out your first reason, summarizing and evaluating the arguments that each side is likely to make. ■ If you have additional reasons, set out those additional reasons, summarizing and evaluating the arguments that each side is likely to make.
3. Broader policy arguments ■ Set out the plaintiff's or moving party's assertions and support for those assertions. ■ Set out the defendant's or responding party's assertion and support for those assertions. ■ Set out your mini-conclusion.	3. Broader policy arguments ■ Set out your conclusion. ■ Set out your first reason, summarizing and evaluating the arguments that each side is likely to make. ■ If you have additional reasons, set out those additional reasons, summarizing and evaluating the arguments that each side is likely to make.

Drafting E-Memos, Email, and Text Messages

On the one hand, the practice of law seems timeless. No matter what the era, clients ask their lawyers questions, and lawyers — often with the help of an intern or a newer associate — answer those questions. On the other hand, the practice of law is constantly changing. Instead of going to the library to do their research, most attorneys turn to their computers, using free and fee-based websites to find the information that they need. In addition, shorter, less formal memos are becoming more common, and instead of letters, sometimes attorneys send emails or, occasionally, text messages.

In this chapter, we focus on these last three changes in practice, providing you examples of e-memos and reminders about email and text messages.

§ 10.1   E-Memos

While some attorneys still want the types of formal memos described in Chapters 6 through 9, other attorneys want what we call an e-memo: a shorter, less formal memo that is often, but not always, sent by email. This section explains the audience, purpose, and conventional formats for such memos and, at the end, sets out three samples.

§ 10.1.1   Audience

Like more formal memos, the primary audience for an e-memo is another attorney in the same firm or office: A more senior attorney asks an intern or a newer attorney to research and analyze an issue. In addition, like more formal memos, e-memos may be sent to the client. As a consequence, make sure that your writing is clear, concise, and correct and that you follow the conventions of formal writing. For example, as a general rule, do not use contractions, colloquialisms, or abbreviations. Be professional.

§ 10.1.2 Purpose

As with more formal memos, your primary purpose in writing an e-memo is to provide other attorneys in your office with the information that they need to evaluate a case, advise a client, or draft another document, for instance, a complaint, an answer, a motion, a brief, or a contract. To meet this purpose, the e-memo must be objective: You must set out the law objectively, you must give appropriate weight to each side's arguments, and your advice must be candid.

§ 10.1.3 Conventional Formats for E-Memos

Just as the format of more formal memos varies from law firm to law firm and attorney to attorney, so does the format of e-memos.

At one end of the continuum are e-memos in which the attorney asks a question for which there is an easy answer, for example, the attorney asks what the statute of limitations is in Illinois for actions to recover damages to personal property. In such instances, simply set out the question and the applicable law.

EXAMPLE 1   **Short E-Memo**

You asked me to research Illinois law and determine what the statute of limitations is on actions to recover damages to personal property. The applicable statute is 735 ILCS 5/13-205, which states that the statute of limitations is five years:

> [A]ctions on unwritten contracts, expressed or implied, or on awards of arbitration, or *to recover damages for an injury done to property, real or personal,* or to recover the possession of personal property or damages for the detention or conversion thereof, and all civil actions not otherwise provided for, *shall be commenced within 5 years next after the cause of action accrued.*

(Emphasis added.)

If you need additional research, please let me know.

At the other end of the continuum are the more formal memos that we described in Chapters 6 through 9: The only difference is that instead of handing your supervising attorney a paper copy of the memo, you email a copy of the memo, usually as an attachment. For examples of more formal memos, see section 6.4.

Many e-memos fall somewhere in between the short memo set out above and the more formal memo described in Chapters 6 through 9. In most instances, these memos deal with a relatively narrow issue. For example, instead of discussing all of the elements of a cause of action, they discuss only one element. While these e-memos will be shorter than more formal memos, the analysis still needs to be sophisticated.

Although the format and content of e-memos vary depending on the office and the issue, most e-memos have the following information.

a. Introductory sentence or paragraph
b. Summary of the applicable law
c. Application of the law to the key facts

a.   Introductory Sentence or Paragraph

Unlike a more formal memo, shorter e-memos do not have a formal statement of facts, a formal statement of the issue, or a separate section setting out a brief answer. Instead, the writer begins the e-memo with a sentence, paragraph, or block of paragraphs that identifies the client, the writer's task, the issue, and the key fact or facts. In addition, in most instances, the writer sets out his or her conclusion, the issue, and, sometimes, the key fact or facts. Compare the following examples.

EXAMPLE 2   **Introductory Sentence in Which the Writer Identifies the Client and the Issue**

You have asked me to research whether our client, Pacific Oil Company, LLC (Pacific), properly terminated a franchise under the Petroleum Marketing Practices Act (PMPA) after the franchisee frequently ran out of various grades of motor fuel.

EXAMPLE 3   **Introductory Paragraph in Which the Writer Identifies the Client, the Issue, and the Key Facts and Sets Out His Conclusion**

You have asked me to determine whether our client, Ms. Dunn, can state a valid claim under the Consumer Protection Act (CPA) when she contracted Salmonella from a burrito she purchased from a food truck. Specifically, you have asked whether we can use the amount that Ms. Dunn paid for the burrito or the amount that she spent for medical care to establish an injury to business or property. Given the current case law, the answer to both questions is no.

Note that in many e-memos, the "statement of facts" is much shorter: The number and type of facts depends on the question asked and who will be reading the memo. If the question is a legal question and the intended audience for the memo is the partner who has spent the last year working on the case, just set out the facts that are relevant to the issue that you were asked to research. Do not include background facts. If, however, the question is a factual question and you know that the e-memo will go to several attorneys, some of whom are not familiar with the case, set out the relevant facts and put those facts in context.

To see how writers set out the relevant facts, compare the three e-memos set out in section 10.1.7 below. In Example 8, the writer includes only a few facts, and she integrates those facts into her statement of the issue. Similarly, in Example 9, the writer includes only a few facts. However, unlike Example 8 in which the facts were at the beginning of the e-memo, in Example 9 the facts are near the end of the memo in the paragraph in which the writer applies the law to the facts. The e-memo in Example 10 is very different. Because the issue required an analysis of the specific facts of the case, the writer goes into detail in setting out the facts.

b.   Summary of the Applicable Law

In most e-memos, the next "section" is the summary of the applicable law: Depending on the issue, this section may be a single sentence or several paragraphs.

The key to writing this section is to give your readers just the information that they need, no more and no less. To do this, you need to have a sophisticated understanding of the applicable law and the issue that you were asked to research. For example, you need to understand the steps in the analysis, you need to be able to determine which rules apply at each step and which of those rules your readers need to know, and you need to make good decisions about when to include descriptions of analogous cases and what to include in those descriptions.

1. Steps in the Analysis

If there are several steps in the analysis, walk your reader through those steps in order. For example, if there is a two-part test, tell your reader that the courts use a two-part test and then discuss the two parts in order. Similarly, if there are different legal theories, identify those theories and then discuss each in turn. See, for example, the e-memo in Example 10, which is set out at the end of this section.

2. The Rules

As in a more formal memo, you need to set out the applicable rules, and you need to include a citation to authority for each of those rules. The primary difference is in focus: In an e-memo, the focus is usually narrower and sharper. As a practical matter, this means that you will be more selective in quoting statutes and regulations and in discussing the rules set out in cases. While you do not want to mislead your readers by leaving out relevant rules, do not give your readers more than they need.

In setting out the rules, remember the principles discussed in sections 7.8.2 and 7.8.4. First, set out more general rules before more specific rules and exceptions. Second, keep the focus on the rules by putting the citations to authority for those rules in a separate citation sentence following your statement of the rule and not in the sentence setting out the rule. Finally, set out the rules clearly and concisely and avoid overquoting.

3. The Analogous Cases

Do not include case descriptions just to include case descriptions. Instead, think about what your readers need. Do your readers need case descriptions to understand how the courts are applying a particular rule or to understand a line of argument? If they do, include the case descriptions. If, however, your readers can understand the rule and arguments without case descriptions, move directly from your discussion of the rules to your application of those rules to the facts of your client's case.

While the case descriptions in e-memos are similar to the case descriptions in more formal memos, they are usually shorter, and parentheticals are more common. In some instances, it may be enough to set out a rule and then, following the citation to the case or cases, parentheticals setting out the key facts.

EXAMPLE 4	**Rule Followed by Citations to Authority with Parentheticals Setting Out Key Facts**

Although the statute does not specify the period of time an individual must occupy a home to be regarded as "residing therein," the courts do not require extended habitation. *Compare Magazine v. Bedoya*, 475 So. 2d 1035 (Fla. Dist. Ct. App. 1985) (six-week stay sufficient to establish residency), *with Gamboa v. Jones*, 455 So. 2d 613 (Fla. Dist. Ct. App. 1985) (ten-day visit not sufficient to establish residency).

EXAMPLE 5	**Rule Followed by Citations to Authority with Parentheticals Setting Out Key Facts**

In other cases in which the employee had a connection to more than one worksite, the courts have held that the location of the employee's worksite was a question of fact. *See, e.g., Podkovich v. Glazer's Distrib. of Iowa, Inc.*, 446 F. Supp. 2d 982, 1000-02 (N.D. Iowa 2006) (concluding that there was an issue of fact when a traveling saleswoman physically reported to one worksite but received her assignments from another site); *Collinsworth v. Earthlink/Onemain, Inc.*, CIV.A. 03-2299GTV, 2003 WL 22916461, at *4 (D. Kan. Dec. 4, 2003) (concluding that there was an issue of fact when the plaintiff worked from home, sometimes used a branch office with fewer than 50 people within 75 miles, yet received and delivered her work product to the main office with more than 50 people within 75 miles.)

PRACTICE POINTER   The rules about citing unpublished decisions are different for memos than they are for other legal documents, such as appellate briefs. While some attorneys will instruct you not to cite to an unpublished decision in an in-house memo, other attorneys will instruct you to cite to an unpublished decision if the decision is directly on point and no other equally applicable published decision is available. In addition, some attorneys will want you to include a citation to an unpublished decision when the judge who wrote the decision is the judge who has been assigned to hear the client's case. The bottom line is that you should ask your supervising attorney whether he or she wants you to include citations to unpublished decisions.

If you need to provide your readers with more information about a case or a group of cases, go through the same steps that you went through to draft the analogous case section for a more formal memo: (1) identify the analogous cases, (2) sort the analogous cases, (3) analyze and synthesize the analogous cases, (4) draft the sentence introducing the analogous cases, and (5) draft your case descriptions. See section 7.8.4. While making sure that you do not misrepresent the facts of the case or the court's holding or reasoning, keep your case descriptions as focused and as short as possible.

EXAMPLE 6   **Sentence Introducing Analogous Cases and Short, Focused Case Descriptions**

In recent cases, the courts have either held that the service was invalid or remanded the case for an evidentiary hearing when the defendant produced evidence establishing that he was not living at the house where the summons was served. *See, e.g., Busman v. State, Dep't of Revenue*, 905 So. 2d 956, 958 (Fla. 3d DCA 2005); *Thompson v. State, Dep't of Revenue*, 867 So. 2d 603, 605 (Fla. 1st DCA 2004). For example, in *Busman*, the Third District Court of Appeals held that the service was not valid when the defendant presented a lease agreement that corroborated his testimony that he had moved out of his half brother's house two and one-half months before his half brother was served. 905 So. 2d at 958. Likewise, in *Thompson*, the First District Court of Appeals reversed and remanded the case for an evidentiary hearing when the defendant submitted an affidavit in which he stated that he was separated from his wife, that he had not resided at that address for more than three years, and that he did not authorize anyone to accept service of process on his behalf. 867 So. 2d at 605.

For more examples of how to discuss analogous cases, see Examples 8 through 10 set out at the end of this section.

c.   Application of the Law to the Key Facts

In an e-memo, you can either "apply the law as you go" or you can set out your summary of the applicable law and then, in a separate paragraph or block of paragraphs, apply that law to the key facts. While there are always exceptions, as a general rule, apply the law as you go when the analysis uses a number of steps and each step builds on the prior one. If, however, the analysis uses only one step or if your readers need to see the "big picture" before you begin your discussion of the individual pieces, summarize and then apply the law. In other situations, use your judgment about what will work best for your particular reader or readers.

You also have a choice about where to put your conclusion. As noted above, sometimes you can put your conclusion at the end of your introductory paragraph. Set out the question that you were asked to research and then answer that question. At other times, you will want to save the conclusion for your application section. When you put your conclusion in your application section, you can use either deductive or inductive reasoning: If you use deductive reasoning, set out your conclusion and then your reasoning; if you use inductive reasoning, set out your reasoning and then your conclusion. Neither approach is inherently better: Some attorneys prefer one approach, and others prefer the other approach. Thus, write for your particular audience.

Regardless of which approach you use, your analysis must be objective, focused, and sophisticated. Because e-memos are objective memos, make sure that your analysis is not one-sided. Your readers need to know both what they can argue on behalf of your client and what the other side is likely to argue. Do not, though, lose your focus. Save the discussion of related issues, arguments, or strategies for the very end of your e-memo or for another conversation or memo. Finally, remember that even if your discussion of an issue is short, your analysis needs to be sophisticated. While it is hard to define "sophisticated," e-memos with sophisticated analysis have the following characteristics:

- The analysis indicates that the writer understands the legal system and the area of law.
- The writer identifies the determinative issue or the key question and gets to that issue or question quickly.
- The writer is specific in applying language from the applicable statute to the facts of the client's case.
- The writer sees not only the obvious arguments but also the less obvious ones and uses good judgment in choosing which arguments to present.
- The writer uses the rules and cases that he or she set out earlier in the memo, using terms consistently and making connections.
- The conclusions that the writer sets out are candid and follow logically from the analysis.
- In setting out advice, the writer considers not only the law but also the client's practical needs and the larger context.

§ 10.1.4   Writing Style

While e-memos are less formal than the memos discussed in Chapters 6 through 9, they still need to be professional in appearance and in register, that is, in the level of formality. Therefore, pause before hitting "send" and view what you have written through the eyes of your supervising attorney and, if the e-memo may go to the client, through that client's eyes. Does the memo look like and read like it was prepared by a knowledgeable and careful individual who communicates clearly and concisely? If your memo meets this standard, send it; if it doesn't, make the necessary changes.

PRACTICE POINTER	The rules that apply to writing effective and correct formal memos also apply to writing e-memos. Consequently, make sure that your paragraph divisions are logical and that your paragraphs are

neither too short nor too long; use roadmaps, signposts, and transitions to explain the connections between paragraphs and sentences; write most of your sentences using the active voice and concrete subjects and action verbs; be precise and concise; and proofread your e-memo to make sure it does not contain any grammar, punctuation, or citation errors.

§ 10.1.5   Client Confidentiality

In-house memos are part of an attorney's work product and are, therefore, protected if you take the necessary precautions: Include a statement in the email that the attached document represents your work product and is confidential; when possible use encryption; and check and double check the email addresses to which you are sending the e-memo. In addition, make sure that you know your local rules relating to the use of email.

EXAMPLE 7   **Statement that Email Contains Confidential Information**

This electronic message contains information from the law firm of Jones and Jones, LLP. The contents are privileged and confidential and are intended for the use of the intended addressee(s) only. If you are not an intended addressee, note that any disclosure, copying, distribution, or use of the contents of this message is prohibited. If you have received this email in error, please contact me at _____.

PRACTICE POINTER   Attorneys do, however, need to warn clients, that emails received on or sent from employer-owned devices may not be protected. See ABA Comm. on Ethics & Prof'l Responsibility, Formal Op. 11-459 (2011), *available at* http://www.americanbar.org/content/dam/aba/adminis trative/professional_responsibility/11_459_nm_formal_opinion.authcheck dam.pdf.

§ 10.1.6   Checklist for Critiquing E-Memos

I. Organization

- The information has been presented in a logical order: In most e-memos, an introductory paragraph is followed by a summary of the applicable law and the application of that law to the facts of the client's case.

II. Content

- The writer has made good decisions about what information to include in the e-memo.
  - The writer includes an introductory sentence or paragraph that identifies the client and the issue that the writer was asked to research.
  - The writer includes only the relevant facts.
  - The writer includes descriptions of analogous cases only when the cases will help the attorney understand how the courts have applied the rules or understand a line of argument.
  - The writer includes a section applying the law to fact.
  - The statement of the research question is accurate and appropriately focused.

- The facts are set out accurately and objectively.
- The rules are supported by appropriate citations to authority.
- The descriptions of the analogous cases are accurate and objective.
- The analysis is objective and sophisticated.

III. Writing

- The attorney can understand the e-memo with just one reading.
- The paragraph divisions are logical, and the paragraphs are neither too long nor too short.
- Transitions and dovetailing are used to make the connection between ideas clear.
- In most sentences, the actor is the subject, and the subject and verb are close together.
- The writer varies the length of the sentences and the sentence patterns so that each sentence flows smoothly from the prior sentence.
- The writing is concise and precise.
- The writing is grammatically correct and correctly punctuated.
- The discussion section has been proofread.

§ 10.1.7 Sample E-Memos

| EXAMPLE 8 | **E-Memo to Attorney Familiar with the Underlying Law and the Facts of the Case** |

To: Supervising Attorney
From: Intern
Date: January 30, 2014
Re: Dunn CPA Claim: Can we use amount paid for medical care or for the burrito to prove an injury to business or property?

You have asked me to determine whether our client, Ms. Dunn, can state a valid claim under the Consumer Protection Act (CPA) when she contracted Salmonella from a burrito she purchased at a food truck. Specifically, you have asked whether we can use the amount that Ms. Dunn paid for medical care or the amount she paid for the burrito to establish the requirement under RCW 19.86.090 that the plaintiff prove an injury to business or property. Given the current case law, the answer to both questions is no.

The Washington courts have consistently stated that plaintiffs cannot use the amounts paid for medical care to establish an injury to business or property. *See, e.g., Stevens v. Hyde Athletic Indus.*, 54 Wn. App. 366, 370, 773 P.2d 871 (1989). For example, in *Stevens,* a case in which the plaintiff sued the store that sold her defective softball cleats, the court rejected Stevens's argument that her medical expenses constituted an injury to property, stating that actions for personal injury do not fall within the coverage of the CPA. *Id.*

In a more recent case in which the plaintiff sued the surgeon who had operated on her shoulder, the court restated the rule set out in *Stevens* and concluded that the plaintiff could not use the amount she paid for subsequent medical care to establish an injury to business or property. *Ambach v. French,* 167 Wn. 2d 167, 179, 216 P.3d 405 (2009). In addition, the court did not allow the plaintiff to use the amount that she had paid for the original surgery to establish an injury to business or property. *Id.* According to the court, "[w]here plaintiffs are both physically and economically injured by one act, courts generally refuse to find injury to 'business or property.'" *Id.* at 174.

Given the courts' decisions in *Stevens* and *Ambach*, we will not be able to establish an injury to business or property. In both *Stevens* and *Ambach*, the courts stated that the plaintiffs could not use medical bills to establish injuries to business or property. In addition, because the *Ambach* court did not allow the plaintiff to use the amount she paid for the original surgery to establish an injury to business or property, it is unlikely that we can persuade a court to use the amount Ms. Dunn paid for the burrito. Finally, like the claims in *Stevens* and *Ambach*, our claim is, at its core, a personal injury claim, and the courts have held that the CPA does not apply to such claims.

If you have any questions or would like me to do additional research, please let me know.

EXAMPLE 9	**E-Memo to an Experienced Attorney About an Issue of Law**

You have asked me to research the scope of 11 U.S.C. § 1301 to determine whether the co-debtor stay applies not only to consumer debt but also to commercial debt. Specifically, you have asked me to determine whether, once the other debtor has filed for a Chapter 13 bankruptcy, a creditor is stayed from enforcing a judgment against a co-debtor on a personal guaranty that arose out of a commercial debt. In short, section 1301 applies only to consumer debts; thus, a creditor should be able to enforce a judgment arising out of a commercial debt against a co-debtor even after the other debtor has filed his/her bankruptcy petition.

Under 11 U.S.C. § 1301, "after the order for relief under this chapter [has been filed], a creditor may not act, or commence or continue any civil action, to collect all or any part of a *consumer* debt of the debtor from an individual that is liable on such debt with the debtor, or that secured such debt, unless such individual became liable on or secured such debt in the ordinary course of such individual's business." 11 U.S.C. § 1301(a)(1) (emphasis added). "The automatic stay under [11 U.S.C. § 1301] pertains only to collection of a *consumer* debt." S. Rep. No. 95-989, at 138 (1978) (emphasis added). Consumer debt means "debt incurred by an individual *primarily* for a personal, family, or household purpose." 11 U.S.C. § 108 (emphasis added.) Thus, "not all debts owed by a Chapter 13 debtor will be subject to the stay of the codebtor, particularly those business debts incurred by an individual with regular income, as defined by section 101[(30)] of this title, engaged in business, that is permitted by virtue of section 109(b) and section 1304 to obtain chapter 13 relief." S. Rep. No. 95-989, at 138.

Accordingly, the automatic stay under 11 U.S.C. § 1301 is inapplicable to commercial debt. *See, e.g., In re Demaree*, 27 B.R. 1 (Bankr. D. Or. 1982) (holding that since it was admitted that the primary reason for the loan was for a business purpose and funds were, in fact, primarily used for a business purpose, loan was not a consumer debt and co-debtor stay was inapplicable); *In re Chrisman*, 27 B.R. 648 (Bankr. S.D. Ohio 1982) (holding that the automatic stay of section 1301 was inapplicable because the proceeds of the loan were used for training for a business opportunity and thus did not constitute consumer debt). Moreover, debts incurred with a profit motive generally are not consumer debts. 8 *Collier on Bankruptcy* 1301.03 (Mathew Bender 15th ed. rev.) (citing *In re Booth*, 858 F.2d 1051 (5th Cir. 1988)).

In this case, the debt was not incurred for personal, family, or household purposes; instead, the debt was incurred for commercial or business purposes. Furthermore, the co-debtor became liable on the debt in the ordinary course of the company's business: The personal guaranty was entered into to benefit the company. Thus, because the debt is not a consumer debt, the creditor may proceed with enforcing its judgment against the co-debtor without moving for relief from the stay.

Please let me know if you have any questions.

EXAMPLE 10	**Example 10 Longer E-Memo**

To: Supervising Attorney
From: Associate
Date: April 10, 2013
Re: Pacific Oil Co., LLC: Termination of Franchise Agreement

You have asked me to research whether our client, Pacific Oil Company, LLC (Pacific), properly terminated a franchise under the Petroleum Marketing Practices Act (PMPA) after the franchisee frequently ran out of various grades of motor fuel. A court is likely to conclude that Pacific properly terminated the franchise relationship with ABC under all three statutory grounds enumerated in the PMPA.

ABC, Inc. (ABC) operated Forest Service Station (Forest), a service station, from 1998 to November 23, 2012. ABC leased the premises from Pacific pursuant to a Retail Facility Lease (the Lease). ABC sold Pacific-branded motor fuel at the premises pursuant to a Retail Sales Agreement with Pacific (the Sales Agreement).

Under the Sales Agreement, ABC agreed that Pacific could terminate ABC's franchise if ABC failed to "comply with any provision of th[e] Agreement, which provision is both reasonable and of material significance to the relationship under this Agreement" **or** if ABC "failed to maintain a sufficient amount of all grades of Products for resale at Retailer's station, or Retailer's failure to operate Retailer's Station, for . . . such lesser period [than 7 consecutive days] which under the facts and circumstances constitutes an unreasonable period of time." Sales Agreement, ¶ 22.

Similarly, the Lease permitted Pacific to terminate ABC's franchise if ABC failed "to operate the Premises for 7 consecutive days, or such lesser period which under the facts and circumstances constitutes an unreasonable period of time," or because of "termination of the [Retail Sales Agreement]," **or** upon "[a]ny other ground for which termination is provided for in this Lease or is otherwise allowed by the PMPA or other applicable law." Lease, ¶ 18(a).

ABC began a pattern of running out of one or more grades of motor fuel. In response to ABC's habitual fuel outages, Pacific sent ABC three notices of violation. In these notices, Pacific outlined the outages at Forest and warned ABC that ongoing product outages or returned drafts would result in termination of the franchise agreements and the franchise relationship "pursuant to provisions of the supply agreement, lease (if applicable) and the [PMPA]." Ignoring these warnings, ABC continued to run out of various grades of motor fuel at its service station.

Pacific sent ABC a "Notice of Termination" pursuant to the Sales Agreement, the Lease, and the PMPA and stated that it would take possession of the retail premises. In the Notice of Termination, Pacific noted ten instances from April 25, 2012, through August 11, 2012, in which Forest had run out of various grades of motor fuel for time periods ranging from 11 hours to 96 hours in duration. ABC failed to take any action with respect to Pacific's Notice of Termination, except to file a Complaint on November 22, 2012.

A franchisor may terminate a franchise when the franchisor has a statutory basis for termination, and the franchisor's notice of termination comports with the requirements of the PMPA. *E.g., Zipper v. Sun Co.*, 947 F. Supp. 62, 67 (E.D.N.Y. 1996). In this case, Pacific has three bases for terminating ABC's franchise based upon fuel outages under the PMPA. These bases are not mutually exclusive. *See Lyons v. Mobil Oil Corp.*, 884 F.2d 1546, 1548 (2d Cir. 1989).

Pacific properly terminated ABC's franchise based upon 15 U.S.C. § 2802(b)(2)(A). This statutory provision permits Pacific to terminate a franchise if a franchisee fails "to comply with any provision of the franchise, [a provision] which . . . is both reasonable and of material significance to the franchise relationship." *See N.I. Petroleum Ventures Corp. v. Gles, Inc.*, 333 F. Supp. 2d 251, 256-57 (D. Del. 2004). Although the PMPA does not define what types of provisions of the franchise are of "material significance to the franchise relationship," a "failure" is not one that is "technical or unimportant to the franchise relationship," "beyond the reasonable control of the franchisee," or invalid under state law grounds. 15 U.S.C. § 2801(13).

The first issue is whether the franchise provision that required ABC to "maintain a sufficient amount of all grades of Products for resale" is reasonable. A court defers to the franchisor's "legitimate business judgment" when it reviews franchise provisions. *Gruber v. Mobil Oil Corp.*, 570 F. Supp. 1088, 1093 (E.D. Mich. 1983) (Mobil's legitimate business judgment entitled to considerable weight so long as decision made in good faith and in the normal course of business); *Crown Central Petroleum Corp. v. Waldman*, 515 F. Supp. 477, 483 (M.D. Pa. 1981), *aff'd*, 676 F.2d 684 (3d Cir. 1982) (court's role is not to discern the economic advisability of a particular term if there exists a reasonable basis for it). A provision is reasonable if it is "not absurd, ridiculous, extreme, or excessive[.]" *See, e.g., Texaco Ref. & Mktg. Inc. v. Davis*, 835 F. Supp. 1223, 1228 (D. Or. 1993) (citation omitted). However, in some jurisdictions, courts apply an objective standard. *See, e.g., Doebereiner v. Sohio Oil Co.*, 880 F.2d 329, 334 (11th Cir. 1989) (reasonableness determined from standpoint of neutral observer).

Under either the subjective or objective standard, the franchise provision that required ABC to "maintain a sufficient amount of all grades of Products for resale" likely is reasonable. Sales Agreement, ¶ 22. Not only does the provision satisfy legitimate business needs of Pacific, *i.e.*, to provide all grades of motor fuel at all times to the motoring public, which is the purpose of a gas station, but it is also neutrally rational to require a franchisee to carry all grades of motor fuel at all times. A court would be unlikely to characterize this term as "absurd, ridiculous, extreme, or excessive," especially in light of a recent opinion from a District Court in California, in which the court observed, " [i]t is difficult to imagine a contractual requirement more material to the franchise than requiring the franchise to actually sell . . . gasoline." *Harara v. ConocoPhillips Co.*, 377 F. Supp. 2d 779, 791 (N.D. Cal. 2005).

The second issue is whether the franchise provision that required ABC to "maintain a sufficient amount of all grades of Products for resale" is material. With respect to whether fuel outages are material, the *N.I. Petroleum Ventures* court stated that "[t]he frequency with which fuel run outs occurred is relevant to whether plaintiff's breach was material. A single run out, for example, may only be a technical breach and not a basis for nonrenewal." 333 F. Supp. 2d at 261 n.18. In this case, the number of fuel outages significantly exceeded a single run out because ABC ran out of a particular grade of motor fuel on at least 21 occasions preceding the notice. A court may find this fact persuasive and determine that Pacific properly terminated ABC's franchise under 15 U.S.C. § 2802(b)(2)(A).

Pacific also properly terminated ABC's franchise under section 2802(b)(2)(B). The PMPA also permits a franchisor to terminate a franchise when a franchisee fails "to exert good faith efforts to carry out the provisions of the franchise if . . . the franchisee was apprised by the franchisor in writing of such failure and was afforded a reasonable opportunity to exert good faith efforts to carry out such provisions." 15 U.S.C. § 2802(b)(2)(B).

The Sales Agreement required ABC "to maintain a sufficient amount of all grades of Products for resale[.]" Sales Agreement, ¶ 22. On at least 21 occasions in the 120 days preceding Pacific's Notice of Termination, ABC ran out of at least one grade of motor fuel. On two previous occasions prior to the termination, Pacific notified ABC in writing that ABC's conduct lacked "good faith efforts in complying with the terms of the supply agreement." Indeed, the February 2, 2005, "Final Notice of Violation" cited to "PMPA Section 2802(b)(2)(B) and provided that "termination would also be justified based upon Retailer's failure to exert good faith efforts to carry out the provisions of the franchise."

Pacific also properly terminated ABC under 15 U.S.C. § 2802(b)(2)(C) and (c)(9). Subsection (b)(2)(C) permits Pacific to terminate a franchise relationship should one of the enumerated, but not exclusive, events in section 2802(c) occur. One such event is the "failure of the franchisee to operate the marketing premises . . . for such lesser period [than 7 consecutive days] which under the facts and circumstances constitutes an unreasonable period of time." 15 U.S.C. § 2802(c)(9). Importantly, at least one court has found that only those run outs occurring in the 120 days preceding the notice may be evidence of failure to operate. *N.I. Petroleum Ventures Corp.*, 333 F. Supp. 2d at 261 (refusing to grant summary judgment where disputed issues as to whether plaintiff maintained adequate supplies of fuel).

In our case, ABC ran out of fuel on at least 21 occasions in the 120-day time period preceding the Notice of Termination. Therefore, the question is whether these run outs constituted an "unreasonable period of time" under section 2802(c)(9)(B). While the procedural posture of *N.I. Petroleum Ventures Corp.* limits its usefulness with respect to that question, three other cases may inform a court's analysis in this case.

In one of these cases, *Harara v. ConocoPhillips Co.*, the plaintiff ran out of 89 and 91 octane gasoline in January or February of 2004. 377 F. Supp. 2d at 784. The plaintiff argued that the defendant oil company constructively terminated his franchise by "making untimely and late deliveries of gasoline" and "canceling his credit privileges and putting him on 'Cash in Advance' status," among other reasons. *Id.* at 790 n.11. The defendant oil company "specified three reasons for termination: (1) plaintiff's failure to stock 76-branded motor fuel, (2) plaintiff's failure to pay $13,163.18 in rent and other charges, and (3) plaintiff's failure to take reasonable steps to control the operations of the station." *Id.* at 791. While it is unclear how many days prior to the notice of termination that the plaintiff ran out gasoline, the court remarked, "[i]t is difficult to imagine a contractual requirement more material to the franchise than requiring the franchise to actually sell 76-branded gasoline." *Id.; see also Rodgers v. Sun Ref. & Mktg. Co.*, 772 F.2d 1154, 1155 (3d Cir. 1985) (concluding that franchisor was entitled to terminate the franchise under section 2802(b)(2)(C) when the franchisee ran out of one or more grades of gasoline products at least 20 times over an approximately two-year period due to cash flow problems); *Crown Cent. Petroleum Corp.*, 515 F. Supp. at 486 (concluding that franchisor was entitled to terminate the franchise under the PMPA where franchisee failed to operate franchise for 10 out of 60 days after repeated warnings even though franchisee did not fail to operate franchise for 7 consecutive days).

The risk if we rely on *N.I Petroleum Ventures* is that some commentators suggest that the case stands for the proposition that fuel outages equate to a failure to operate and must be brought under section 2802(c)(9), rather than brought under section 2802(b)(2)(A). 333 F. Supp. 2d at 260-61; 2 *Franch. and Dist. Law & Prac.* § 15.7. However, our case is distinguishable because the Sales Agreement contains a provision directed at the failure to stock all grades of motor fuel, unlike the provision upon which the defendant oil company in *N.I. Petroleum Ventures* relied, which involved only operations. *Id.* (paragraph 14(j) of the agreement required franchisee to operate business for 24 hours a day, 7 days a week). Thus, the provision at issue in this case imposes a duty on the franchisee to both operate the service station and maintain sufficient amounts of all grades of motor fuel. A court may find this fact dispositive and distinguish our case from *N.I. Petroleum Ventures*.

There are few cases that directly address 15 U.S.C. § 2802(c)(9)(B) and delineate how many fuel outages constitute an unreasonable number so that a franchisor can terminate a franchise under that section. However, Pacific likely will prevail on at least one of the three enumerated grounds for termination set forth in its Notice of Termination to ABC.

Please let me know if you would like additional research on any of these points.

§ 10.2   Email[1]

Most attorneys have an email horror story. A client who is a manager sends another manager an email suggesting that the company could save money by forcing all of the employees who are over the age of 60 to retire. Another client unthinkingly hits "Reply All" and sends a message to more than a dozen people in which she essentially admits that she committed a crime. A new associate

---

1. The material about email first appeared in an article written by Anne Enquist and Laurel Oates, *You've Sent Mail*, 15 Perspectives 127 (Winter 2007).

attaches the wrong file to an email, accidentally sending opposing counsel a copy of an office memo that outlines the firm's trial strategy.

The horror stories confirm what most of us know: Email is both a blessing and a curse. It has made communication easier and faster, but like most new tools, email has a learning curve. Most people are still figuring out how to use it appropriately in professional settings, and in the meantime, many lawyers are discovering that careless or ineffective use can cause serious problems.

Many of the serious and not so serious email problems can be avoided by using a little common sense. Below are several tips that many professionals, particularly lawyers, find helpful for their work-related emails.

Tip 1: Do Not Include Anything in an Email that You Would Not Want Read Aloud in Court

No matter what types of statements about confidentiality that you insert in your email, there are no guarantees that your email will remain confidential. Although the ABA has stated that there is a reasonable expectation of privacy in emails, emails (and text messages, for that matter) may be discoverable. Consequently, the safest policy is not to include anything in an email that you do not want shared with the rest of the world.

When you do include confidential information in an email, consider the following precautions. First, consider obtaining client consent that it is acceptable to communicate confidential information via email. Second, always include a confidentiality in your emails. Third, draft emails with sensitive information in a Word document first. Once you are satisfied with the document, you can cut and paste it into the email. This process will prevent discovery of metadata (edits made to a document that are deleted). Fourth, be sure that your office's encryption programs are up to date.

Tip 2: Use the Same Professional Language that You Would Use in an Office Memo, an Opinion Letter, or a Business Letter

Sending an office email is not the same thing as text messaging a friend. No matter how well you know the person to whom you are writing a work-related email, use the same language that you would use drafting an office memo, an opinion letter, or a business letter. Do not use abbreviations, code words, slang, or emoticons such as ☺.

EXAMPLE 1	**Example 1 Inappropriate Language**

BTW, if you have questions, feel free to call me 24-7.

Edited: Appropriate Language

Finally, if you have questions, please feel free to call me.

Tip 3: Make Sure that the Tone of the Email Is the Tone that You Intend

"Flaming" in email is the equivalent of shouting at a person. Messages written in all caps, boldface, or other attention-getting fonts should be used with extreme care.

EXAMPLE 2   **Inappropriate Tone**

I got your request for the meeting with Chong. ARE YOU SERIOUS ABOUT WANTING AN HOUR WITH HIM?

Edited: Appropriate Tone

I got your request for the meeting with Chong. An hour meeting seems excessive. Would a shorter meeting work for you?

Notice, too, that while some people view very short emails as efficient, others may read in a curt or rude tone. In addition, it is often a good idea to follow up a request for information with a quick note of thanks so that colleagues and employees know you have received their emails and that their follow-up was appreciated.

EXAMPLE 3   **Tone May Be Interpreted as Curt or Rude**

Original Email

Do you want to review the draft before I submit it to O'Brien?

Answer

No.

Original Email

Do you want to review the draft before I submit it to O'Brien?

Edited Answer

No, that won't be necessary. Thanks for your hard work on this project.

In addition, in drafting an email, keep cultural differences in mind. If you are emailing a person from a culture where it is customary to begin a conversation with an exchange of pleasantries, include the same kind of opening pleasantries in an email to that person.

Tip 4: Before Hitting "Send" or "Reply," Reread Your Email, Including the Address Lines

Although it takes a bit of extra time, rereading an email before sending it is time well spent. Before sending an email, take a few minutes to proofread the email and to double check the address lines. While many people are forgiving of small typos in emails, others are not. In addition, some typos can lead to serious miscommunication. Remember, too, that if you are using a tablet or smart phone that tries to predict what word you intend as you type, you may end up sending gibberish if you do not proofread your messages before sending them.

Tip 5: Do Not Misuse the "High Importance" or the "Read Receipt" Functions

Marking every email as being of high importance is a bit like calling "wolf" every time you hear a noise in the bushes. At some point, no one pays any attention to emails that come from you with the high importance mark. Therefore, limit your use of the mark to those emails that are, in fact, of high importance.

In addition, do not ask for a read receipt for every email you send. At best, most individuals find the process annoying; at worst, it sends the message that you do not trust the individual to whom you are sending the email. If you would like a response, you can ask for such a response in the text of your email. If you need proof that someone received information, use one of the more traditional methods: Send the information through a delivery service or by some type of registered mail.

Tip 6: Be Selective in Attaching Large Files to an Email

If you know that someone uses a tablet or smart phone to retrieve email, do not attach large files without first checking with the recipient to make sure that he or she will be able to receive and open the file. Similarly, if the person to whom you are sending the email is traveling in a country where email access is limited, do not send large files without first checking with that individual.

Tip 7: Make Sure the Subject Line Accurately Reflects the Topic or Topics Discussed in the Email

If, in sending email back and forth, the topic changes, change the subject line so that it matches the topic or topics discussed in the email. Also try to select labels that will increase the chance that the recipient will open the email and that will allow you and the recipient to store the email in appropriate folders or easily retrieve the email.

Tip 8: As a General Rule, Do Not Copy or Forward an Email Message or Attachment Without the Author's Permission, But Be Aware that Others May Forward Your Emails Without Asking Your Permission

In most instances, ask for the original author's permission before forwarding an email or an attachment to an email. Asking for permission demonstrates your personal integrity and can help prevent misunderstandings. Do, however, use common sense. You do not, for example, need to ask for permission to forward an email to a colleague who is working on the same project.

Remember, too, that when you forward an email, the recipient may read the whole string of exchanged emails in the message, not just the last message that was sent.

Unfortunately, though, not all recipients of your emails will return the favor and ask your permission before forwarding an email you have written. Some may do so without any malicious intent. They just assume that it is fine to pass along the information. If you have concerns about an email you are writing getting forwarded, you may want to begin the email with a strong request asking the recipient not to forward the email to others, or you may want to reconsider whether email is the best way to communicate the message.

Tip 9: There Is No Such Thing as "Delete"

Many people mistakenly assume that they can eliminate the paper trail they have created through email by simply deleting old messages. While computer experts may have the necessary skills to permanently delete old emails, they also have the skills to recover emails that the typical user believes he or she has deleted.

Tip 10: When in Doubt, Sleep on It or Get a Second Opinion Before Hitting "Send"

Emails allow us to respond to someone else's ideas or comments almost instantaneously. Sometimes in the heat of a situation, that is not a good thing. Use the speed and convenience of email to your advantage, but remember that in some situations, it may be to your advantage to take a breath, slow down, and not respond immediately.

§ 10.3   Text Messages

If email is the modern update for snail mail, then text messaging is the modern update for the phone call. Although phone calls and voice mail are still commonplace in all work settings, text messages are growing in popularity, and with that growth has come a number of issues regarding effective use.

Because text messages have a fair amount in common with emails, many of the tips and cautions about use of email in section 10.2 apply to text messages as well. And just like email, text messages have both advantages and disadvantages.

The principal advantages of text messages over phone calls are that they can be less intrusive and more efficient. Text messages can be sent and read when it is convenient for both sender and receiver, and messages can be sent and read silently, without interrupting another meeting with all the sounds attendant to a phone call.

Text messages also tend to be shorter and thus more efficient than phone calls. Probably because the screen size is small, most recipients expect text messages to be short, even cryptic. In addition, incomplete sentences are not uncommon. Consequently, there is less of a chance that a short text message will be interpreted as curt or rude.

An additional advantage of text messages over phone calls may be cost, especially for international communications. While international phone calls can be very expensive, text messages are not.

Capitalizing on the advantages of text messaging, then, a lawyer might well use a text message for short communications, such as changing a meeting location. The message can be sent and received with minimal interruption, and the recipient can be in transit and still receive it. While a phone call might have a more personal touch, a phone call will inevitably be more of an interruption and take longer to convey the message. Note, though, that the assumption is that the recipient of the communications not only has a cell phone that is set up to receive text messages but also that he or she would prefer a text message over a call.

The main disadvantage of text messages is that most people consider them to be an informal form of communication that works best among family members and close friends. Indeed because so many people use text messaging for their personal lives, there is a tendency to bring an inappropriate level of informality to text messages in the work place. The sort of shorthand phrasing or spelling such as "R U coming?" or "Thx" that is commonplace in text messaging close friends may be inappropriate with colleagues at work and certainly with clients.

One additional consideration is that some cell phone users have not set up password protection for their text messages so confidential information sent in a text message may be read by anyone who answers the phone.

Chapter 10 Quiz

Draft answers for each of the following questions. Make your points clearly and concisely, and write sentences that are easy to read and that are grammatical and correctly punctuated.

1. How are e-memos the same as more formal memos? How are they different?
2. In writing an e-memo, when should you include descriptions of analogous cases?

3. What are some of the characteristics of a memo in which the analysis is sophisticated?
4. Are emails confidential?
5. What is the appropriate "tone" for an email or text message?

Drafting Letters

Some clients love their attorney and recommend him or her to their business associates, friends, relatives, and people they meet at the gym and on the golf course. Unfortunately, other clients do not give their attorneys the same rave reviews. As a new attorney, how do you make it more likely that you fall into the first and not the second category? While "by winning" seems like the obvious answer, it is not the only answer. Even though clients tend to like attorneys who win or who tell the clients what they want to hear better than attorneys who lose or who have to give them bad news, many clients are looking for more: They want an attorney who listens to them, who explains the law to them in language they can understand, who gives them good advice, and who does not make promises that are not kept. In addition, they want an attorney who is professional. They want someone who dresses professionally, who has a professional demeanor, and who creates professional documents.

Thus, in writing a letter to a client, keep in mind that you are doing more than just telling the client what the law is or what you think your client should do. You are establishing a relationship with your client and building, or destroying, your professional reputation.

§ 11.1   The Assignment

As an attorney, you will write many different types of letters to clients. You will, for example, write letters confirming that you have agreed to represent a particular individual, letters updating your client about the status of his or her case, demand letters, and letters like the ones that we describe in this chapter: opinion letters that explain the law and your client's options.

> **PRACTICE POINTER**
>
> Before you write your first demand letter, read Bret Rappaport's article, *A Shot Across the Bow: How to Write an Effective Demand Letter,* 5 JALWD 32 (2008).

For the purposes of this chapter, assume that you are an attorney in Austin, Texas, and that you represent Mary Corner, who has just purchased a restaurant in a historic building in the Austin Historic District. On September 13, 2013, Ms. Corner filed an application for a permit to install two six-foot by four-foot painted signs on the front of her new restaurant, the Corner Café, which is located in the corner of a building that has been designated as a Historic Landmark. One sign would be on the north side of the building, and the other sign would be on the west side of the building. Each sign would extend eighteen inches above the roof line and would have a beige background and green lettering. At night, the signs would be lit by a small light installed under the signs. On October 1, 2013, the Historic Landmark Commission denied Ms. Corner's application and gave her fourteen days to appeal its decision. Ms. Corner is thinking about appealing and has asked for our advice.

§ 11.2   Know Your Audience and Your Purpose

Before you begin writing, ask yourself two questions: Who is my audience? What is my purpose?

§ 11.2.1   The Audience for an Opinion Letter

Although the primary audience for an opinion letter is the client, there may be a secondary audience. The letter may be read not only by the client but also by an interested third party. Consequently, in writing the letter, write both for the client and for anyone else who may read the letter.

In the Corner Café sign case, the primary audience for your opinion letter will be Mary Corner. Ms. Corner may, however, show the letter to another small business owner, to friends and relatives, or even to a city official.

§11.2.2   The Purpose of an Opinion Letter

Assume for a moment that the audience is the client and no one else. In writing to that client, what is your purpose? Is it to inform? To persuade? To justify your bill? Should you be giving the client only your conclusions, or should you include the information that the client needs to reach his or her own conclusions?

Your role is determined, at least in part, by your state's Rules of Professional Conduct. For example, in Texas attorneys are bound by the following rule and comments.

EXAMPLE 1	**Texas Disciplinary Rules of Professional Conduct**

1.03 Communication

(a) A lawyer shall keep a client reasonably informed about the status of a matter and promptly comply with reasonable requests for information.

(b) A lawyer shall explain a matter to the extent reasonably necessary to permit the client to make informed decisions regarding the representation.

Comment:

1. The client should have sufficient information to participate intelligently in decisions concerning the objectives of the representation and the means by which they are to be pursued, to the extent the client is willing and able to do so. For example, a lawyer negotiating on behalf of a client should provide the client with facts relevant to the matter, inform the client of communications from another party and take other reasonable steps to permit the client to make a decision regarding a serious offer from another party. A lawyer who receives from opposing counsel either an offer of settlement in a civil controversy or a proffered plea bargain in a criminal case should promptly inform the client of its substance unless prior discussions with the client have left it clear that the proposal will be unacceptable. See Comment 2 to Rule 1.02.

2. Adequacy of communication depends in part on the kind of advice or assistance involved. For example, in negotiations where there is time to explain a proposal the lawyer should review all important provisions with the client before proceeding to an agreement. In litigation a lawyer should explain the general strategy and prospects of success and ordinarily should consult the client on tactics that might injure or coerce others. . . .The guiding principle is that the lawyer should reasonably fulfill client expectations for information consistent with the duty to act in the client's best interests, and the client's overall requirements as to the character of representation.

Accordingly, under the Texas rules, your primary purpose in writing the letter would be to give Ms. Corner the information that she needs to make an informed decision about whether to appeal the Historic Landmark Commission's decision.

§ 11.3   Prepare the First Draft of the Letter

Just as convention dictates the content and form of the objective memorandum, convention also dictates the content and form of the opinion letter. Most opinion letters have (1) an introductory paragraph identifying the issue and, most often, the attorney's opinion; (2) a summary of the facts on which the opinion is based; (3) an explanation of the law; (4) the attorney's advice; and (5) a closing sentence or paragraph. Note the similarities between a formal memorandum and the opinion letter.

Objective Memorandum	**Opinion Letter**
Heading	Name
	Address
	File
	Reference
	Salutation
Question presented	Introductory paragraph
Brief answer	Opinion
Statement of facts	Summary of facts on which opinion is based
Discussion section	Explanation
Conclusion	Advice
	Closing

§ 11.3.1   The Introductory Paragraph

In writing the introductory paragraph, you have two objectives: to establish the appropriate relationship with your client and to define the issue or goal. In addition, you will often include substantive information. For example, when the news is favorable, you will usually set out your opinion in the introductory paragraph.

Because the introductory paragraph is so important, avoid "canned" opening sentences. For instance, do not begin all of your letters with "This letter is in response to your inquiry of . . ." or "As you requested . . . ." Instead of beginning with platitudes, begin by identifying the issue or goal. Compare Examples 1, 2, and 3.

EXAMPLE 1   **Canned Opening Sentence**

This letter is in response to your inquiry of October 3, 2013. The information that you requested is set out below.

EXAMPLE 2   **Better Opening Sentence**

After our meeting yesterday, I researched the Austin ordinances governing signs in the Austin Historic Districts.

EXAMPLE 3   **Even Better Opening Sentence**

During our meeting yesterday, you asked me whether you should appeal the Historic Landmark Commission's decision denying your request for a permit to install two signs above the entrance to your new restaurant, the Corner Café. To answer your question, I have reviewed the facts and the Austin ordinances on signs in Historic Landmark Districts.

Because Example 1 could be used to open almost any letter, it subtly suggests to the reader that he or she is just one more client to whom the attorney is cranking out a response. Consequently, most successful attorneys avoid opening sentences like the one in Example 1 and, like the authors of Examples 2 and 3, personalize their openings.

§ 11.3.2 Statement of the Issue

Although you need to identify the issue, you do not want to include a formal issue statement. In most instances, the "under-does-when" and the "whether" formats used in formal memos are inappropriate in an opinion letter.

In deciding how to present the issue, keep in mind your purpose, both in including a statement of the issue and in writing the letter itself. In most letters, your purpose is twofold: You want the client to know that you understand the issue, and you want to protect yourself. Consequently, you include a statement of the issue for both rhetorical and practical reasons. You use it to establish a relationship with the client and to limit your liability.

In the Corner Café sign case, there are a number of different ways and places to set out the issue: You can incorporate your issue statement into your introductory paragraph; you can combine your statement of the issue with your statement of your opinion; or you can set out the issue at the beginning of your explanation of the law.

EXAMPLE 4   **Issue Statement Incorporated into the Introductory Paragraph**

During our meeting on Tuesday, you asked whether you should appeal the City's decision denying your request to install two signs above the entrance to your new restaurant, the Corner Café.

EXAMPLE 5   **Issue Statement Combined with Your Opinion**

I have completed my review of the ordinances governing business signs in the Austin Historic Districts. Based on this review, I recommend that you appeal the City's decision denying your request to install two signs above the entrance to your new restaurant, the Corner Café.

EXAMPLE 6   **Issue Used to Introduce Explanation of the Law**

[Introductory paragraph and facts go here.]

Before deciding whether to appeal the City's denial of your application for a permit to install two signs above the entrance to your new restaurant, you should consider the following ordinances and the procedures and costs that are involved in appealing a decision. [Explanation of the law goes here.]

---

§ 11.3.3 Opinion

When the client has asked for your opinion, set out your opinion in the letter. When the news is good, you will usually put your opinion in the introductory paragraph; having had his or her question answered, the client can then concentrate on the explanation. You may, however, want to use a different strategy when the news is bad. Instead of putting your opinion "up front," you may choose to put it at the end, in the hope that having read the explanation, the client will better understand your opinion.

Whatever your opinion, present it as your opinion. Because you are in the business of making predictions and not guarantees, never tell clients that they will or will not win. Instead, present your opinion in terms of probabilities: "It is unlikely that you would win on appeal." "It is unlikely that the City Council will overturn the decision of the Historic Landmark Commission and grant your application for a permit."

§ 11.3.4   Summary of the Facts

There are two reasons for including a summary of the facts. As with the statement of the issue, the first is rhetorical. You want the client to know that you heard his or her story. The second is practical. You want to protect yourself. Your client needs to know that your opinion is based on a particular set of facts and that, if the facts turn out to be different, your opinion might also be different.

Just as you do not include all of the facts in the statement of facts written for an objective memorandum, you do not include all of the facts in an opinion letter. Include only those facts that are legally significant or that are important to the client. Because the letter itself should be short, keep your summary of facts as short as possible. For instance, in the Corner Café sign case, your statement of facts might look like this.

EXAMPLE 7   **Summary of Facts**

You submitted your original application on September 13, 2013. In that application, you requested a permit that would have allowed you to install two six-foot by four-foot painted wood signs on the front of your building. One of the signs would have been installed on the north side of the building, and the other would have been installed on the west side of the building. Both signs would extend about eighteen inches above the top of the building and would be beige with green lettering. At night, the signs would be lit by a light installed under the signs. The Historic Landmark Commission denied your application on October 1, 2013, giving you fourteen days to appeal its decision to the City Council.

---

§ 11.3.5   Explanation

Under the rules of professional responsibility, you must give the client the information that he or she needs to make an informed decision. It is essential, therefore, that you give not only your opinion but also the basis for your opinion. The explanation section is not, however, just a repeat of the discussion section from an objective memorandum. It is usually much shorter and much more client-specific.

When the explanation requires a discussion of more than one or two issues, you will usually want to include a roadmap. Having outlined the steps, you can then discuss each step in more detail. The amount of detail will depend on the question, the subject matter, and the client. Although there are exceptions, as a general rule, do not set out the text of ordinances or statutes or include references to specific cases. Instead, just tell the client what the ordinances, statutes, and cases say, without citations to authority.

After explaining the law, apply the law to the facts of your client's case. If a particular point is not in dispute, explain why it is not in dispute; if it is in dispute, summarize each side's arguments. The difference between the analysis in an objective memorandum and in an opinion letter is a difference in degree, not kind. In each instance, give the reader what he or she needs — nothing more and nothing less. For examples of explanations, see the sample letters set out at the end of this chapter.

§ 11.3.6　Advice

When there is more than one possible course of action, include an advice section in which you describe and evaluate each option. For example, if there are several ways in which your client could change its business operations to avoid liability, describe and evaluate each of those options. Similarly, if your client could choose negotiation over arbitration or arbitration over litigation, describe and evaluate each option. Having described the options, you can then advise the client as to which option you think would be in his or her best interest.

§ 11.3.7　Concluding Paragraph

Just as you should avoid canned openings, also avoid canned closings. Instead of using stock sentences, use the concluding paragraph to cement the relationship that you have established with the client and to confirm what, if anything, is to happen next. What is the next step and who is to take it?

§ 11.3.8　Warnings

Some firms will want you to include explicit warnings. They will want you to tell the client that your opinion is based on current law and on the facts currently available and that your opinion might be different if the facts turn out to be different. Other firms believe that these warnings, when set out explicitly, set the wrong tone. Because practice varies, determine which approach your firm takes before writing the letter.

In writing your letter, you can use any of the standard formats for business letters. For examples of accepted formats, see the sample letters at the end of this chapter.

§ 11.4　Revising, Editing, and Proofreading the Opinion Letter

It is not enough that the law be stated correctly and that your advice be sound. Your letter must be well written and the tone must be the one that you intend.

§ 11.4.1　Drafting a Well-Written Letter

Like other types of writing, a well-written letter is well organized. As a general rule, present the information in the order listed above: an introductory paragraph in which you identify the issue and give your opinion followed by a summary of the facts, an explanation of the law, your advice, and a concluding sentence or paragraph. You will also want to structure each paragraph carefully, identifying the topic in the first sentence and making sure that each sentence builds on the prior one.

In addition, take care in constructing your sentences. You can make the law more understandable by using concrete subjects and action verbs and relatively short sentences. When longer sentences are needed, manage those sentences by using punctuation to divide the sentences into shorter units of meaning.

Finally, remember that you will be judged by the letter you write. Although clients may not know whether you have the law right, they will know whether you have spelled their names correctly. In addition, many will notice other mistakes in grammar, punctuation, or spelling. If you want to be known as a competent lawyer, make sure that your letters provide the proof.

§ 11.4.2   Using an Appropriate Tone

In addition to selling competence, you are selling an image. As you read each of the following letters, picture the attorney who wrote it.

EXAMPLE 1

Dear Mr. and Mrs. McDonald:

This letter is to acknowledge receipt of your letter of February 17, 2013, concerning your prospects as potential adoptive parents. The information that you provided about yourselves will need to be verified through appropriate documentation. Furthermore, I am sure that you are cognizant of the fact that there are considerably more prospective adoptive placements than there are available adoptees to fill those placement slots.

Nonetheless, I will be authorizing my legal assistant to keep your correspondence on file. One can never know when an opportunity may present itself and, in fact, a child becomes unexpectedly available for placement. If such an opportunity should arise, please know that I would be in immediate contact with you.

Very sincerely yours,

Kenneth Q. Washburn III
Attorney at Law

EXAMPLE 2

Dear Bill and Mary,

Just wanted you to know that I got your letter asking about adopting a baby. I can already tell that you two would make great parents. But, as you probably know, there are far more "would be" parents out there than there are babies.

But I don't want you to lose hope. You might be surprised. Your future little one may be available sooner than you think. It has happened before! And you can be sure that I'll call you the minute I hear of something. Until then, I'll have Marge set up a file for you.

All the best,

Ken Washburn

EXAMPLE 3

Dear Mr. and Mrs. McDonald:

Your letter about the possibility of adopting a baby arrived in my office yesterday. Although the information in your letter indicates that you would be ideal adoptive parents, I am sure that you realize that there are more couples who wish to adopt than there are adoptable babies. For this reason, you may have to wait for some time for your future son or daughter.

Even so, occasionally an infant becomes available for adoption on short notice. For this reason, I will ask my legal assistant to open a file for you so that we can react quickly if necessary. Because we do not know exactly when an infant will become available, I recommend that we begin putting together the appropriate documentation as soon as possible. In the meantime, please know that I will call you immediately if I learn of an available infant who would be a good match for you.

Sincerely,

Kenneth Washburn

§ 11.4.3 Checklist for Critiquing the Opinion Letter

I. Organization

- The information has been presented in a logical order: The letter begins with an introductory sentence or paragraph that is followed, in most instances, by the attorney's opinion, a summary of the facts, an explanation, the attorney's advice, and a concluding paragraph.

II. Content

- The introductory sentence identifies the topic and establishes the appropriate relationship with the client.
- The attorney's opinion is sound and is stated in terms of probabilities.
- The summary of the facts is accurate and includes both the legally significant facts and the facts that are important to the client.
- The explanation gives the client the information that he or she needs to make an informed decision.
- The options are described and evaluated.
- The concluding paragraph states who will do what next and sets an appropriate tone.

III. Writing

- The client can understand the letter after reading it once.
- The paragraph divisions are logical, and the paragraphs are neither too long nor too short.
- Transitions and dovetailing have been used to make the connections between ideas clear.
- In most sentences, the writer has used the actor as the subject of the sentence, and the subject and verb are close together.
- The writer has varied the length of the sentences and the sentence patterns so that each sentence flows smoothly from the prior sentence.
- The writing is concise and precise.

■ The writing is grammatically correct and correctly punctuated.
■ The letter has been proofread.

Chapter 11 Quiz

Draft answers for each of the following questions. Make your points clearly and concisely, and write sentences that are easy to read and that are grammatical and correctly punctuated.

1. In writing an opinion letter, what is your purpose?
2. As a general rule, what types of information should be included in an opinion letter and in what order should that information be presented?
3. In general, what is the appropriate tone for an opinion letter?

§ 11.5   Sample Client Letters

| **EXAMPLE 1** | **Sample Client Letter** |

Confidential
Attorney-Client Communication

Mary Corner
101 Main Street
Austin, Texas 73344

Dear Ms. Corner:

During our meeting yesterday, you asked me whether you should appeal the Historic Landmark Commission's decision denying your request for a permit to install two signs above the entrance to your new restaurant, the Corner Café. To answer your question, I have reviewed the facts and the Austin ordinances on signs in Historic Landmark Districts.

You submitted your original application on September 13, 2013. In that application, you requested a permit that would have allowed you to install two six-foot by four-foot painted wood signs on the front of your building. One of the signs would have been installed on the north side of the building, and the other would have been installed on the west side of the building. Both signs would extend about eighteen inches above the top of the building and would be beige with green lettering. At night, the signs would be lit by a light installed under the signs. The Historic Landmark Commission denied your application on October 1, 2013, giving you fourteen days to appeal its decision to the City Council.

City of Austin ordinances prohibit certain types of signs in Historic Landmark Districts. For example, the ordinances specifically prohibit roof signs and any sign, or any portion of a sign, that rotates. Although your signs would not rotate, they might fall within the definition of a roof sign, which is defined as a sign that is "installed over or on the roof of a building." In determining whether to grant a permit for other types of signs, the Historic Landmark Commission considers a number of other factors, including the following:

(1.)   the proposed size, color, and lighting of the sign;

(2.)   the material from which the sign is to be constructed;

(3.)   the proliferation of signs on a building or lot;

(4.)   the proposed orientation of the sign with respect to structures; and

(5.)   other factors that are consistent with the Historic Landmark Preservation Plan, the character of the National Historic Register District, and the purpose of historic landmark regulations.

If the Commission denied your application for a permit because your proposed signs fall within the definition of a roof sign, it is unlikely that the City Council would overturn the Commission's decision. Our only hope would be to persuade the City Council that a sign that extends above the top of the building does not fall within the definition of a roof sign.

If, however, the Commission denied the permit for some other reason, the City Council might overturn the Commission's decision, particularly if your proposed signs are consistent in size, color, lighting, and material with other signs in the area and if there are not already a number of other signs on the building.

To preserve your right to appeal, I recommend that you file a notice of appeal within the time limits set out in the letter that you received from the Commission. I would then schedule a meeting with a member of the Commission to determine the reason that the Commission denied your application. If the Commission denied your application because your signs would extend beyond the roof line, the Commission may be willing to approve your application for a permit if you agree to change the size and/ or locations of your signs so that they do not extend beyond the roof line. Similarly, if the Commission denied your application because of the signs' size, color, or lighting, you may be able to work with the Commission to modify your application so that your proposed signs meet the Commission's criteria. If, however, you cannot find out from the Commission why it denied your application or you cannot reach an agreement with the Commission about an application that would meet its criteria, you can then proceed with your appeal to the City Council.

Although you do not need an attorney to file an appeal with the City Council or to schedule meetings with the Commission, I would be glad to assist you with either or both actions. If you would like me to act on your behalf, please call me by Wednesday, October 9, 2013, so that I can submit the appeal before the deadline. If you would like to file the appeal without my assistance, please see the instructions that are set out in the letter that you received from the Commission. In addition, you can request an appointment with a Commissioner by calling the following number: (512) 974-2680. If you have any further questions or concerns, please feel free to call me. Please keep in mind that you must file your appeal no later than Monday, October 14, 2013.

Very truly yours,

Your name

| EXAMPLE 2 | **Sample Client Letter** |

Confidential
Attorney-Client Communication

September 30, 2013

Ms. Marian Walter
1234 Main Street
Wichita, KS 67218

File No. 0192002

Dear Ms. Walter:

Thank you for contacting me about whether you can vacate your current location before the expiration of your lease. After researching the issues, I have determined that, if you decide to move out before the end of your lease and your landlord, Valley Antiques, files a lawsuit to collect the unpaid rent, you can probably win the lawsuit. You should, however, consider some of your other options.

Because my opinion is based on the following facts, please contact me if I have left out a fact or misstated a fact.

In June 2012, you received a brochure advertising an "elegant antiques mall" that was certain to attract "the most discriminating clients." When you met with the leasing agent, Joann Carter, she told you that the mall would house antique stores and that the mall was designed to attract adults, not children. In August 2012, you signed a five-year lease. The lease stated that the remaining spaces would be rented to antique stores or other retail businesses.

Between August 2012 and November 2012, five other upscale antique stores moved into the mall. The landlord was, however, unable to rent the remaining eight spaces to antique dealers. As a result, between February and April 2013, the landlord leased four of the remaining spaces to other types of businesses. It leased one of the spaces to a video arcade and three others to secondhand stores. Since these stores moved into the mall, there have been children with skateboards in the mall area, and you have experienced a 20 percent decrease in profits. In addition to making oral complaints, on April 30, 2013, you sent a letter to the landlord notifying it that you believe that it violated the terms of your lease when it leased spaces in the mall to the video arcade and secondhand stores.

If you vacate the premises and default on the lease, Valley Antiques may file a lawsuit against you to recover the rent due for the remaining months of the lease. If this happens, you can argue that Valley Antiques "constructively evicted" you when it leased to the arcade and secondhand stores. A constructive eviction is different from an actual eviction: While an actual eviction occurs when the landlord literally takes the premises away from the tenant, a constructive eviction occurs when the landlord interferes with a tenant's right to use the premises for their intended purpose. It would be up to the jury to decide whether the circumstances surrounding your case constitute constructive eviction.

To establish that you have been constructively evicted, you will need to prove four things. First, you must prove that Valley Antiques violated the lease agreement. Valley Antiques will argue that, under the lease, it had the right to lease to retail stores and that an arcade and thrift shops are retail stores. Although the lease does allow Valley Antiques to lease to retail stores, you can argue that both parties understood the language in the lease to mean that Valley Antiques could lease to antique stores and other "upscale" retail establishments, for example, an upscale jewelry store or restaurant. Based on the language in the brochure and the statements made by the leasing agent, a jury should conclude that the landlord violated the lease by leasing the other spaces to the video arcade and secondhand stores.

Second, you must prove that when Valley Antiques leased the vacant spaces to a video arcade and secondhand stores it substantially interfered with your ability to use your leased space. Although there have been cases in which the courts have found that a landlord substantially interfered with a tenant's use of its leased space when the landlord rented to an incompatible business, there are other cases in which the court found that the landlord did not substantially interfere. The key seems to be whether the landlord's act caused a loss of profits. As a consequence, to prove substantial interference, we will have to show that Valley Antiques caused your loss of profits when it leased the vacant spaces to the arcade and the secondhand stores. Even though we should be able to do this, Valley Antiques will try to prove that your losses are the result of other factors, such as the seasonal nature of your business, the current economic climate, or your own business practices.

Third, you must prove that you gave Valley Antiques notice of the problem and an opportunity to correct it. You should be able to meet this requirement: in addition to making oral complaints, you also sent a letter, and you have given Valley Antiques several months to correct the problem.

Finally, you must prove that you vacated the premises within a reasonable amount of time after complaining to the landlord. If you vacate the premises by November 1, 2013, the jury will most likely find that you have met this requirement.

Although you should be able to prove that you have been constructively evicted, litigation is expensive and stressful, and there are no guarantees. As a result, you should consider some of your other options.

One option is to stay and pay rent. Although this option avoids the expense and stress of litigation, you may lose your right to claim that you have been constructively evicted. As I indicated earlier in this letter, one of the requirements for constructive eviction is that you move out within a reasonable time. In addition, if your loss in profits continues, it may be impractical to stay in business.

A second option would be to try to sublease your space to another business. Even though your lease requires that you obtain Valley Antiques' approval before you sublet your space, the courts have said that a landlord cannot withhold approval except for good cause. The risk associated with this option is that you may be liable for unpaid rents if the new tenant fails to make payments.

A third option is to try to negotiate an early termination of the lease on the grounds that Valley Antiques has violated the lease by leasing to the arcade and secondhand stores. I can do this for you or, if you want to minimize your costs, you can do it on your own.

A fourth option would be to file a lawsuit against Valley Antiques for breach of contract. Although you should be able to win this lawsuit and recover your lost profits, such a lawsuit would be expensive and, once again, there are no guarantees.

Unfortunately, none of these options is very good. As a result, you need to balance your desire to move out of the mall against the potential costs. Although there is a good chance that your landlord will not sue you, under our state's statute of limitations it has six years to file a lawsuit. Therefore, you would have to live under the cloud of potential litigation for a number of years.

Please contact my office to schedule an appointment to talk in more detail about your options. I look forward to meeting with you.

Sincerely,

Name
Attorney at Law

EXAMPLE 3   **Sample Client Letter**

Confidential
Attorney-Client Communication

September 20, 2013

Onlinebooks.com
6524 Industrial Parkway South
Tampa Bay, Florida 33607

Dear Mr. Brooks:

You have asked if Onlinebooks may ask job applicants whether they have back problems or have used more than five days of sick leave during the past year. My research indicates that the Americans with Disabilities Act (ADA) prohibits the asking of such questions. You can, however, ask questions that will help you determine whether an applicant can perform the essential job requirements. Because my opinion is based on current law and my understanding of the facts, I have set out those facts so that you can review them for accuracy. Please note that a change in the facts might change my opinion.

Onlinebooks employs "pickers," that is, individuals who pick books off shelves, place them in a box, and then place the box on a conveyor belt. Pickers must be able to climb, reach, and lift boxes weighing up to thirty pounds. In the past, some of the individuals you have hired as pickers have not been able to do all parts of the job or have used substantial amounts of sick leave for back or other health problems. Thus, you want to ask job applicants about whether they have back problems and about how they use sick leave.

The ADA prohibits employers from discriminating against qualified job applicants who are disabled. More specifically, the ADA prohibits employers from asking applicants questions that are designed to "weed out" individuals who have a disability or who suffer from a chronic illness. As a result, Onlinebooks cannot ask job applicants about whether they have back problems or about their use of sick leave.

The ADA does not, however, prohibit an employer from asking job applicants whether they can, with or without reasonable accommodations, perform the essential functions of the job for which they are applying. Therefore, Onlinebooks may describe the essential functions of the job and then ask applicants whether they can perform those functions. For example, you may tell applicants that pickers must be able to climb, reach, and lift thirty-pound boxes and then ask them whether they can perform each of these tasks. In addition, Onlinebooks may ask applicants to demonstrate that they can do each of these tasks.

If an applicant asks for a reasonable accommodation, Onlinebooks must grant that accommodation unless doing so would impose an unreasonable burden on Onlinebooks. For example, if an applicant asks to be allowed to wear a back support or to use a handcart to move heavy boxes longer distances, you should grant the request unless doing so would create an unreasonable burden on the company. You would not, however, need to grant an employee's request to be exempted from carrying boxes weighing over, for example, ten pounds.

In addition, the ADA does not prohibit employers from asking applicants about their work histories. Consequently, although you may not ask applicants how much sick leave they used in the last year, you may ask them about their attendance records. In doing so, you just need to make sure that the questions are designed to collect information about the applicants' work records, not to determine whether the individual is disabled or suffers from a chronic illness.

To summarize then, although you may not ask applicants whether they have back problems, you may ask them whether they can, with or without reasonable accommodations, perform the essential functions of the job. In addition, although you may not ask applicants about their use of sick leave, you may ask them about their attendance records as long as your questions are not designed to collect information about whether the person is disabled or suffers from a chronic illness.

If you have any additional questions, please feel free to contact me.

Sincerely,

Name
Attorney at Law

Index